The American Theological Library Association

Essays in Celebration of the First Fifty Years

Edited by
M. Patrick Graham
Valerie R. Hotchkiss
Kenneth E. Rowe

The American Theological Library Association
1996

Copyright © 1996
By The American Theological Library Association

Published in the United States by The American Theological Library Association, 820 Church Street, Suite 300, Evanston, Illinois 60201

Prepress production, including text and cover, by Albert E. Hurd.

ISBN: 0-524-10300-3

ATLA Cataloging in publication:

> The American Theological Library Association : essays in celebration of the first fifty years / edited by M. Patrick Graham, Valerie R. Hotchkiss and Kenneth E. Rowe. -- Evanston, Ill. : American Theological Library Association, 1996.
>
>   p. ; cm.
>
> Includes bibliographical references.
> Contents:
> ISBN 0-524-10300-3
>
> 1. American Theological Library Association. 2. Library science--Societies, etc. 3. Theological libraries. 4. Theology--Study and teaching. I. Graham, Matt Patrick. II. Hotchkiss, Valerie R., 1960- III. Rowe, Kenneth E. IV. American Theological Library Association
> Z675.T4A62 1996

Printed on 50# Natural; an acid free paper
by
McNaughton & Gunn, Inc.

Contents

THE THEORY AND PRACTICE
OF THEOLOGICAL LIBRARIANSHIP

Acknowledgments

The editors would like to express their appreciation to Albert E. Hurd for inviting them to undertake the preparation of this volume, encouraging them along the way, and lending a hand to bring the project to completion. We extend our thanks as well to the contributors of the essays for their willingness to accept writing assignments or prepare articles on the basis of research already under way. Finally, we want to acknowledge our indebtedness to our colleagues in ATLA who have lent their time and energies to the organization over these first fifty years of its life. They have nurtured our professional development, assisted our efforts to offer our constituencies the very best in the way of theological and religious library resources, and enabled us to accomplish things together that none of us could have done on our own.

—The Editors

Preface

Albert E. Hurd

The genesis of this *Festschrift*—in celebration of the American Theological Library Association's (ATLA) first fifty years—has two sources. First, at the 1993 Annual Conference members attending the Publication Section enthusiastically endorsed Drew Kadel's idea for this work by forwarding a recommendation to the ATLA Board of Directors that it " . . . adopt and fund the *Festschrift*."[1] The Board of Directors concurred with this recommendation and passed it onto the Executive Director to implement. Second, several ATLA members had at about the same time raised with me the possibility of a special publication that would update the many organizational changes within the Association, since its official incorporation in 1972, and those within theological librarianship. With the convergence of these two independent initiatives within the Association, with the single goal of a publication representing contributions by members and friends of the Association, I was faced with the question of how best to proceed.

One of my concerns as Executive Director of ATLA has been to foster opportunities for new and younger members to advance into leadership roles within member libraries as well as within the Association. Therefore, in selecting the editorial direction of the *Festschrift* I wished to bridge the membership generations within ATLA. On this basis, I appointed an editorial committee made up of two of ATLA's newer members, M. Patrick Graham and Valerie Hotchkiss, along with a more senior member, Kenneth Rowe, who has served ATLA in many capacities and is presently the most senior member of the Publication Section/Committee.

The regular appearance of new titles in the ATLA Monograph and Bibliography Series and new volumes of the *Methodist Union Catalog* testify to Ken's dedication as a bibliographer of Methodism and to his prowess as an editor. My task in the *Festschrift* was to prepare this preface and the camera-ready copy to produce the book in hand. This has been a learning experience in merging many papers, submitted in various word processing programs, into a single document.

Indeed this is not the first *Festschrift* published by ATLA. In 1980 we published, under the editorial direction of Peter De Klerk and Earle Hilgert, *Essays on Theological Librarianship Presented to Calvin Henry Schmitt*. Cal Schmitt had served as librarian of McCormick Theological Seminary from 1940–1980 and as General Director of Jesuit-Krauss-McCormick Library from 1975 until his retirement in 1980. He also served as chair of the ATLA Board of Indexing for twenty years (1959–1979). The Schmitt *Festschrift* contained not only personal tributes to Cal from his colleagues, but it also dealt with the role of theological librarians and libraries in the educational process, the importance of collection development, the role of bibliography and bibliographical control of monograph and periodical literature, and the place of rare books in denominational libraries. One essay, that proved to be the precursor of the ATLA Monograph Preservation Program was titled, "An Analysis of Paper Stability and Circulation Patterns of the Monographic Collection of Speer Library, Princeton Theological Seminary." The author of this essay—Louis Charles Willard—is the only person to have contributed to both *Festschriften* published to date by ATLA .

As *Festschriften* are published, their usefulness for readers is enhanced by author and subject access provided by indexing services. In the early 1970s many voices in ATLA were urging the then Board of Indexing to do two things: apply computer technologies to the production of *Religion Index One: Periodicals* (previously, *Index to Periodical Literature in Religion*) and to undertake a new index to provide access to collected works, that is, essay literature, conferences, congresses, and *Festschriften*. (I am certain that the essays in this *Festschrift* will appear in the 1996 volume of *Religion Index Two*, thus bringing the task of original and secondary publication full circle.) Historically, the bibliographic service side of the ATLA has been well-served. First, in response to these members concerns, the then Board of Indexing and G. Fay Dickerson, general editor of the Religion Indexes for more than twenty-five years, issued the 1975-1976 volume of the *Index to Periodical Literature in Religion* as the first computer compiled and photocomposed ATLA publication, and soon thereafter the first volume of *Religion Index Two: Multi-Author Work*, popularly known to theological librarians as RIT appeared. Second, by popular demand, indexing coverage of journal and essay literature in RIO and RIT, respectively, has steadily increased and been augmented since the early 1980s. Third, and in keeping with the prevailing technologies, since 1993 all of the Religion Indexes, comprising the ATLA Religion Database from 1949 to current, have been available on a single CD-ROM.

RIT actually had its origins from several sources. It was preceded by two independent efforts within ATLA. John Sayre and Roberta Hamburger compiled and published an *Index to Festschriften* (Enid, Oklahoma: Haymaker Press 1970, and in 1973). Concurrently, Elmer and Betty O'Brien compiled a substantial index to *Festschriften* contained in journal issues from 1960-1969, which was published in 1980 by ATLA as *Religion Index Two: Festschriften, 1960-1969*. Elmer and Betty O'Brien have over many years contributed other important publications to the field. Under a grant from the United Methodist Board of Higher Education and Ministry, Elmer, with Betty's assistance, produced and ATLA published, the two volume *Methodist Reviews Index* (volume 1: Periodical Articles [1989]; and volume 2: Book Review Index [1991]), which provided author/editor, title, and subject heading access to five Methodist journals from 1818 through 1985. In addition, Betty served as editor of the *ATLA Proceedings* from 1981 to 1991, providing in the 1986 issue an invaluable comprehensive index to the ATLA *Proceedings* from 1947 through 1986.

In preparing this preface I am struck by the paucity of journal and monograph literature on North American theological libraries and librarianship from the 1940s through the 1990s. On the other hand, since the 1960s many of our members have well documented the history of ATLA, a number of its member libraries and collections, as well as the theory and practice of theological librarianship in their masters papers and doctoral dissertations. Beyond these graduate papers or dissertations, most of the source literature on theological libraries and librarianship is contained within the ATLA *Proceedings*, or is scattered throughout journal literature in library/information science or religion. Indeed, our long-standing partner in theological education, the Association of Theological Schools in the United States and Canada (ATS), has supported our professional concerns by assisting us with obtaining grants and by devoting several issues of *Theological Education* to the interests of theological libraries and librarianship.

The theme of the Autumn 1969 issue of *Theological Education* was "Theological Libraries: Assets or Liabilities." Although published more than twenty-five years ago, its topics have a contemporary ring for the status of the profession today: the cultural context for theological education and the role of the theological librarian in the educational process (reflect on the 1993-1995 ATLA conference program segments dealing with the revised ATS accrediting standards, which will be voted on in June 1996); the implications of the early stages of newer technologies and their impact on the management of theological libraries (then referred to as systems analysis); the importance of cooperative resource sharing (then known as "geographic proximity clustering" with all of its institutional impediments making it, as Newland Smith observes in his essay, a noble but elusive goal of the participants; today resource sharing and cooperation have been given new life and meaning with the application of the new technologies to the Internet); and, finally, a host of perennial library issues, such as bibliographic control, library buildings, and economic support for libraries. Despite the persistence of these issues faced by theological librarians, we can celebrate the major advances that inclusiveness of race and gender has brought to our profession, the seminaries, and theological education in the past twenty-five years. Thus, some of the language contained in the editor's introductory remarks to this special issue are now inappropriate, such as:

> Theological educators are becoming polarized in their response to the role of the library in educating men for ministry. Some are still struggling to make the library the center of the educational endeavor. Their goal is to achieve or maintain the high academic standard long considered requisite to a learned ministry. Theological research remains their watchword. Others increasingly question the possibility of training men for ministry in a period of massive change primarily through lectures and library research.[2]

Ten years prior to these essays—and toward the end of ATLA's first fifteen years—its first generation of founders and leaders took stock of theological librarianship on the North American continent. In 1960 a special issue of *Library Trends* titled, "Current Trends in Theological Libraries,"[3] appeared under the editorship of Niels Sonne, Librarian of General Theological Seminary (NY). The list of contributors reads like a who's who to the formative years of ATLA: Robert Beach (Union Theological Seminary, NY), John Harrington (Archbishop Corrigan Memorial Library, St. Joseph's Seminary, NY), I. Edward Kiev (Hebrew Union College, Jewish Institute of Religion Library), Frank Price (Mission Research Library, NY), Kenneth Gapp (Princeton Theological Seminary), Edgar Krentz (Concordia Seminary, St. Louis, MO), Roscoe Pierson (College of the Bible, now Lexington Theological Seminary), Jules Moreau (Seabury-Western Theological Seminary), Ernest Schwiebert (Foundation for Reformation Research), Ruth Eisenhart (Union Theological Seminary, NY), Connolly Gamble, Jr. (Union Theological Seminary, Richmond, VA), and Decherd Turner, Jr. (Bridwell Library, Southern Methodist University).

One may find many similarities in the content of "Current Trends in Theological Libraries" and this anniversary *Festschrift*. In the earlier work, three essays discuss the unique characteristics of theological libraries that serve Protestant, Catholic, and Jewish seminaries. Kenneth Gapp documents ATLA's formative years, initial publications, and the founding of the index and preservation programs. Other articles explore the roles and importance of monograph and periodical collections, bibliographical control and classification of theological literature, microfilming and preservation, and the seminary library's role in the continuing education of ministers.

Decherd Turner, charged by the editor with summarizing the thirteen essays, made several timely observations about their content.

> Theological libraries are indelibly tied to theological education. Analysis and judgment in every paper in this issue springs from the ever-present question: "What is the content, structure, and purpose of theological education?" So sensitive to this foundation have been the contributors that no portion of the picture could be developed without some expression concerning the nature of theological education.[4]

Turner continues:

> The theological librarian works within the context of an historic spread of materials of incredible depth and breath. . . . The extensive literature of theology makes far more fundamental an expertise in subject matter than in library science, although theological librarians have both taken from and given to the central common core of experience known as library science.[5]

As theological librarianship moves toward the twenty-first century it is being challenged by the newer technologies and their influence on educational theory and context to reinvent its long-standing role as keeper and interpreter of the tradition and its *corpus*.

In the early 1980s ATS again expressed its commitment to improving the place and role of theological libraries and librarians in the educational process. ATS obtained a Lilly Foundation grant and engaged our colleague Stephen Peterson (Yale Divinity School Library) to reassess the role of libraries in theological education. Published as a special supplement to *Theological Education*, Peterson's, "Theological Libraries for the Twenty-First Century: Project 2000 Final Report,"[6] was widely circulated to theological librarians and faculties. The Peterson report remains insightful and contains a number of timely recommendations for the transformation of theological libraries as well as fostering a renewed relationship between ATLA and ATS.

At the conclusion of the report, a joint ATS and ATLA committee was appointed to implement various recommendations in the Project 2000 report. Unfortunately, the committee's work remained obscure to most of the Association and its final report was not as widely distributed as was the Project 2000 report, but included in Part 6 of the ATS *Bulletin*. Peterson provided a timely update to his Project 2000 report with a somewhat tongue-in-cheek title: "The More Things Change—the More Things Change: Theological Libraries in the 1990s."[7] As members are faced with many of the forces and changes identified by Peterson, they would be well served by revisiting the observations and recommendations contained in the two reports and his follow up article.

The essays included in this 1996 ATLA *Festschrift* are organized under three sections: the history of ATLA and its programs and services; the application of information theory to the development of bibliographies, reference tools, acquisition and organization of collections, and the management of archives; and the theory and practice of theological librarians and the role of theological libraries in theological education. The first and last essays are written by senior members of the Association. Who better than Elmer and Betty O'Brien to provide us with an opening essay bringing forward from the 1960 Gapp article our progress as an Association at its fiftieth anniversary? Who better to bring to conclusion the *Festschrift* than Louis Charles Willard, who continues with his article to demonstrate his energy, ideas, vision, and leadership for improving the profession and preserving its heritage?

Between these first and last essays are sixteen additional essays that testify to the diverse interest within the profession and our libraries. Together they portray who we are and what we have been about in practicing our profession. The Bollier, Chace, and Stuehrenberg articles document ATLA's historic and contemporary programs and our efforts in the areas of internationalization, preservation, and collection development. Harking back to similar essays in the "Current Trends in Theological Libraries," the Krieger and Derrenbacker articles update the growth of the richness and diversity within the membership.

The importance of the acquisition of special collections and the organization of theological collections are represented in the common thread of the Burke Library of the Union Theological Seminary (NY), as Milton Gatch describes how Union acquired the library of Leander van Ess and Richard Spoor assesses Julia Pettee's contribution to the organization and classification of the Union collection. Brian Carter, in turn, makes a number of critical observations on the impact of changing collection development policies, fiscal resources, and the influence of the "virtual library" for the acquisition of special collections by libraries since 1971. Martha Lund Smalley stresses enhancing the value and usefulness of denominational archival and manuscript collections by attending to their organization, documentation, and conservation.

The articles by Schrodt, Keck, and Crocco revisit the contemporary role and perceptions of the theological librarian within the theological education process and seminary. The Graham and Choquett articles strengthen our perceptions about the continuous challenge for developing bibliographies and reference tools that respond to both the traditional and contemporary needs of scholars and students. James Pakala's article, based on his 1995 survey of technologies extant in member libraries, ably benchmarks the level and kinds of automated computer systems found within our member libraries. It is regrettable that more contributions on the impact of newer technologies on our libraries and theological education were not submitted for inclusion in this volume.

Finally, I owe a debt of gratitude to all of the authors for their high quality contributions. I need to thank my colleague at ATLA, Don Haymes, for his suggestions regarding layout, his careful editorial eye, and for reading this preface, which has also benefited from his suggestions. I also want to thank my colleague John Bollier for his support during this project and his suggestions on the preface. Thanks to Judy Knop for preparing ATLA CIP information for all who are eager to get this book into circulation. Thanks also to Karen Anderson for assisting with the cover design. I appreciate Pat Graham's ability to chair the editorial committee, to handle numerous administrative details, and to deliver the *Festschrift* on time. For the time and contributions made to each piece by the coeditors, Valerie Hotchkiss and Kenneth Rowe, many thanks. Together, the labors of editors and contributors have produced for the Association an excellent appraisal of its first fifty years.

Endnotes

1. David Himrod (Secretary), "Publication Section [Report]," *Summary of Proceedings* 47 (1993): 94-95.
2. "Editorial Introduction," *Theological Education* 6 (Autumn 1969): 5.
3. Niels H. Sonne (ed.), "Current Trends in Theological Libraries," *Library Trends* 9 (October 1960).
4. Decherd Turner, Jr., "Summary," *Library Trends* 9 (October 1960): 281.
5. Ibid, 282.
6. Stephen L. Peterson, "Theological Libraries for the Twenty-First Century: Project 2000 Final Report," *Theological Education* 20:3 (Suppl. 1984).
7. Stephen L. Peterson, "The More Things Change—The More Things Change: Theological Libraries in the 19990s," *Theological Education* 26 (Spring 1990).

THE DEVELOPMENT OF THE AMERICAN THEOLOGICAL LIBRARY ASSOCIATION

From Volunteerism to Corporate Professionalism: A Historical Sketch of the American Theological Library Association

Elmer J. O'Brien and Betty A. O'Brien

Background and Beginnings[1]

Education for Christian ministry in North America, particularly its contemporary form as expressed in the formation of theological seminaries, is a relatively recent development dating back no earlier than 1784.[2] It was not until the mid-nineteenth century, however, that an appreciable number of graduate professional schools were established to train clergy. Their establishment was a significant development as it represented a developing professional status for ordained ministry in America. Theological libraries, in nascent form, emerged with the establishment of theological seminaries. As Glenn T. Miller notes:

> In the place of the gentleman scholar, who worked long hours in his garret and invested his meager finances in a private library, the seminary offered substantial facilities. Although seminary libraries were small, they were much larger than a private individual could collect. Moreover, the better seminaries purchased significant libraries in Europe that bolstered their collections.[3]

It is well to remember, however, that the seminary library of today with its own quarters and trained staff is very recent. Even Yale Divinity School Library was not organized in its present form until 1932, as the theological holdings were, prior to that time, a part of Yale University's Sterling Memorial Library.[4]

Early in the nineteenth century voluntary associations such as the American Tract Society and the American Sunday School Union developed the mass production and distribution of literature to an expanding nation. An important role in the distribution of these materials was played by itinerant circuit riders, who supplemented the numbers of pastors trained by the seminaries. (Before the Civil War many clergy were trained by an apprentice system, augmented by reading and examinations; rapid development of graduate professional theological schools occurred in the second half of the nineteenth century.) All of this underscores the place that books and reading have always enjoyed as an integral component of ministry and church life in North America.

Theological schools once established were slow to set standards, concentrating instead on the maintenance of particular confessional traditions. It was not until 1918 that theological seminaries formed a national organization, the Conference of Theological Seminaries and Colleges of the United States and Canada, reorganized in 1936 as the American Association of Theological Schools (AATS).[5] It was this body, known today as the Association of Theological Schools in the United States and Canada (ATS), that sponsored the organization of the American Theological Library Association (ATLA).

In 1934 Mark A. May, Professor of Educational Psychology at Yale University, and colleagues issued a report on theological education, concerned that the library was not playing the role in theological education that was needed. Raymond P. Morris of the Yale Divinity Library wrote the section on libraries and offered six recommendations as standards for theological libraries.[6] Two decades later, the Niebuhr-Williams study of 1956-1957, gave considerable attention to the library, including a chapter on "Theological Teaching in Classroom, Field and Library." It stressed the importance of the library and the librarian fulfilling a teaching function.[7] These studies stimulated AATS and seminary communities to think constructively about and lend support to the development of standards for the theological library.

4

The earliest efforts to organize theological librarians centered in the American Library Association (ALA).[8] As early as 1884 Ernest Cushing Richardson, assistant librarian at Hartford Theological Seminary, was ALA Reporter representing theological libraries.[9] In 1916, the Round Table for Theological Libraries was founded when representatives from twenty-one libraries met. This group, which changed its name to the ALA Religious Books Round Table, continued to meet over many years.

Immediately following World War II, interest in convening a meeting of theological librarians led AATS to authorize the first national conference of seminary librarians. It issued a call for a meeting of the librarians of 110 member institutions and appointed a committee to prepare a program and convene the conference. The 1946 AATS biennial also voted to adopt as their primary objective, during the biennium 1948-1950, the study of theological libraries.

The Convening Committee planned the first conference via correspondence, exchanging more than 650 communications over a six-month period. The conference met June 23-24, 1947, at Louisville Presbyterian Seminary with fifty librarians, one president, and one dean in attendance. Ernest White was the host librarian. Committees met "and business sessions were held, so that on the afternoon of the second day," L. R. Elliott noted, "a permanent organization was effected by adopting a name, tentative constitution, and a slate of officers with an executive committee."[10] The group of librarians came together as strangers but over the brief two days together, respect and appreciation for one another grew and they departed as friends. That spirit of mutual association, sharing, and fellowship engendered at the beginning remains, fifty year later, one of the attractive and enduring characteristics of the Association. It had taken thirty years of dreaming, anticipation, and effort to realize the establishment of a theological library association.

The Formative Years

The librarians who met at Louisville faced problems that were formidable and complex. They represented institutions with very limited resources. The Constitution of the Association specified that one purpose of the group was "to study the distinctive problems of theological seminary libraries."[11] The members immediately set about identifying their concerns and appointed committees to study them. Through focused effort new opportunities for cooperation, hitherto unknown, presented themselves.

Several problems emerged immediately. The recruitment and training of personnel, for example, was particularly difficult, since the seminaries had little salary or status to encourage potential recruits to undertake a long and expensive process of education. It was not until 1959 that a grant of $9,000 was received from the Lilly Foundation for fellowships and scholarships to assist persons seeking training in theological librarianship.

The lack of adequate indexing for religious periodical literature had surfaced as early as 1938 at the ALA Religious Books Round Table. A Committee on Religious Periodical Indexing was appointed in 1947, and by 1952 the committee had devised a cooperative effort whereby twenty libraries would do the indexing. One year later, Stillson Judah, editor of the *Index to Religious Periodical Literature (IRPL)*, reported that the first volume was nearing completion. It included thirty-one titles covering the years 1949-1952. He and Leslie Joan Ziegler "worked day and night averaging about four or five hours sleep for a number of weeks to complete all the necessary proof reading and often trouble shooting ahead of the typists . . . in time to deliver copy to a printer with cheap prices before the printer went out of business!"[12] It would be 1956 before sufficient funding was secured to ensure the stability and future of this undertaking.

Partially because of a lack of standards there was concern about the three classification systems in general use among member libraries: Dewey Decimal, Library of Congress, and the Union Theological Seminary (New York). This led, by 1951, to the appointment of a Committee on Cataloging and Classification.

AATS had encouraged the organization of ATLA, in part, to improve its accrediting process. A Joint Committee of the two associations worked for two years, 1950-1952, drafting the revised accreditation standards adopted by AATS in 1952.[13] The new standards shifted the emphasis on adequacy away from quantitative measurement to a focus on the educational process. Following the adoption of the standards, ATLA developed (at the request of AATS) a syllabus of questions and checklists of library holdings for the use of accrediting teams.

Based on presentations at the 1949 annual conference, which noted (among other things) the value of microforms for obtaining out-of-print publications, the ATLA appointed a Committee on Microphotography.[14] Not all the members of ATLA were initially convinced that micrographic publication in theology was feasible. After the successful publication of a "Microcard Theological Studies" series and other titles, however, the Board of Microtext was organized in 1957. The result was a greatly expanded program of microtext publications in the following years.

The funding of the Association and of its projects was a pervasive problem. The Executive Committee debated raising dues, appointed a Finance Committee, and turned down good project proposals for lack of funds. Since the libraries of ATLA were minimally funded and since the Association had little opportunity to generate capital resources, it required some years before ATLA would succeed in securing external funding to augment its limited resources.

Apart from these problems, the Association achieved some notable successes during its formative years. One of these was in the field of publication. The *Summary of Proceedings*, initiated by Secretary Robert F. Beach and issued as a byproduct of the annual conference, continues to the present. In 1950 *A Bibliography of Post-Graduate Master's Theses in Religion* was issued under the leadership of Niels H. Sonne. At the 1953 annual conference, the Association voted to publish a newsletter, and Donn Michael Farris was appointed to serve as editor for one year. Under his capable direction the *Newsletter* met an enthusiastic reception, and Farris continued as editor an additional thirty-nine years!

The annual conference programs were a success from the beginning. A series of bibliographical-historical papers were offered at each conference over many years, as were papers on the literature of denominations and religious movements. Other standard components of the conferences have included worship services, committee reports, round tables, business sessions, and denominational caucuses. This structure has been modified considerably over these fifty years, but the basic outline of organization is recognizable even today. The periodical exchange program, begun in 1948, has operated efficiently and been highly successful in its efforts to move duplicate periodical issues from one library to fill the gaps in another library's holdings. The Committee on Library Buildings and Equipment operated informally as a consultative service from 1948-1969.

During its formative years the Association, while evolving as a professional organization in its own right, maintained close ties with AATS, the parent organization. It met jointly with AATS six times over the first eleven years. Also, over many years ATLA maintained cordial relationships with and was a member of ALA.

The organization of ATLA met a need whose time had arrived. Within two years of its founding, seventy-six percent of seminary libraries affiliated with the AATS had joined, and a united attack on theological library problems had begun.[15] In the first history of ATLA (1961), Marcia Lee Tuttle concluded that the Association "is fulfilling the objectives stated in the Constitution by means of its publications, its committee activity, and indeed, through its very existence."[16]

Growing and Maturing Years

The beginning and formative years of the Association, characterized by idealistic visions and volunteer service on the part of members, laid the foundation for substantial gains and fledgling progress during the first ten years. However, idealism, heroic effort, and muscular volunteerism proved inadequate to such challenges as preserving theological materials and bringing theological literature under bibliographic control. Realizing that the future of the periodical index and the microphotography program would depend upon subsidization from external sources, a Committee on Financial Assistance from Foundations, chaired by Robert Beach, was appointed. In December 1956 ATLA received a grant of $110,000 from the Sealantic Fund, Inc. to support the two programs: $80,000 for microtext and $30,000 for indexing. L. R. Elliott, first ATLA President, viewed this as a major achievement: "The approval in many ways of the American Association of Theological Schools and the recent grant of the Sealantic Fund mean that we have passed the experimental stage. We are now accepted within the community of American Protestant theological institutions, as well as abroad."[17]

The Board of Microtext was organized in 1957 in conformity with the structure proposed in the Sealantic grant request. Raymond P. Morris was appointed chair of the Board and, in effect, became its chief operation officer with his wife, Jean, as volunteer office staff. The microtext program began modestly with six serial titles filmed in 1958. By 1965, 150,000 linear feet of microfilm had been produced, utilizing the facilities at the University of Chicago Department of Photoduplication under the direction of Cosby Brinkley. Both Jean Morris and Brinkley were recognized for their generous services to the program with the bestowal of honorary memberships in 1969 and 1972, respectively.

The Board on Religious Periodical Index, like the Board of Microtext, was organized in 1957. Jannette E. Newhall was appointed chair of the new board, and Lucy W. Markley was employed as editor. In 1960 Calvin Schmitt was appointed chair of the board, and G. Fay Dickerson was employed as a full-time indexer and office manager. When Markley resigned in 1959, members of the Index Board assumed editorial oversight of the Index, a pattern that continued until 1965, when Dickerson was appointed editor. The growth of the indexing program was steady and incremental. By 1969 the Board could report the accumulation of financial reserves and the successful publication of *IRPL* volume eight (1967-1968).

The recruitment and education of persons for theological librarianship continued to concern the association in the late 1950s and through the 1960s. In 1959 the Committee on Financial Assistance from Foundations announced a grant of $9,000 from the Lilly Foundation to improve the educational qualifications of theological librarians. By 1960 the Lilly Endowment awarded a three year extension of the grant at $27,000. Similar extensions in 1964, 1966, and 1968 brought funding for the scholarship program to a total of $108,000. In July 1966 a grant of $35,000 was received from the Sealantic Fund, "designated to improve the professional and academic qualifications of Head Librarians."[18] These efforts of recruitment and training were successful and witnessed the presence of a "new breed" of librarians trained with managerial, library science, and theological skills. By the 1970s the older pattern of a faculty member, without library training, functioning as librarian of a staff with library science training but little or no theological training had been displaced by staffs possessing better and more adequate qualifications.

One of the unmistakable indications of ATLA's maturation was the receipt, in 1961, of an $875,000 grant from the Sealantic Fund to support the Library Development Program. The primary objective of the grant was to increase book purchases, thereby strengthening the book collections of the libraries. Each institution was challenged to match dollar-for-dollar grants up to a maximum of $3,000 per year for three years. Raymond P. Morris, as chair of the program, administered the grant. By the third year of the program all eighty-five eligible AATS institutions participated either fully or in part. In the initial three years of the program, library expenditures at these schools rose from $2,800,000 to over $3,877,000.[19] In consequence of this strong response, the Sealantic Fund extended the program two years with additional funding of $436,750.

The Sealantic and Lilly grants, while enormously beneficial to member institutions, did nothing to provide for the Association's general expenses. There was strong resistance to increasing dues either for institutions or individuals. Apparently it was felt that if funds were needed for projects they could best be secured from external sources. The Association relied on income from book exhibits at the annual conferences to augment the general fund. Alec R. Allenson and his son, Robert, ran an exhibit for many years. In 1962 receipts from these annual exhibits amounted to $1,068. Receipts from dues, by comparison, were $1,622.[20]

A concern about securing out-of-print books led ATLA to seek ways of reprinting scarce titles. In 1957 it worked through the ALA Committee on Reprinting, but in 1961 ATLA established its own program, funded by a grant of $1,800 received from John Workman of Delaware, OH. Over a period of six years the Committee on Reprinting issued fourteen works and ended the program with a balance of some $3,000.[21]

From its inception ATLA needed to gather basic data about its institutional members and to help meet this need it established a Committee on Statistical Records, which issued its first report in 1962. The first compilation and summary of ATLA library statistics, a feature that has appeared in the *Summary of Proceedings* each year since, appears in the 1965 issue.

One of the chief strengths each library brought to the Association was its denominational affiliation. At the early annual conferences at least one major bibliographic paper was devoted to the resources of a particular denomination or religious movement. This tradition continued for many years and remains a part of each conference. Denominational groups met informally in the early years, but by 1966 a listing of denominational group meetings appeared in the *Summary of Proceedings* as part of the annual conference program. Until the late 1960s ATLA remained a predominantly Protestant organization. In 1964 an Ecumenical Periodical Exchange was begun, which included fifteen Roman Catholic and twenty-one ATLA libraries. By 1970 Catholic seminary librarians had joined the Association, and that same year ATLA Index representatives met with the *Catholic Periodical and Literature Index* Committee in a first conversation to explore feasible ways of cooperation.

Relationships with AATS remained cooperative, and representatives from ATLA participated in drafting a set of new library accrediting standards, which were adopted in 1958. Closing out the decade of the 1960s the Association appointed a Committee on Appraisal "to study the projects of ATLA and determine the present and future needs of theological librarianship."[22] The committee issued a set of recommendations that were incorporated into a new constitution adopted in 1970: a provision for relationship to other associations; an expansion of membership beyond AATS institutions to include accredited institutions with post-graduate theological programs; creation of the office of Executive Director; a provision for chapters of the Association; and clarification of committee structure. Revised bylaws were adopted in 1971.

Years of Unrest and Change

A series of far reaching social, ecclesiastical, educational, and technological developments during the late 1960s and the 1970s affected all institutions of higher learning. Theological schools were not immune from the essential changes that these developments prompted. The Civil Rights Movement and the Vietnam War challenged the social conscience of the United States. Vatican Council II (1962-1965) inaugurated a new era of relations between Roman Catholics and other Christians. The women's liberation movement made a significant impact on the churches and on theological education. In 1972 there were 3,358 women enrolled in all degree programs of theological schools in the United States and Canada. By 1983 this number had increased to 13,451.[23] This challenged educators to rethink gender roles and the meaning of human sexuality, the use of inclusive language, and the importance of social justice. Education for all professions came under scrutiny and began to change. Students demanded training that would involve them in the actual work of ministry. Denominational bodies began formulating continuing education requirements for clergy, prompting alumni/ae to look to their alma maters for post-graduate courses and programs. One response of seminaries was to begin offering the Doctor of Ministry (D.Min.) degree. There was also a strong movement toward consolidation and the formation of consortia. AATS became pro-active, encouraging this development out of a belief that adequate resources and a rational distribution of them was essential to the health of theological education.

Technological change had been introduced in libraries during the 1890s when typewriters and card catalog 3x5 cards came into use. Following World War II, microfilm was accepted as a feasible and economic means of storing texts. The photocopy machine became a standard piece of reproduction equipment in most libraries by the mid-1960s. University and large public libraries began experimenting with the use of computers in the early 1960s, but it was not until the next decade that automation became financially feasible for theological libraries.[24]

Two developments in relation to automation, occurring almost simultaneously, made it possible for libraries to make use of this new electronic technology. The first came in 1969 with the development of the machine readable bibliographic or MARC record by the Library of Congress. The second was the founding in 1971 of OCLC, a centralized library network accessible from remote locations via terminals, which was successful in making automation feasible for all types and sizes of libraries.

By 1975 many ATLA libraries were automating their cataloging operations, and the annual conference that year featured automation as its theme. During this period ATLA was also moving toward the automation of its indexing services. Richard H. Lineback, founder and editor of *Philosopher's Index*, wrote and tested the programs that were used to produce the first two semi-annuals of *IRPL* for volume 12 (1975-1976) and subsequent volumes.

The convergence of all these social, ecclesiastical, educational, and technological changes in the late 1960s and the 1970s created a pervasive sense of uneasiness in academia. One symptom of the unease was the tendency of institutions and organizations to structure themselves to work through ad hoc groups. ATLA was not immune from this institutional configuration, appointing a number of ad hoc groups in the 1970s. Since the future appeared to be uncertain, a tentativeness seemed appropriate.

During the period 1970-1983, ATLA struggled to initiate new strategies and programs, as well as to engage in strategic planning and restructuring. A 1972 Task Force on Strategy for Seminary Libraries and Learning Materials Centers worked hard to frame an ambitious two-year program addressing a wide range of educational concerns. In 1976 and 1977 an Ad Hoc Committee on ATLA Needs was appointed "to stimulate and collect the thinking of ATLA on its needs and to encourage the appropriate committees and agencies of the ATLA to seek solutions and undertake projects that have grown out of this thinking."[25] Program needs, identified by both personal and institutional members, clustered around fund raising, collection development, instructional materials, and descriptive lists of archival materials in theological libraries.

In 1970 AATS embarked on drafting the new set of standards for accreditation that were adopted in 1972. While individual libraries were consulted by the Revision of Standards Committee, there was no direct consultative process established with ATLA. Unhappiness with this situation prompted ATLA to appoint a Committee on Standards of Accreditation in 1973. It drafted an adaptation of the "Joint Statement on Faculty Status," issued by the Association of College and Research Libraries and other professional groups, for inclusion in AATS standards. The relationship with AATS on accreditation standards had changed dramatically since 1947.

As part of the 1970 reorganization of ATLA and the adoption of a new constitution and bylaws, the Executive Committee acted to incorporate the Association. President Peter VandenBerge (1972-1973) was the catalyst behind incorporation, convinced that it was essential to the viability and unity of the Association. In 1973 the Association approved both the Certificate of Incorporation and the adoption of revised bylaws.[26] The dust had hardly settled when President John D. Baker-Batsel (1973-1974) proposed a second reorganization with a full-time staff, central office, and a unified publications and communications program.[27] In 1979 the Board of Directors initiated an increase in dues and brought the Boards of Microtext and Periodical Indexing into closer alliance with its oversight of the Association.

Following close on these changes, President Simeon Daly (1978-1981) set out to improve communications in the Association and to identify ways of improving program elements of the annual conference. Task forces in 1980 and 1981 proposed a number of organizational changes: production of the annual *Proceedings* was entrusted to an editor; a Recording Secretary was to record minutes for the Board of Directors and the Association; the office of Executive Secretary was restructured along the lines of an executive director; and a Program Committee was created to plan the annual conference. These changes were put in place by the Board of Directors. Changes in the bylaws provided three-year terms on the Boards of Microtext and Periodical Indexing with no member serving more than two consecutive terms, and a section was added to provide an article on indemnification for any director, officer, employee, or agent of the Association.

The Periodical Indexing program continued to expand during the 1970s. By 1978 subscriptions to *Religion Index One* (*RIO*), previously the *IRPL*, exceeded the 1,000 mark. The computerization of the indexing operations made possible publication in computer-compiled photocomposed format and the creation of new products and projects. In 1976 the first volume of *Religion Index Two: Multi-Author Works* (*RIT*) was issued, followed in 1980 by a volume on *Festschriften, 1960-1969*, a project prepared by Elmer and Betty O'Brien. To fill the gap between the *Festschriften* volume and *RIT*, a retrospective project, *RIT: Multi-Author Works, 1970-1975*, partially supported by a National Endowment for the Humanities (NEH) grant, was completed and published in 1982. Two major personnel changes during this period were the retirements of Calvin H. Schmitt as chair of the Board in 1979 and of G. Fay Dickerson as editor in 1983.

The Board of Microtext was reorganized in 1972 with the retirement of Raymond P. Morris, who had served as chair since 1957. Morris served an additional two years as Executive Secretary, being succeeded as chair by Charles Willard. By 1974 the Board could report that there were approximately fifteen manuscripts, 250 periodicals, and 400 monographs in the microtext program, as well as fifteen continuations. In 1982 an aggressive program of filming added over 100 additional serials to the program. Microfiche production began in 1979 and was destined to become a major production format when, later, the Preservation Program was begun. Also, during this period the Board began contributing bibliographic records for its products to the OCLC database, facilitating the provision of cataloging to member libraries.

The Committee on Publication was appointed in 1968 by President Maria Grossmann as an ad hoc committee to formulate a publication policy for ATLA. Reorganized in 1972 as a standing committee, it launched two scholarly series in religion and theology—a monograph series and a bibliographic series—published by Scarecrow Press with ATLA as the sponsoring body. By 1977 the committee could report that sales on each of the first eight volumes in the monograph series had exceeded 500 copies with some titles selling over 1,000. Kenneth E. Rowe has served as editor for both series from their inception. Since 1972 modest grants-in-aid have been awarded to encourage scholars in the preparation of annotated bibliographies for publication.

In 1974 the Publication Committee investigated the possibility of developing a union list of periodicals maintained by ATLA libraries. This effort resulted in the appointment of an Ad Hoc Committee on Serials Control. The committee developed a well-conceived program and ran a successful pilot project, but it proved impossible to secure the needed funds to develop a permanent program, and the ad hoc committee was disbanded. The concern for a union list was not dropped, however, and was referred to the Bibliographic Systems Committee where John Meuther worked on it for several years.

Other standing committees of the Association provided continuity of purpose and opportunities for members to express their concerns and interests. The Committee on Cataloging and Classification urged member libraries to report their holdings to the *National Union Catalog* and *New Serials Titles*, published a series of newsletters, and represented ATLA interests on the AACR code revision committee. At the 1980 reorganization its concerns were transferred to the Bibliographic Systems Committee. A Reader Services Committee was formed in 1972. One of its popular projects was the operation of an Instruction Clearinghouse, which made materials in bibliographic instruction available for circulation to member libraries. In 1977 the Periodicals Exchange Committee became the Library Materials Exchange Committee, and since 1980 this popular program has been administered by the office of the Executive Secretary. The Membership Committee of many years standing, its responsibilities also transferred to the Executive Secretary's office, recruited members for the Association. This activity has been crucial to the vitality of ATLA, since there is typically an annual turnover of about 150 members.[28] The Library Consultation Program, established in 1971, typically scheduled two to six consultations each year through 1982. Its purpose was "to share the expertise and experience of its membership and other qualified librarians with institutions contemplating improvements in library resources and services." Over many years there has been a concern for archives and archival work among member libraries but no committee or group organized to address this interest. By 1970, however, ATLA appointed a Committee on Archives to care for its own records, established an archives for the Association at the Presbyterian Historical Society in Philadelphia, and conducted an oral history program.

Two significant projects were formed in the period 1978-1983. They were what came to be known as the Preservation Project and Project 2000. The former dealt with developing a program to preserve books printed between 1860 and 1929, while the latter dealt with an analysis of theological libraries and an assessment of their role in theological education. The Ad Hoc Committee on the Preservation of Theological Materials was appointed in 1978 and asked to study the cooperative possibilities for the storage and preservation of theological materials. The initial study and definition of the problem were based on investigations conducted by Andrew Scrimgeour and Charles Willard. The committee recommended a program to film some 259,000 volumes of theological materials known to be in advanced states of deterioration.[29]

Congruent with the 1980 Association reorganization, Leon Pacala, Executive Director of ATS, had been convinced that the 1980s were an opportune time to reassess the role of libraries in theological education. He secured a grant from the Lilly Foundation to conduct a study, appointing Stephen L. Peterson, Yale Divinity School librarian, as director. Peterson conducted hearings with regional groups and consortia within ATLA as well as at the 1982 annual conference, presenting a final report at the 1984 conference just prior to the report's publication.[30] The response of theological schools to Project 2000 was disappointing: only half of ATS member institutions reported general faculty discussion of the report. The document itself, however, remains provocative and is often cited in library reports and discussions.

Through the years ATLA has maintained relationships with a number of groups sharing similar interests: ALA; the United States Book Exchange, later named the Universal Serials and Book Exchange (1964-1977); the Council of National Library Associations, later named the Council of National Library and Information Systems (1951-1995); the American National Standards Committee (ANSI, 1977-); and the Council on the Study of Religion (1972-1979?).

A New Organization: Revised, Enlarged and Improved

While many in ATLA may have thought that reorganization had been completed in 1983, only one year later President Martha Aycock-Sugg appointed an Ad Hoc Committee on Financial Management to recommend an improved financial program. For various reasons the committee moved forward with a study of organizational management concurrent with the development of a financial plan. This strategy ultimately led to major organizational changes in the Association. The committee proposed to use the New York firm of Peat, Marwick, Mitchell and Co. (PMM) as consultants. In March 1985 a grant of $25,000 was received from the Lilly Endowment to underwrite a recommended study. The Board of Directors approved the PMM report in January 1986 and appointed a Financial Management Committee to carry out its recommendations. One of the committee's first actions was to employ Patricia Adamek as

Controller and to create a unified accounting system based on accrual methods, effective with the 1987-1888 budget year. The committee continued its work through 1991, helping to guide the third major reorganization of the Association.

The Interim Board for the Preservation of Theological Monographs, appointed in 1983 to proceed with the preservation of theological monographs, was, together with the Board of Microtext, reorganized in 1984 as a nine member Preservation Board. It was responsible to run two programs: a serials program, much as had existed under Microtext, and a preservation filming program for monographs. The latter effort got underway in September 1985, when Robert P. Markham was hired as full-time Director of Programs with his wife, Letha, as Administrative Assistant. A grant of $100,000, the first of several, was received from the NEH to help underwrite filming costs for 1987.

Over the next six years, 1987-1992, the preservation program received nine grants totaling $1,524,330. Despite this magnanimous support from NEH and other foundations, the program sustained a $263,500 deficit by August 1987, largely because a recession hit theological schools and undermined subscription support from libraries.

In early 1989 the Index Board and the Preservation Board voted to work together under a Joint Executive Committee and with one Executive Director, sharing facilities and staff whenever feasible. Albert Hurd could report two years later, when the Executive Board was terminated, that "Of the 250,000 volumes published between 1850 and 1916 which need preservation, we have done preservation filming of 19,000 titles."[31]

It should be noted that in addition to having received over $1,500,000 in grants to preserve monographic literature, the member libraries of ATLA had, as of April 1995, provided $3,750,000 of subscription income. To these impressive figures should be added four grants totaling $640,486, which the Association received for preserving in microformat 300 carefully selected periodical titles published 1850-1950.[32]

The other program of the Association, indexing, has had an evolutionary, continuous growth. In accordance with the recommendations on administrative reorganization proposed by PMM, the indexing program was restructured to provide for an Executive Director, an editor, and two assistant editors. Albert Hurd was appointed to this new position, effective February 1985.

As for new products and services, the indexing program made signif-

17

icant gains during this period. The retrospective upgrading of the first four volumes of *IRPL* was published under the title *Religion Index One: Periodicals, Volumes 1-4 (1949-1959)*, in 1985, and a new product, *Index to Book Reviews in Religion (IBRR)*, was launched in 1986 with better than anticipated sales. By May 1989 *Religion Index Two: Multi-Author Works, 1976-1980*, a cumulated and augmented edition, was issued. This project was funded with a 1987 NEH grant of $124,749.[33] Also during this time 214,500 records from the database were available online through BRS (Bibliographic Retrieval System). Later, in 1989, the index databases were available through the H. W. Wilson Company's WILSONLINE system.[34] The index program continued to issue *Research in Ministry* (*RIM*), published the *Methodist Reviews Index* on contract from the United Methodist Board of Higher Education and Ministry, issued a thesaurus of index descriptors for use with its indexes, and created subject indexes/bibliographies on special topics.

The year 1990 proved to be pivotal for the two program boards. Having operated since 1988 under a Joint Executive Committee with an Executive Director and a unified staff, members of the Association voted that year for a plan of reorganization that placed both programs directly under the Board of Directors. The merged programs outlined ambitious developments, including the development of the International Christian Literature Documentation Project with a three-year $375,000 Pew Charitable Trust grant; a ten-year project to begin filming denominationally specific materials; and the development of the Religion CD-ROM in cooperation with the H. W. Wilson Company.

The 1990 reorganization of ATLA began with the creation of the Task Force for Strategic Planning appointed by the Board of Directors at its 1988 winter meeting. Its charge was "to engage in the process of looking at the structure of the association and to develop a strategic planning process." After careful study the task force identified several organizational weaknesses: (1) the program boards and the Board of Directors functioned by combining policy formation and management roles; (2) the standing committees were hampered by their inability to enlist active membership support or to effectively address the emerging interests of theological librarianship; and (3) the lack of a chief executive officer (CEO) hampered the organization's work.

Subsequently, the Board of Directors appointed Albert Hurd CEO of ATLA, effective July 1, 1991. With the restructuring, the CEO was now responsible for all staff appointments, which marked a dramatic change from the previous practice of the Board of Directors making all staff appointments. In line with this restructuring the new CEO appointed Patricia Adamek as Director of Finance; John A. Bollier as Director of Development; and began the search for a Director of Member Services. The reorganization of the Association construed the Board of Directors as a policy making body and vested the management of the Association in the CEO and his/her staff. Whereas the Board had operated with ten directors, under the new plan there were twelve. Under the 1990 reorganization the Board elects its own officers for one year terms: a president, vice-president, and secretary. With a single Board of Directors all the programs and activities of ATLA were brought under the authority of a single, governing body. Both of these changes were major developments for the Association and a substantial, essential change from the organizational structure that had prevailed for forty-three years. It is probably fair to say that they moved ATLA toward being more of an economically driven organization, more responsive to market forces. This movement would seem to be consistent with the larger cultural trend toward the increasing commercialization of higher education.

A major change in organization that directly affected individual members was the provision for interest groups, formed around professional concerns, to replace the former committee structure. This change was not adopted without anxiety, since some members feared it was a move to withdraw support from or give less recognition to the work previously done by committees and sections. By 1994, however, there were nine Interest Groups, representing a wide range of interests and professional concerns.

The 1991 annual conference at Toronto was the time when the reorganization of the Association coalesced, and all the pieces of a large effort came together. On Friday morning, June 21, the Strategic Planning Committee report presented the outline of reorganization. The following afternoon the bylaw amendments necessary to effect the changes were approved by the membership.

Over the years ATLA has been fortunate to have members who were able and willing to devote considerable volunteer time and energy to the Association. Officers of the Association have given exemplary service, especially those with extended years of tenure: David Wartluft as Executive Secretary (1971-1981); Robert Olsen, Jr., as Treasurer (1974-

1992); Betty O'Brien as Editor of the *Proceedings* (1981-1991); Joyce Farris as Recording Secretary (1980-1994); and Donn Michael Farris as Editor of the *ATLA Newsletter* (1953-1993). Kenneth Rowe, Martha Aycock-Sugg, Linda Corman, Sarah Miller, Channing Jeschke, Ronald Deering, Dorothy Thomason, and Lucille Hager have served on innumerable task forces, committees, and boards of the Association. Who can forget Rosalyn Lewis and her singular work on bylaws revision? Or Richard Spoor with his inimitable study of ATLA's structure, done with such grace and good humor?

Upon recommendations from the Financial Management Committee, the Executive Director acted to create a Development Program, including the establishment of an endowment fund. One of John A. Bollier's first tasks as Director of Development was to move quickly to institute a three part program that included an Annual Giving Fund to receive gifts for supporting the programs of member services, indexing, and preservation; an Endowment Fund to seek larger gifts; and Grant Support to seek grants from government and private foundations for special projects.

The integrated development plan produced results in the first year with twenty-eight donors giving $3,025 to the annual fund. The endowment fund received its first substantial gift, valued at $10,400 from Jean Kelly Morris, in memory of her late husband, Raymond P. Morris. Three grants totaling $777,986 were received from the Pew Charitable Trust, the Henry Luce Foundation, and the NEH.

Another aspect of the Association's development program has concentrated on the globalization of theological education. In 1993 Bollier visited nine theological schools and three universities in Puerto Rico, Costa Rica, and Jamaica to open conversations on possible cooperative projects. The following year he gave particular attention to the development of international partnerships between ATLA and European indexing agencies and publishers. The Trinity Grants Program of the parish of Trinity Church in New York awarded a grant of $7,700 in April 1995 to fund a partnership between ATLA and the Seminario Biblico Latinoamericano in San José, Costa Rica, for making available resources for theological education using electronic technology.

In 1993 ATS launched a three-year project, ATS Quality and Accreditation Project, "intended to provide the basis for the redevelopment of its accrediting standards." ATS anticipates the adoption of new standards at its 1996 biennial meeting. A Joint ATS-ATLA committee is working on library standards, and Sara Myers serves on the Steering Committee of the project, which is guiding the development of the new standards. From remarks made at the 1995 annual conference, Daniel Aleshire of ATS made it clear that the new standards would place strong emphasis on academic competency of librarians and libraries embracing electronic technology and resources to support curriculum and research.

In addition to ATLA's record of service in theological education, the Association established the first major program to preserve monographic literature in theology and religion, has greatly expanded the scope of its indexing program with the development of new products, and secured major funding to underwrite these efforts through subscription and grant income. In addition to restructuring itself to become more flexible and responsive to both its members and to its external environment, it has launched a development program to undergird its future. The annual conferences have become a significant source of continuing education and professional development. It is now extending its services beyond North America to become a global partner with bibliographic services and theological institutions in South America, Africa, and Europe.
Over the five decades since its founding, ATLA has evolved from being an accrediting appendage of its parent, ATS, to become a professional organization in its own right. Part of this evolution has included the incorporation of the Association to facilitate the production and marketing of its microtext, indexing, preservation, and publishing programs, as well as to provide services to its institutional and personal members. The transition from volunteerism to corporate professionalism has been accomplished in a series of three Association reorganizations. In the beginning, members were intimately involved in the daily operation of the organization, volunteering hundreds of hours annually to its projects, programs, boards, and committees. In more recent years, members have relied upon a staff of professional managers and others to care for the Association's affairs, leaving the members free to turn their attention to professional concerns and concentrate on serving the bibliographic and information needs of the theological community.

1. A valuable resource for the historian of theological education is Heather Day, *Protestant Theological Education in America* (Metuchen, NJ: Scarecrow Press, 1985).

2. New Brunswick Theological Seminary traces its origin to 1784.

3. Glenn T. Miller, "God, Rhetoric, and Logic in Antebellum American Theological Education," in *Communication and Change in American Religious History*, ed. Leonard I. Sweet (Grand Rapids: Eerdmans, 1993), 183. Miller's volume, *Piety and Intellect: The Aims and Purposes of Ante-Bellum Theological Education* (Atlanta: Scholars Press, 1990), is the most recent history of U.S. theological education for the years prior to the Civil War.

4. "YDS Library Adds Volume 400,000," *Spectrum* 16 (November 1995): 16.

5. AATS became, in 1975, the Association of Theological Schools in the United States and Canada (ATS). For a history of AATS in recent years see Jesse H. Ziegler, *ATS Through Two Decades: Reflections on Theological Education, 1960-1980* (Vandalia, OH: Jesse H. Ziegler, 1984). Ziegler was Associate Director, 1959-1966, and Executive Director of ATS, 1966-1980.

6. William Adams Brown, Mark A. May, and Frank Shuttleworth, *The Education of American Ministers* (New York: Institute of Social and Religious Research, 1934), 4 vols. The chapter by Morris, a condensed edition of his Columbia University master's dissertation, "The Libraries of Theological Seminaries," appears in vol. 3: 149-91.

7. See especially H. Richard Niebuhr, Daniel Day Williams, and James M. Gustafson, *The Advancement of Theological Education* (New York: Harper, 1956), 112-44. The other volumes are: H. Richard Niebuhr and Daniel D. Williams, *The Ministry in Historical Perspective* (New York: Harper, 1956); and H. Richard Niebuhr, *The Purpose of the Church and Its Ministry: Reflections on the Aims of Theological Education*, in collaboration with Daniel Day Williams and James M. Gustafson (New York: Harper, 1956).

8. See Marcia Lee Tuttle, "A History of the American Theological Library Association: A Master's Paper Prepared for Librarianship 397" (master's thesis, Emory University, 1961); and Warren Roy Mehl, "The Role of the American Theological Library Association in American Protestant Theological Libraries and Librarianship, 1947-1970" (Ph.D. diss., Indiana University, 1963). A summary about theological libraries in Canada is T. G. Kier, "Theological Libraries in Canada Today," *Summary of Proceedings* 4 (1950): 8-13. Since Roman Catholic participation in ATLA began in the late 1960s, the first twenty-five years of the Association history is predominantly Protestant.

9. Lewis C. Branscomb, *Ernest Cushing Richardson: Research Librarian, Scholar, Theologian, 1860-1939* (Metuchen, NJ: Scarecrow, 1993), 67.

10. *Summary of Proceedings* 5 (1953): 4.

11. *Summary of Proceedings* 1 (1947): 75.

12. J. Stillson Judah, "Bits of Oral History of My Association with the American Theological Library Association," mss. dated April 25, 1994, 4, Archives of the American Theological Library Association, Presbyterian Historical Society, Philadelphia, PA.

13. For ATLA's views on accreditation see Raymond P. Morris, "Standards for Accreditation for the Theological Library," *Summary of Proceedings* 5 (1951): 1-10.

14. See Myron B. Chace's article, "ATLA's Preservation Microfilming Program: Growing Out of Our Work," in the present volume.

15. R. Pierce Beaver, "The Religious Library and the Professor's Attitude," *Special Libraries* 40 (February 1949): 61.

16. Tuttle, "A History of the American Theological Library Association," 83.

17. *Summary of Proceedings* 10 (1956): 105.

18. *Summary of Proceedings* 22 (1968): 18.

19. *Summary of Proceedings* 19 (1965): 52.

20. *Summary of Proceedings* 16 (1962): 40. In recognition for his contributions over the years, Alec Allenson was elected an honorary member in 1971.

21. *Summary of Proceedings* 21 (1967): 61.

22. *Summary of Proceedings* 23 (1969): 9.

23. Marvin J. Taylor (ed.), *Fact Book on Theological Education, 1983-84* (Vandalia, OH: Association of Theological Schools in the United States and Canada, n.d.), 10.

24. Cf. Doralyn J. Hickey's address, "Machines in the Library Age," in *Summary of Proceedings* 16 (1962): 104-15.

25. *Summary of Proceedings* 31 (1977): 45.

26. Transcript of oral history interview with David Wartluft, interview no. 1, ATLA Archives.

27. *Summary of Proceedings* 28 (1974): 101-108.

28. In 1976, for example, ninety-four new members were admitted but there was also a loss of eighty-three members. See *Summary of Proceedings* 30 (1976): 17.

29. *Summary of Proceedings* 35 (1981): 162-206.

30. Stephen L. Peterson, "Theological Libraries for the Twenty-First Century: Project 2000 Final Report," *Theological Education* 20:3 (Suppl. 1984).

31. *Summary of Proceedings* 45 (1991): 27.

32. See reports by John A. Bollier, *Summary of Proceedings* 48 (1994): 165-66; and Albert E. Hurd, *Summary of Proceedings* 46 (1992): 32-40.

33. *Summary of Proceedings* 41 (1987): 37-38.

34. *Summary of Proceedings* 43 (1989): 32-33.

The Internationalization of the
American Theological Library Association

John A. Bollier

The American Theological Library Association (ATLA) was founded in 1947 as an "American" (i.e., "contiguous with the United States of America") professional organization, and today it still numbers its largest constituency in this country. But shortly after its founding, ATLA started reaching out to serve the needs of theological librarians and libraries beyond the boundaries of the United States. This outreach has continued for a half-century, albeit with some interruptions and disappointments, so that today ATLA provides its products and services throughout the world and works with partners in North and South America, Europe, and Africa and will soon open discussions with potential partners in Asia. This paper will describe five distinct stages in the development of ATLA's internationalization and will then examine three significant factors that contributed to this process.

The first step in ATLA's internationalization was the early inclusion of Canadian theological librarians and libraries in its membership. As Canadian members have been such an integral part of ATLA almost since its beginning, this important first step in ATLA's internationalization may easily be overlooked. The first Canadian member of ATLA was Patricia G. Kier, Librarian of Divinity Hall at McGill University, whose name first appears on the membership role in 1950.[1] In the decade following her joining ATLA, three major papers concerning Canadian theological libraries, seminaries, and churches were presented at ATLA annual conferences.[2]

Although Canadians have constituted less than ten per cent of ATLA's membership, they have consistently made significant contributions to the organization. For example, Eric Schultz of Waterloo Lutheran University (name later changed to Wilfrid Laurier University) served two terms as President, 1975-1977; Grant Bracewell of Toronto School of Theology served on the Index Board, 1971-1983 and as its chair, 1979-1983; and Linda Corman of Trinity College has served on the Board of Directors, 1991- , as Vice President, 1993-1995, and as President, 1995-1996. Moreover, Canadian member institutions to date have hosted six of ATLA's fifty annual conferences, including three in Toronto (1959, 1982, 1991), two in Vancouver (1977, 1993), and one in Waterloo (1973). ATLA has refrained from recruiting members outside the United States and Canada in order not to diminish support for other national and regional theological library associations. However, theological librarians and libraries from approximately twenty countries around the world have chosen to become members of ATLA.

The second step in the ATLA's internationalization was its participation with European theological librarians from 1954 through 1961 to establish the ambitious, but short-lived, International Association of Theological Libraries (IATL). One of the chief aims of this organization was to publish an international and interfaith quarterly journal of religious and theological bibliography, for which it anticipated receiving funding from UNESCO. IATL also hoped to become a unit of the International Federation of Library Associations.

At the invitation of the Standing Conference of Theological and Philosophical Libraries of London, ATLA appointed a committee to work with its European counterparts for establishing this new organization. ATLA committee members J. Stillson Judah of the Pacific School of Religion and L. R. Elliott of Southwestern Baptist Theological Seminary attended a meeting of the organizing committee convened by the World Council of Churches in Brussels on September 10, 1955. By 1957, though, it became clear that UNESCO funding would not be forthcoming, and so IATL dropped it plans for a major bibliographic journal in favor of a more modest journal devoted to "bibliographies of significant theological writers or subjects, 1500 to the present."[3] ATLA was opposed to this revised plan, as it considered such a journal unnecessary and also unable to attract financial support.

For the next three years, in 1958, 1959, and 1960, ATLA's committee reported to each ATLA annual conference that the fledgling IATL continued to lack any unified cooperative program or any members beyond the English and American sections. Finally, in 1961 ATLA voted to discontinue its participation in IATL, and thus IATL was no longer viable.

Although IATL had but a brief life span, nevertheless it succeeded in promoting internationalization among theological libraries on both sides of the Atlantic. John V. Howard of New College Edinburgh in an address to ATLA at its 1983 annual conference said that the International Association of Theological Libraries "failed to get the endorsement of UNESCO and died after a few years, but there is now a flourishing international federation of European theological library associations . . . ."[4] He was referring to the Conseil International des Associations de Bibliothèques de Théologie, which today includes theological library associations from Western and Central European countries in its membership.

ATLA's seven years of participation in this failed venture also stimulated considerable international interest and service among many ATLA members. For example, Raymond L. Morris of Yale Divinity Library made a four month trip in 1958 through Southeast Asia under the auspices of the Board of Founders of Nanking Theological Seminary and the Theological Education Fund of the International Missionary Council. In addition to providing consulting services to many theological libraries in Southeast Asia, he conducted a three week workshop at Silliman University in the Philippines for library workers, who came from sixteen schools in eight countries.[5]

Likewise, Jannette Newhall of Boston University School of Theology spent a sabbatical in 1960 in Korea at Yonsei University and Ewha Women's University. Subsequently, both before and after her retirement, she made several other international tours to serve as a consultant for theological libraries. She also wrote a manual for workers in seminary libraries in Africa, Asia, and Latin America.[6] Other prominent ATLA members of that period, such as Ruth Eisenhart, Niels Sonne, Calvin Schmitt, Roscoe Pierson, and Charles Johnson, also accepted special consulting assignments abroad.

This same tradition of international service by ATLA members continues to the present, with scores of members having served or presently serving libraries outside North America, either as short-term consultants or as long-term staff members. The Library of Union Theological Seminary in Virginia also provides an important service to theological libraries abroad that are in need of materials by collecting and shipping books and journals to them.

The third stage in ATLA's internationalization was its participation from 1987 to 1991 in the International Association for Mission Studies' Documentation, Archives and Bibliography project (IAMS-DAB). The aim of this ambitious project was "to coordinate the documentation and research work done on mission studies throughout the world. It plans to develop a common cataloguing standard, and a common set of subject headings (thesaurus), all tailored to an affordable and simple computer system for a small library. A further aim has been to extend the documentation work to areas within the Two-Thirds World that do not currently have projects, using the standard package that IAMS will provide. All data produced would then be exchangeable."[7]

Upon invitation, ATLA sent staff to attend IAMS-DAB planning meetings in 1987 at Paris and in 1990 at Basel. ATLA was also represented at the IAMS conference in 1991 at Honolulu. However, ATLA was never optimistic concerning the success of IAMS-DAB because of the project's over-arching goals, the diverse requirements of its many national and regional constituencies, its meager funding, and its lack of full-time technical or support staff. Nor could ATLA lay aside its work on the Automated Indexing Data Entry (AIDE) system it was developing for the production of the International Christian Literature Documentation Project (ICLDP) and the *Religion Indexes* in order to contribute to a proposed system that had no database, no firm completion date, and little hope of success. Therefore, ATLA found it necessary to withdrew from the IAMS-DAB project.

After several years of delay and disappointment, the IAMS-DAB leadership also became convinced that it could not complete this project. Therefore, in 1991 it turned over the development and distribution rights for the project to the Global Mapping Institute (GMI), a not-for-profit independent mission agency located in Colorado Springs. As of mid-1995, GMI has not announced the release of this projected bibliographic system.

While the IAMS-DAB project did not attain its original goals, it did succeed in stimulating ATLA to consider international outreach once again as an important part of its mission. Through its participation in IAMS-DAB meetings, ATLA recognized the increasing need abroad for its expertise and experience in the use of computer technology to provide wider access to theological literature and documentation. Moreover, through contact with IAMS-DAB, ATLA began developing a world-wide network of scholars, bibliographers, and editors, who could provide invaluable help to ATLA as it began working in an international environment.

The fourth stage in ATLA's internationalization occurred during 1989-1993, when it undertook the International Christian Literature Documentation Project (ICLDP). Funded by a $375,000 grant from the Pew Charitable Trusts, this project's aim was "to index works in North American library collections from non-western countries and non-western cultural groups in western countries, as such literature proves to be germane to research about and documentation of Christian life in those countries and groups."[8]

ICLDP focused its indexing efforts particularly upon publications such as conference proceedings, congresses, collections of essays, working papers of corporate bodies, catechistical collections, and ephemeral materials, such as pamphlets, irregular runs of periodicals, and booklets, which are often gathered together and bound with other like materials, but have no bibliographic details about the separate items. Thus, ICLDP intended to facilitate bibliographic and physical access to resource materials important for theological schools as they were integrating globalization into their curricula.

One of the most challenging components of ICLDP was ATLA's development of indexing software that would enable both ATLA staff in Evanston and participating libraries off-site "to enter data easily, evaluate it, correct it, transfer it to other systems, provide for various output formats (print, digital, and electronic) and distribute it electronically to users in a fashion parallel to the MARC tagged record format." [9] This software, known as AIDE (Automated Indexing Data Entry), was successfully developed for ICLDP and is now also used extensively by ATLA in the production of *Religion Index One: Periodicals* and *Religion Index Two: Multi-Author Works*.

Responding to ATLA's invitation to member libraries to participate in ICLDP were eight libraries, although only two (Yale Divinity Library and Speer Library of Princeton Theological Seminary) used the AIDE software to index retrospective materials: the other six submitted cataloging records produced with their OCLC or RLIN systems for currently acquired materials in scope for ICLDP. Nevertheless, this cooperative effort resulted in the enrichment of the ATLA database with 18,635 bibliographic records of monographs and pamphlets and indexing for 6,774 new essays, contained in 1,843 multi-author works. ATLA published these records in 1993 in two volumes, totaling 1,715 pages. Volume 1 is a subject index and volume 2 is an author/editor and corporate name index, which also provides library location symbols.[10]

Although changing priorities at the Pew Charitable Trusts precluded ATLA's receiving grant support for this project beyond four years, ICLDP certainly moved ATLA further along the path of internationalization. The ICLDP print indexes were widely distributed at a moderate price in western countries and at a deeply discounted price in the non-western world, thanks to the Pew grant underwriting much of the editorial production cost. Thus, ATLA's reputation as an indexer of non-western, as well as western, materials was considerably enhanced throughout the world.

Moreover, from the service of several extremely able missiologists on an ICLDP Advisory Committee, ATLA's network of friends and advisors with international expertise continued to expand. But most significantly, the ICLDP development of the AIDE software and its successful use for indexing, both at ATLA headquarters and at two off-site participating libraries, demonstrated that this software could be used by potential ATLA indexing partners anywhere in the world where PCs operating with DOS were available.

Thus, ATLA was ready to enter the fifth and current stage in its long process of internationalization: the development of global partnerships for the electronic indexing and distribution of bibliographic records to facilitate access to the literature of religion/theology world-wide. The need for such partnerships with ATLA was first expressed in 1987 by the director of the Latin American index, *Bibliografia Teologica Comentada del área iberamericana* (BTC), which is published by the Institutio Superior Evangelico de Estudios Teologicos (ISEDET) in Buenos Aires. At that time he appealed to ATLA for financial and technical assistance to enable BTC to automate its manual production and close its several years lag in publication. However, ATLA had neither the financial resources nor the personnel to respond positively to this request, even though the BTC director persistently renewed his appeal, including one time when he was visiting the ATLA indexing operations in Evanston.

In 1992 ATLA received a grant of $30,000 from the Trinity Grants Program of Trinity Parish in New York for undertaking this project, which is the first of ATLA's international partnerships. Although subsequent personnel changes and financial problems at BTC and ISEDET have delayed its completion, the project is still viable and progressing. Three years later, ATLA received a second grant from the Trinity Grants Program for $7,700 to begin working with another partner, the Library of the Biblical Seminary of Latin America in San José, Costa Rica. ATLA's purpose in this alliance is to assist in the development of a Latin American Theological Information Network (LATIN).

When ATLA was developing its AIDE indexing software in connection with the grant-supported International Christian Literature Documentation Project (ICLDP), it was concurrently developing, with the investment of its own resources, the capacity to produce its electronic database in CD-ROM format. Thus, with its in-house CD-ROM production capacity begun in 1993 and since steadily improved, ATLA is now able to offer CD-ROM production, as well as the AIDE software, to indexing partners world-wide.

In 1996 ATLA plans to bring on-line an ATLA Internet node, hosted at the computer center of a major university. This new capacity will enable ATLA to make available on-line its own database, currently containing more than 870,000 records, as well as the databases of its partners throughout the world. This new capacity will also enable ATLA to implement its plans for an electronic document delivery system.

Currently, ATLA's domestic partners are the Catholic Biblical Association, for producing an *Old Testament Abstracts* CD-ROM, and the Catholic Library Association, for producing a *Catholic Periodical and Literature Index* CD-ROM. Abroad, ATLA is working with the University of South Africa in Pretoria for producing a CD-ROM of the *South African Theological Bibliography*. ATLA is also in the final stages of contract discussion with the Pontifical Biblical Institute in Rome for the electronic production and distribution of the *Elenchus of Biblica*. Moreover, ATLA is continuing it partnership discussions with the University of Tübingen Library for the distribution of the recently automated *Zeitschrifteninhaltsdienst Theologie* on CD-ROM and online.

In ATLA's partnerships, the producers of the databases continue to own the copyright to their data, but they grant to ATLA the rights for producing and distributing their data on CD-ROM and online. The major portion of royalties from the distribution of these materials in electronic formats will go to the database owners, with ATLA receiving a sufficient percentage to cover its costs. Thus, producers of indexing databases in religion/theology need not duplicate ATLA's investment in high cost technology and staff for the electronic distribution of their records but may use ATLA as a vendor for this purpose.

In addition to the partners and potential partners in Latin America, Europe, and the United States already cited, ATLA is in partnership discussions with other libraries, theological faculties, and producers of religion/theology databases in Rome, Basel, Warsaw, Budapest, Bratislava, and Prague. ATLA also expects to open such discussions with the leadership of the *Australasian Religion Index* in the fall of 1995.

This review of ATLA's internationalization reveals that the first two stages of this process (i.e., Canadian membership and participation in the International Association of Theological Libraries) occurred during ATLA's first 15 years (1947-1961) and that the last three stages (i.e., participation in the International Association of Mission Studies' Archives, Documentation and Bibliography Project, undertaking the International Christian Literature Documentation Project, and developing international partnerships) occurred during the last ten years (1987-1996). Between these two periods of international activity, there was a period of twenty-five years (1962-1986) when ATLA had little international engagement.

Three factors can be cited in explanation of the current period of intense international activity: technology, globalization, and the restructuring of ATLA. Ironically, the first factor may also be cited as contributing significantly to ATLA's long period of international disengagement.

Technology in the last decade has provided the universal availability of increasingly powerful computers at decreasing costs and also the rapid advance of global telecommunications. As libraries have widely adopted the new technology and have agreed on international bibliographic standards, they can now transcend national borders and make known their resources world-wide. Because ATLA began adopting this new technology early on and has kept current with it, ATLA in recent years has been able to take a leadership role among theological libraries and religion indexing agencies throughout the world.

On the other hand, technology may also account for ATLA's little progress in internationalization during the 1970s and most of the 1980s.

For during these years ATLA, like many of its member libraries, was so fully engaged with the heavy financial, technical, and administrative demands of adopting the new technology that it had little time or resources for developing international initiatives. However, within the last decade as ATLA has successfully employed the power of technology and is reaping its benefits, ATLA has again renewed its commitment to international outreach.

The second important factor contributing to ATLA's recent international engagement is globalization, as it has been understood both in theological education and in the business community.[11] As American and Canadian theological schools in the 1980s began developing a global dimension to their curricula, ATLA and its member libraries experienced an increasing demand for resources documenting the life and thought of religious communities outside North America. And as the business world began to see globalization as a strategy for economic growth—and even survival—ATLA, as a not-for-profit publisher of religion/theology bibliography, also began to look abroad for strategic partnerships and new markets.

The third factor enabling ATLA to make rapid progress in internationalization in recent years was the thorough restructuring of ATLA's governance, programs, finances, and staff from 1985 to 1991. The catalyst for this restructuring was a Lilly Endowment grant of $25,000 in 1985 to support a thorough financial management study of ATLA by Peat, Marwick, a major accounting and management consulting firm. ATLA's gradual restructuring process consolidated all its operations, which previously had been widely dispersed between such places as Chicago, IL, Princeton, NJ, and St. Meinrad, IN, with all bank accounts in Fort Worth, TX, incorporation in the State of Delaware, and executive responsibility, which was lodged with the president, changing location each year anywhere within the United States or Canada, depending upon the residence of the president for that year. By merging ATLA's two semiautonomous program boards, the Index Board and the Preservation Board, with the Board of Directors, ATLA then had a single Board of Directors, with the power to define the association's mission and to set policy. Moreover, by appointing an executive director/chief executive officer, gathering the dispersed staff together at one headquarters location, adopting a unified budget, and following approved accounting procedures, ATLA was able to use its considerable resources more effectively to make timely decisions required for participating in a global environment and to attract foundation support for many special initiatives.

The internationalization of ATLA during its first half century has produced a record of solid achievement through the dedicated service of its members, officers, and staff. The new era of strategic partnerships that is now dawning offers ATLA considerable opportunities in the next half-century to continue its progress in internationalization and expand its service throughout the world.

Endnotes

1. ATLA, *Summary of Proceedings* 4 (1950): Appendix B.
2. Patricia G. Kier, "Theological Libraries in Canada Today," *Summary of Proceedings* 4 (1950): 8-13; Kenneth H. Cousland, "Church Union in Canada: an Historical and Bibliographical Study," *Summary of Proceedings* 13 (1959): 83-101; A. B. B. Moore, "Theological Education in Canada," *Summary of Proceedings* 13 (1959): 147-51.
3. *Summary of Proceedings* 11 (1957): 49. For ATLA's actions concerning IATL, see also *Summary of Proceedings* 8 (1954): 40-41; 9 (1955): 4-6; 10 (1956): 63-64; 12 (1958): 52; 13 (1959): 25; 14 (1960): 50; 15 (1961): 10.
4. John V. Howard, "British Theological Libraries, 1983," *Summary of Proceedings* 37 (1983): 199.
5. For trip report, see Raymond P. Morris, "The Place of the Library in Christian Theological Education in Southeast Asia," *Summary of Proceedings* 13 (1959): 152-58.
6. Jannette E. Newhall, *A Theological Library Manual* (London: Theological Education Fund, 1970), 161 p.
7. Norman E. Thomas, "Documentation, Archives and Bibliography (DAB) Progress Report," *Mission Studies* 7 (1990): 238.
8. Albert E. Hurd, "Final [ICLDP] Report to Pew Charitable Trusts," August 14, 1993: Appendix B. See also Douglas W. Geyer and Sharon Vlahovich, "Where is It? A New Index to Non-Western Christian Literature," *International Bulletin of Missionary Research* 16 (1992): 110-14.
9. Hurd, "Final Report," 3.
10. *International Christian Literature Documentation Project* (Evanston, IL: ATLA, 1993), 2 vols.

11. See Don S. Browning, "Globalization and the Task of Theological Education," *Theological Education* 23 (1986): 43-59; William E. Lesher, "Globalization and its Significance for Theological Librarians," *Summary of Proceedings* 44 (1990): 137-45; Robert J. Schreiter, "Globalization and Theological Libraries," *Summary of Proceedings* 44 (1990): 146-59; *The Globalization of Theological Education*, ed. Alice Frazer, Robert A. Frazer, and David A. Roozen (Maryknoll, NY: Orbis Books, 1993), 366 p.

From the Outside In: A History of Roman Catholic Participation in the ATLA

Alan D. Krieger

In looking back at the Conference of Theological Librarians held in Louisville, June 23-24, 1947, the meeting that really produced our American Theological Library Association, L. R. Elliott of Southwestern Baptist Theological Seminary noted accurately that it "was the first meeting on a national scale of the librarians of American Protestant theological schools."[1] In the early years, the association saw itself principally as a crucial partner in the mission of Protestant theological education; indeed that first conference was convened under the auspices of the American Association of Theological Schools. Elliott, who would become the ATLA's first president, noted in his "Introductory statement of the convening committee" that "there is a growing recognition . . . of the value of a closer integration of the library and the educational program of the institution,"[2] and it is instructive that even at that first meeting there was a session entitled "Accreditation—what is adequacy?"[3]

This close tie between the genesis of the ATLA and the evolving goals of American Protestant theological education goes far in explaining the virtual absence of Catholic influence in the association's first decade of existence. Until the 1960s, "the Roman Catholic seminaries had looked within their own tradition for approval or disapproval of seminary programs. As long as priests served their own congregations only, there was little need for outside supervision of the institutions that provided their schooling."[4] Thus, without a real incentive to develop standards of quality in conjunction with their Protestant counterparts, Roman Catholic institutions were simply not a part of the ATLA landscape in the fifties. A brief look at association membership figures for the period confirms this. The registration roll at the 1948 conference lists fifty-seven attendees, none from Catholic institutions.[5] By 1949, the association had grown to ninety-two active individual members, thirteen associate members, and seventy-seven institutional members; again, no Catholics.[6]

The first ATLA member from a Catholic school would appear to be Miss Katharine Skinner, from St. Meinrad's Abbey, St. Meinrad, IN. Miss Skinner was an active member from 1953-56, although she apparently attended only the 1953 conference.[7] W. Charles Heiser, S. J., known to many in the association as the longtime editor of the *Theology Digest* "Book Survey," is listed first as an associate member in 1957, and he retained that status for a number of years.[8] Nevertheless even in 1960, the ATLA membership lists reveal only one identifiable Catholic (Paul-Emile Filion, S. J.) among 172 full members and not a single Catholic school in the list of 111 institutional members.[9]

Given the state of Protestant-Catholic theological relations during this period, it is perhaps understandable that references to Catholic theology in the published *Proceedings* were scarce and, where present, not always flattering. One paper presented at the 1958 conference stated that "Roman Catholic and Eastern Orthodox theologians continue to defend their formulas long adopted, while generally ignoring completely the problems posed by historical studies of the Bible and freely invoking their doctrines of absolute authority." The author goes on, however, to grudgingly concede the growing influence of Catholic Thomism at the time.[10] But there was a hint of changes to come the next year: one author praised the role of Roman Catholics in the field of historical liturgics,[11] while Edgar Krentz's "The Literature of the Roman Church and the Protestant Seminary Librarian" represented the first comprehensive treatment of Catholicism offered at an ATLA conference.[12]

Another milestone was reached during the 1961 conference at Wesley Theological Seminary in Washington, D.C., when a major Catholic theologian, Gustave Weigel, S. J., addressed the association,[13] but generally Catholic participation in the ATLA continued to be quite modest during the first half of the decade. In 1965 there were still no full or institutional members who were Catholic, while only twelve of 152 associate members could be identified as such.[14] It was not until 1967 that the association attracted its first Catholic institutional member, St. Vincent College of Latrobe, PA.[15]

But in the next three years the Catholic presence increased dramatically, and there is no doubt that this must be linked with the issue of accreditation. Simeon Daly, O. S. B. of St. Meinrad's, the first Catholic to serve on the association's Board of Directors and a past president of the ATLA, has pointed out that following the reorganization of the Catholic seminary curriculum, which aligned it with the traditional American system (four years of high school, four years of college, four years of theological studies), "more and more Catholic educational leaders and their Bishops became convinced of the importance, value, even necessity of some form of accreditation." Of the various alternatives, such as the establishment of an accrediting body for Catholic seminaries, most chose to petition the American Association of Theological Schools to include Roman Catholic schools of theology. This was not a difficult decision, given that "the ecumenical climate was much improved in the wake of 2nd Vatican Council. Relationships that would have been unthinkable only a few years before were developing all around."[16]

As Roman Catholic schools of theology began to receive AATS accreditation in 1968,[17] Catholic membership in the ATLA also began to increase. This was especially understandable since the Association had continued to stress the importance of its work within the context of theological education. For example, the ATLA Library Development Program, which ran from 1961-1966 and was made possible by grants from the Sealantic Fund, Inc. totaling more than $1,300,000, had as a primary objective an increase in book purchases for participating libraries; each institution was challenged to match, dollar for dollar, up to $3,000 per year. Systematic studies of the library were also encouraged. "This was to include an examination of the relationships between library service and instruction, of instruction and research in professional theological education, and of the objectives of library service in terms of the purpose of the institution."[18] The 1968 conference featured several AATS-ATLA joint sessions, including one with a Catholic speaker; Bernard Cooke of Marquette gave an address entitled "Essentials in the Theological Curriculum." [19]

Thus, as an important partner in the development of resources for theological education, the ATLA began to attract ever larger numbers of

Catholics. Between 1968-1970, the number of Catholic full members rose from three to twelve to fifteen, and Catholic institutional membership increased from three to five and then to ten.[20] The 1970 conference also witnessed the first Roman Catholic denominational meeting; Father John J. Shellem, the librarian at St. Charles Seminary, Philadelphia, convened the session and delivered a paper that evening.[21]

Catholic membership figures continued to climb through the seventies. By 1975, the association included thirty-one such institutional members,[22] and by 1978 the total had reached thirty-four.[23] As to gauging the degree of actual Catholic influence in the life of the Association, a more telling trend was the steady increase in the number of individual Catholics occupying important leadership roles. Daly, after joining the ATLA in 1969, was elected to the Board of Directors in 1973,[24] and he subsequently served two terms as president of the association in 1979 and 1980.[25] Lawrence Hill of St. Vincent College chaired the Periodical Exchange Committee in 1976,[26] and James Caddy of St. Mary Seminary in Cleveland headed the Standards of Accreditation Committee in 1977.[27] By 1979, Jasper Pennington of St. Bernard's Seminary was chairing the Annual Conference Committee, and Henry Bertels handled the same duties for the Library Materials Exchange Committee.[28] This progress was accompanied by an atmosphere of cordiality that Daly has not failed to note. He could not "recall a single incident of prejudice against the Catholics who now began to swell the membership rolls" and affirmed that "the Roman Catholic brethren were fully accepted . . . ."[29]

Throughout the seventies, Catholics and Catholic topics now regularly formed an important part of conference activities. Examples include the 1972 address by Gregrory G. Baum of St. Michael's College, University of Toronto entitled, "The Opening of Theology to the Social Sciences,"[30] and "Information Retrieval in the Field of Bioethics," an address delivered by LeRoy Walters of the Kennedy Institute at Georgetown in 1975.[31] There were two excellent presentations by Catholics in 1978: Norbert F. Gaughan's "Ratio vs. Auctoritas: The Never-ending Issue" and George M. Barringer's "Historia vero testis temporum: A Survey of Manuscript and Archival Collections Relating to American Catholic History in Catholic Colleges and University Libraries."[32] Finally, Colman J. Barry, O. S. B. offered a timely commentary on spiritual renewal during the 1979 conference entitled, "Spiritual Signs of the Times."[33] Clearly, the ecumenical atmosphere fostered by the Second Vatican Council and its aftermath was reflected in the sheer scope of the Catholic impact on the association during this period.

This trend has continued unabated through the eighties and up to the present day. There has been no shortage of Catholic contributions to the intellectual life of the Association over the last fifteen years. Examples range from Mary Farrell Bednowski's "Women in Religious History"[34] and Fr. George Tavard's "The Contemporary Role of Women in the Catholic Church"[35] to Fr. Cyprian J. Lynch's bibliographical essay on Franciscan spirituality[36] and Bertels' response to a seminal essay by Stephen Peterson on collection development in theological libraries.[37] In 1985, John Eagleson of Orbis Books offered a provocative historical overview on the rise of liberation theology.[38] Matthew Fox, Rosemary Radford Ruether, and Charles Curran have all offered presentations to the association in recent years.[39]

Catholics have also continued to contribute to the organizational vitality of the ATLA, both individually and collectively. Daly served as the association's executive secretary from 1985-1990 and worked diligently to issue the *Summary of Proceedings* promptly, maintain accurate membership rolls,[40] and invite ATS schools who were not ATLA members to join the association.[41] After reaching something of a plateau in the eighties, Catholic institutional membership has also picked up again, increasing from thirty-three in 1985 to a remarkable forty-nine (out of 188) in 1994.[42]

The group meetings of Roman Catholic librarians at the annual conferences have also provided a source of important work as well as good fellowship. Since 1984, when denominational meetings began to be regularly summarized in the *Proceedings*, Catholic attendees have ranged from fifteen to twenty-seven and have tackled numerous projects, including the development of guidelines for the classification of materials on canon law and St. Thomas Aquinas, the treatment of liturgical uniform titles, the development of bibliographies to augment the association's monograph preservation program, and the creation of an acquisitions list exchange for interested group members.[43] As one who has been privileged to convene these meetings for the last several years, this writer is confident that Catholic contributions to the ATLA will continue to be vital and dynamic as we enter the next century.

1. *Summary of Proceedings* 2 (1948): 1.
2. *Summary of Proceedings* (1947): 1.
3. Ibid., 21-22.
4. Simeon Daly, *Mission Expanded: Roman Catholic Presence in ATLA* (S. l.: s. n., 1995), 1.
5. *Summary of Proceedings* 2 (1948): Appendix B.
6. *Summary of Proceedings* 3 (1949): Appendix B.
7. See ATLA's *Summary of Proceedings* 7 (1953): 69, 51, C-3, 81.
8. See ATLA's *Summary of Proceedings* 11 (1957): 110 and subsequent member lists.
9. *Summary of Proceedings* 14 (1960): 107-13, 116-19.
10. L. Harold DeWolf, "Trends and Authors in Contemporary Theology," *Summary of Proceedings* 12 (1958): 54, 62.
11. Jules Moreau, "A Serials Program for Theological Libraries: A Plea for More Cooperation in Cooperative Accession," *Summary of Proceedings* 13 (1959): 54.
12. Ibid., 70-82.
13. Gustave Weigel, "When Catholic and Protestant Theologies Meet," *Summary of Proceedings* 15 (1961): 60-66.
14. *Summary of Proceedings* 19 (1965): 115-32.
15. *Summary of Proceedings* 21 (1967): 194.
16. Daly, *Mission Expanded*, 1.
17. See ATLA Past President Channing Jeschke's tribute to Simeon Daly, O. S. B., *Summary of Proceedings* 44 (1990): 39.
18. Raymond P. Morris, "ATLA Library Development Program: A Summary 1961-1966," *Summary of Proceedings* 21 (1967): 127.
19. *Summary of Proceedings* 22 (1968): xi.
20. Compare *Summary of Proceedings* 22 (1968): 125-33, 141-45; 23 (1969): 145-55, 163-67; 24 (1970): 147-57, 166-70.
21. *Summary of Proceedings* 24 (1970): xxi.
22. *Summary of Proceedings* 29 (1975): 197-203.
23. *Summary of Proceedings* 32 (1978): 192-98.
24. *Summary of Proceedings* 27 (1973): vii.
25. *Summary of Proceedings* 33 (1979): ix; 34 (1980): vii.
26. *Summary of Proceedings* 29 (1975): x.
27. *Summary of Proceedings* 30 (1976): x.
28. *Summary of Proceedings* 32 (1978): ii.
29. Daly, *Mission Expanded*, 2-3.
30. *Summary of Proceedings* 26 (1972): 139-44.
31. *Summary of Proceedings* 29 (1975): 151-62.
32. *Summary of Proceedings* 32 (1978): 104-109; 135-51.

33. *Summary of Proceedings* 33 (1979): 121-32.

34. *Summary of Proceedings* 34 (1980): 102-104.

35. *Summary of Proceedings* 43 (1989): 95-103.

36. Cyprian J. Lynch, "The Bibliography of Franciscan Spirituality: A Poor Man's Legacy," *Summary of Proceedings* 36 (1982): 89-108.

37. Henry J. Bertels, "Reflections on 'Collection Development in Theological Libraries: A New Model—A New Hope' by Stephen L. Peterson," *Summary of Proceedings* 35 (1981): 36-38.

38. John Eagleson, "Orbis Books and Liberation Theology," *Summary of Proceedings* 39 (1985): 130-40.

39. See Fox's "Toward a Living Cosmology: From the Quest for the Historical Jesus to the Quest for the Cosmic Christ: A Summary," *Summary of Proceedings* 41 (1987): 170; Ruether's "Feminist Theology in Global Context," *Summary of Proceedings* 44 (1990): 130-36, and Curran's "Toward 2000: Tensions, Perennial and New, Facing the Church," *Summary of Proceedings* 46 (1992): 201-205.

40. *Summary of Proceedings* 44 (1990): 47, 49.

41. *Summary of Proceedings* 41 (1987): 32.

42. *Summary of Proceedings* 39 (1985): 275-81; and 48 (1994): 290-306.

43. See the summaries of Roman Catholic group meetings published in the *Summary of Proceedings* 38-48 (1984-94).

A Brief Reflection on ATLA Membership

Cindy Derrenbacker

As we approach the golden anniversary of the American Theological Library Association (ATLA), it is fitting to reflect on the members who comprise the Association. While the central administrative office of the Association has not statistically tracked its members in the past,[1] Albert E. Hurd, Executive Director of ATLA, recently noted that ATLA began in 1947 with an assembly of fifty-one theological librarians in Louisville, KY.[2] He likened the emergence of the Association to a "pebble falling into the water and creating ever widening circles."[3] As of July 1995, these circles have expanded to include 590 individual members serving the libraries of theologcal schools, colleges and universities, church libraries, public libraries, government libraries, and other organizations in North America and the world; 201 institutional members representing diverse religious traditions and denominations; and 333 members and friends attending the annual conference and educational seminars.[4] Clearly, the composition of the ATLA membership is broad and reflects the Association's policy on individual membership, which states that membership is "open to all persons interested in the practice, support, or promotion of theological librarianship, information systems, or bibliography."[5]

The incentives for membership are driven by the unique benefits of the Association. For example, individual membership provides opportunities for networking with other library professionals, as well as access to relevant continuing education and job postings. Members receive—and may at times contribute to—the quarterly *ATLA Newsletter* and the *Summary of Proceedings* of the annual conference. Individual members may also participate in the interest groups that have been developed to address specific issues or concerns of the ATLA membership. Currently, there are nine interest groups: the Automation and Technology Section, the Collection Evaluation and Development Section, the College and University Section, the OCLC Theological Users Group, the Online Reference Resources Section, the Public Services Section, the Publication Section, the Special Collections Section, and the Technical Services Section. In addition, the annual conference provides a forum for theological librarians to gather, both formally and informally, for workshops, interest groups, and continuing education seminars. Finally, the ATLA Institute offers intensive training opportunities for individual members on issues pertinent to the management of theological libraries.

Institutions may assume membership in order to receive product discounts on items such as *The ATLA Religion Database on CD-ROM* and the *ETHICS Index CD-ROM*, as well as free subscriptions to the Association's two publications noted above. Institutional members are also eligible to participate in the Library Materials Exchange Program, a program designed for the exchange of duplicate library materials, and the ATLA Consultation Service. The latter service provides an institutional member with the opportunity to apply for limited funds to hire a consultant to provide professional advice on a particular issue or project related to the library of that institutional member. Institutional members also benefit from the cooperative relationship between ATLA and the Association of Theological Schools (ATS), the institutional accrediting agency for theological schools in North America.

The most compelling reasons for joining the Association, however, come from the members themselves. In response to a recent informal survey,[6] individual members disclosed why they initially joined ATLA and how they have since gained from their participation in the Association, both personally and professionally. One member, considering theological librarianship as a career, found the *ATLA Newsletter* and the discussions on ATLANTIS[7] to be essential in her getting a clear picture of who theological librarians are and the particular issues that concern them. Another librarian, whose membership in the Association had lapsed for a time, joined again because he found the expertise of certain members of the Association especially helpful in the preparation of a manuscript for publication. This particular member also subscribed to the ATLANTIS listserv, because he found the cooperative online theological reference help useful. Still another long-time member confided that "ATLA has been the place where I have found my work as a theological librarian most supported and where I have been able to grow most in my profession." This member attributed his loyalty to the Association, in part, to having served on various ATLA committees, where he "learned a great deal, made lasting friendships, and had the most fun in my professional life." Another member commented that the annual ATLA conference is the high point of his year. He returns to his home institution professionally and intellectually "recharged" and has successfully implemented many of the ideas and insights gleaned from other members of the Association attending the conference. Still another member landed her first job as a theological librarian through the Association's network of members. All of these testimonies demonstrate that there are many excellent and varied reasons for information professionals and others to have joined ATLA over the years.

What are the prospects for future membership growth? The Long-Range Marketing Plan for Member Services, developed in February 1995, indicates that substantial increases in individual and institutional membership (28.5% and 30.5%, respectively) have occurred since the last membership census taken in 1981.[8] The Marketing Plan also reveals, however, that the present number of institutional members (201) is expected to remain constant in the United States and Canada. This is due to the fact that ATS currently endorses approximately 225 institutional members. Because libraries of institutions that hold membership in ATS are explicitly granted membership in ATLA,[9] few increases may be expected. In addition, the "downsizing" and restructuring of some seminaries and the mounting financial burdens borne by many theological institutions[10] does not bode well for increased institutional membership in ATLA. As a result, the Plan predicts that the demand for institutional membership will come increasingly from institutions situated outside of North America. As for individual membership, the Plan makes the recommendation that students enrolled in graduate library programs should be more actively recruited as new members of ATLA.

So it is clear that ATLA has been a valuable organization for the fostering of the professional growth of its individual members and facilitating cooperative working relationships among its membership generally.

As the Association commemorates its fiftieth anniversary, it is appropriate for its members not only to celebrate its achievements and note its benefits for theological librarians and their profession, but also to take steps to insure that it continues to flourish and extend its benefits to our successors.

Endnotes

1.   The last comprehensive statistical record of ATLA membership may be found in Jerry D. Campbell, ed., *Summary of Proceedings* 35 (1982): 135-61. The current Director of Member Services at ATLA plans to begin tracking membership annually during the 1995-1996 academic year.

2.   Albert E. Hurd to ATLA Membership, March 3, 1995, ATLA Annual Opportunity Giving Letter.

3.   Ibid.

4.   Melody S. Chartier, Director of Member Services, provided me with the most current membership statistics available by telephone, on July 5, 1995.

5.   Albert E. Hurd, ed., *ATLA Brochure*, (Chicago: American Theological Library Association, 1982).

6.   The author sent an email message via ATLANTIS (see endnote 7 for a description of ATLANTIS) to the ATLA membership on March 29, 1995, asking that members describe their reasons for joining ATLA. Selected responses have been included in this essay.

7.   ATLANTIS is a facility for electronic conferencing intended to aid the "ongoing communication between members of ATLA and the discussion of issues relevant to the Association" (Duane Harbin, "ATLANTIS: An Electronic Conference for ATLA Members," *ATLA Newsletter* 40/1 [1992]: 21).

8.   Campbell, *Summary of Proceedings*, 135-61.

9.   Note that institutions seeking ATLA membership on the basis of accreditation through an agency other than ATS can qualify for institutional membership if such institutions meet the criteria outlined in the Association's By-laws.

10. For further details, see Timothy C. Morgan, "Re-Engineering the Seminary: Crisis of Credibility Forces Change," *Christianity Today* 38 (October 24, 1994): 74-78; and Anthony Ruger, "Growth or Decline: A Look at Seminary Finances," *Christian Century* 112 (1995): 115-19.

ATLA's Preservation Microfilming Program: Growing Out of Our Work

Myron B. Chace

"This project will serve our Association best if it grows out of our work."
—Raymond P. Morris[1]

Introduction

The eve of the American Theological Library Association's fiftieth annual conference provides an opportunity to reflect on ATLA's role in the preservation of theological materials. By even the most cursory review of annual ATLA *Summary of Proceedings* published in more recent years, ATLA's *Newsletter*, and ATLA marketing literature, it is clear that the ATLA Preservation Microfilming Program has made valuable contributions to theological libraries and librarianship.

While a complete summary or listing of what has been reformatted in microform is not the purpose of this essay, it may be instructive to note the topical nature of works now in the custody of ATLA as master negative microforms. Among the thousands of microform monographs are: biblical studies, covering biblical manuscripts, commentaries, and versions of both Old and New Testaments in various languages; theological studies, including historical theology, philosophical theology, systematic and dogmatic theology; ethics; hymnody; devotional and homiletic literature; and world religions. Also represented are historical studies, including histories of Christianity; general histories of denominations, traditions, heresies, and schisms; histories of religion in the United States with works covering denominational developments and traditions, doctrine, liturgy, and governance; and historical works describing revivals and new religious movements. Supplementing this wide variety of monographic literature are many hundreds of serial titles on preservation microfilm, including some titles that have been microfilmed continuously from the early days of the Association.[2] In all, ATLA has produced microforms for approximately 1,800 periodicals and 30,000 monographs.[3]

The above listing, in a cursory way, represents the output from many years of work converting to microform those collections and titles supplied by Association members and institutions. Although these microforms have value in a collections sense, an argument may be made that the initial work to identify the body of theological and religious literature that was and is at risk through deterioration has a greater value to scholarship.

Seminal work to recognize the potential loss of our collective printed and written religious heritage sprang from Association members. An early sampling and investigation took place in 1976.[4] One observation in the 1976 study was that books printed and bound beginning around 1860 and into the 1920s were very likely to be deteriorating. In 1978, another study estimated that about 218,000 theological titles or 259,000 volumes were in advanced stages of deterioration.[5] From these studies came the suggestion and framework for the Association's preservation microfilming program, and in time, bibliographies, which in effect became a preservation microfilming work plan.[6] With this identification process and the resulting bibliographies, there is now documentation of at-risk works of recognized importance to theological libraries.

History

Much of what has been recorded in these prefatory paragraphs could serve as a background for a history of the ATLA Preservation Microfilming Program, particularly what has occurred with the Association's microfilming activities since 1985. There is, however, considerable documentation about the program presently available. Reports appearing in the annual *Proceedings* from the ATLA Board of Microtext, Preservation Board, and more recently from ATLA's Executive Director, provide a good overview of events—triumphs as well as setbacks—in the program.

In addition, specifics about the program are described in some detail in a 1987 *Microform Review* article.[7]

Notwithstanding the potential usefulness of an updated retelling of preservation microfilming work by the Association, a theme of this essay is that from even the very early ATLA microfilming projects, the character and values of the Association were paramount in this work. During its fifty years, ATLA has come to rely on cooperative, member-directed projects that follow high professional standards and that emphasize benefits to more than one library. These noteworthy attributes have been continually present in ATLA's microfilming work, and notes here about the microfilming program highlight the interplay of these values.

Beginnings

Chronologies of ATLA microfilming work generally place its beginnings in 1955.[8] Actually, interest in microfilming and microforms dates from the first Association conference in 1947.[9] Then, there was little acknowledgement of microfilming for preservation purposes. Indeed, the early years saw microforms as a possible way to obtain out-of-print or otherwise unavailable religious books.[10]

The idea of microfilm benefiting more than one library in an acquisition context was presented at the 1949 conference.[11] A principal speaker expressed his view that the existence of a master negative microfilm reduced the need to acquire an item except when actually needed. He further noted that libraries should not make large expenditures to create specialized collections via reproductions when there is no real demand for them. When the need arises for a title not usually in demand and if that publication has been converted to negative microfilm, it means that the item is permanently available.[12]

It is possible to speculate that the concept of an ATLA preservation master negative repository resulted from those remarks. After all, as noted earlier, what the Association possesses today in microform is a comprehensive collection of theological materials ready to meet a wide range of scholarship demands. That speculation, however, bears little resemblance to the way events unfolded.

Many attending the 1949 conference apparently were not persuaded that microforms could offer more than collection building. Attractive then were microcards, and their advantages were outlined in a conference presentation.[13] Somewhat less familiar now, microcards are the size of the usual library catalog card. On the card is photographic paper with microimages of text or book pages arranged in a grid pattern. Bibliographic data is usually available on the card. Generally assumed with microcards is the production of multiple copies, thus taking advantage of economies of scale.

No decision was made at the 1949 conference about microfilm versus microcard. Coming from that conference, however, was a recommendation to consider appointing a special committee on microreproduction.[14] That recommendation resulted in the formation of the Committee on Microphotography. At the outset, microform work by the Association through this committee relied heavily on input from its members.

A first step taken by the microphotography committee was a survey to list book and periodical titles needed but not available.[15] Because Association institutions would be paying for microreproduction work (both microcard and microfilm), it was obviously desirable to reap the benefits from making multiple copies. Since there was initially little agreement on requested titles, there was therefore no immediate systematic production of microforms. In fact, obtaining the requisite number of purchasers (fifteen) for microcards proved to be sufficiently daunting that there was doubt about the need to keep the committee intact.[16]

The first ATLA micropublication was announced in 1953.[17] Probably as no surprise, the first publication was the *ATLA Summary of Proceedings*, 1947-1950. This was one title that had enough appeal to generate sufficient orders for the microcard format. Creating and distributing the first microcard set was the Microcard Foundation (Middletown, CT).

But the Committee on Microphotography was not exclusively tied to microcards. Microfilm also played a role in the Association's nascent microform program. One advantage that the microfilm component enjoyed was requiring fewer copies (five) to defray filming and distribution costs. Like microcards, however, the first microfilm was the result of a cooperative arrangement with an outside organization: the Mittelstelle für Mikrokopie in Göttingen.[18]

While the early efforts of ATLA towards microform production perhaps were difficult—by no means could much of this work be labeled preservation microfilming—they did serve as good preparation for the time when a significant opportunity to stabilize and upgrade the program did appear. That opportunity came in the form of a Sealantic Fund grant in December 1956. The hard experience gained from trying to administer a poorly-funded reformatting program and the firm belief in the potential uses of microforms by Association institutions led ATLA's leaders to apply Sealantic grant monies to meet a recognized need.[19]

In describing the Association's microfilming work to this point, there has been scant mention of ATLA members, who contributed mightily to establishing and administering microfilming activities. This is not an oversight, but those individuals began to play their most prominent roles in the creation of the ATLA Microtext Program using the Sealantic grant. Without question, the values and standards that evolved in the microtext program reflect the efforts of Raymond P. Morris of Yale Divinity School. He prepared the basic proposal:

> to make possible the selective preparation of important religious materials which are either unavailable, or which, for reasons of space and deterioration, should be made available in microtext form . . .
>
> The proposal envisages grants totalling $80,000 spread over a three-year period. Such support would permit a starting program of an estimated sixty serial runs; or, correspondingly, much more extensive material in non-serial form. Production costs include secretarial, editorial, collation, committee expense, manufacture, distribution and collection, equipment, housing and storage, administration, plus a ten per cent contingency item.[20]

The administrative structure selected to bring the proposal to reality was a Board of Microtext. Due more than likely to his work to prepare the original proposal, Morris became Chairman of the Board of Microtext. Joining him on the Board were Jaroslav J. Pelikan, University of Chicago; Decherd Turner, Jr., Southern Methodist University (previously, Chairman of the Committee on Microphotography); Roscoe Pierson, College of the Bible; and Herman H. Fussler, University of Chicago.[21]

This Board served the Association well, although early on there must have been the temptation to plunge into microfilming many attractive items. Fortunately for ATLA, the first Board carefully deliberated how it wanted to proceed and decided what was required to carry out the project: a purpose, general policies, and understanding what kinds of materials are compatible with microfilming.[22]

The purpose of the project was the first component, and the Board saw the purpose as advancing the Association's interest, theological scholarship, and scholarship in general. A general policy was also set out by the Board. Seen as an educational venture, the microtext project was to be nonprofit in nature. Pricing of the finished project was to return the initial capitalization with filming costs based on selling five positive copies. Furthermore, microfilming was seen as publishing, but where service is more important than profit. The goal was to offer a high-quality product, which could be sold at a price consistent with that quality. Filming was to be accomplished with the full cooperation of publications' owners but with selection designed to reflect the library and research needs of the Association. Types of materials to be considered for the project then were items out of print and no longer available; materials that would be difficult or expensive to acquire; deteriorating items important enough to be preserved; items physically difficult to shelve or house; manuscripts or unprinted documents. Morris then stated what could be considered ATLA's guiding principles for its microfilming activities. He believed that the success of the project depended on the care and the wisdom in selecting materials for filming, with the Board taking responsibility for a high-quality and serviceable film product. But he also asked for cooperation by the membership, adding, "Every member of the Association is in some degree responsible for determining . . . what types of material . . . are required by our Association . . . ."[23] In establishing this first, large-scale (for the time) ATLA microfilming project, Morris—consistent with Association values—emphasized its cooperative, member-directed character.

Taking the trouble to construct this framework proved beneficial to the Board of Microtext and the Association, especially during problem periods. And there were problems. Board of Microtext reports in the annual *Proceedings* from 1959 and into the early 1970s note slow production, inability to recover costs, quality concerns, selection issues, and difficulties in obtaining permissions to microfilm. Yet, nearly every report unfailingly repeats the tenets of the program. Usually noted, for example, were the "common cause" of the work (1961), refusal to compromise quality (1962), and being "guided by high ethical standards" (1965).

Annual reports about the microtext endeavor are replete with acknowledgements for assistance and work contributed by institutions and members of the Association. Taken directly, these report entries have the appearance of a common courtesy. But years later, acknowledgements for cooperative efforts were placed in a larger context.

> [Morris] had a strong desire, in addition to the main purpose of the establishment of the Board of Microtext. He wanted to give members of the Association some part in the work of the organization to which they belonged. There were tasks that could be undertaken by individual librarians in their own libraries.... So interest was created in many ways and the efforts of many people furthered the work of the microtext program.[24]

Included among the "many people" were some individuals outside of the Association, such as Cosby Brinkley, Head of the Photoduplication Department, University of Chicago Library. (Microfilming for ATLA and film storage under the microtext program began at the University of Chicago in 1957.) Reports by the Board of Microtext perennially mention Brinkley and salute his technical expertise—"probably the most exacting and best technician in charge of any microfilm project in the United States."[25] He was praised as much for his dedication to the program as for his expertise. For example, Morris noted that Brinkley personally examined every negative microfilm produced—an activity that extended into weekends and was done as contributed labor.[26] One may wonder if he was intrigued by the project's technical challenges and "our work" or inspired by the dedication and values of the Association and its members.

Preservation Program Prologue

Although not identified as such, the early years of Board of Microtext work was a preservation microfilming program primarily because of its strong adherence to microphotographic standards. A preservation purist, however, might object to this view, because the program did not have reformatting of deteriorating or brittle materials as its primary focus. Whether or not ATLA microfilming activities took into account preservation definitions, the project began to change in 1971 with the filming of more "brittle" monographs.[27]

There were other Microtext changes in the early 1970s beyond a change in the makeup of materials reformatted. Some of these changes coincided with the retirement of Raymond Morris, but change was also required because of the increasing complexity of the program's financial and operational administration. The result was a restructuring of the program in 1972.[28] Continuity with the Association remained by recruiting new leadership from its members, including Wilson N. Flemister (Interdenominational Theological Center), Norman G. Wente (Luther Theological Seminary), L. Charles Willard (Princeton Theological Seminary), and Conrad Wright (Harvard Divinity School). (Morris remained on the Board briefly as Executive Secretary, and Willard became Chairman.) Soon joining the Board was Maria Grossmann (Harvard College Library), who served as Chairperson for several years, with Willard becoming Executive Secretary.

Under the new structure, and chiefly through Willard's leadership, the Board began to take up issues clearly directed towards a comprehensive preservation microfilming program.[29] A key element here was the proposal of a more aggressive approach to preserving large numbers of deteriorating monographs. Preventing action on this front, however, was a troubling financial picture. Activities and economic conditions during the previous years had resulted in deficits. It became clear that additional revenue sources would have to be found. Suggestions included encouraging more sales of positive copies, the Board forming alliances with other organizations, and encouraging ATLA member institutions to direct all whole-book copying requests received to the Board so that its facilities could be used.

Another topic that Willard brought to the membership at this same time has been mentioned earlier: reformatting (especially monographs) in both microfiche and microfilm, or one or the other.[30] Early work by the Board of Microtext was aimed at microfilming periodical and serial literature. During those years, *Proceedings* and *Newsletter* reports reflect continuing attempts to locate complete runs of selected titles and what was indicated as missing. Reports reveal less emphasis on microfilming monographs.

Not lost in this discussion was a concern for high standards and quality of work that had been the hallmark of the Board's prior years. Would microfiche compromise those standards? A chief motivation for considering a microfiche format was its potential application to deteriorating monographs. Microfiche may be called a unitized record—i.e., depending on reduction ratio, the entire contents of a monograph may be contained on one or two microfiche sheets. Microfiche is easier to use with reading equipment and is less expensive to duplicate. Among others, these characteristics make microfiche attractive, especially to the library interested in selected monograph titles. In any case, the Board's decision in 1973 was to offer both microfiche and roll film for a trial period. In 1977, the determination was that "microfiche was preferable to roll film for the addition of a substantial number of monographs in the program."[31]

By 1976, several of the issues noted above had been sufficiently explored to warrant a revised policy statement. The new policy reflected a firm commitment to preservation.

> The Board is deliberately expanding its volume of operations, seeking to preserve as much deteriorating material as possible. Titles recommended for filming are added to the program whenever technically possible even though sales potential may be very low. Consequently, sales income is likely to continue to decrease in relation to filming costs, but the Board is prepared to authorize reasonable withdrawals from capital funds to underwrite the expansion.[32]

Implementing the Program

What had been the Association's endeavor of a home-grown nature over the next several years expanded to become a preservation microfilming business. Board of Microtext reports that appeared in the *Proceedings* during the late 1970s and into the early 1980s document what was forcing the expansion: the need to respond to the problem of deteriorating monographs. That this problem was of massive proportions was described in research studies undertaken by Association members and cited above. Concern for the deterioration problem also stemmed from a growing national awareness that all libraries were grappling with "brittle book" problems.

The Board took some business-like and imaginative actions to raise additional capital and to promote greater involvement by ATLA member institutions. One was called COMPORT (Cooperative Microform Project on Religion and Theology), a fee-based program initiated in 1977 and offering borrowing privileges for positive copies of microfilm produced by the Association and discounts when purchases were made.[33] Another effort was to engage in a marketing venture with a private company, Scholars Press. This occurred in 1978, and the agreement featured a microform subscription program based on bibliographies developed within the Association.[34] But by 1979, the most significant change had been proposed: the development of a full-blown micrographic preservation and bibliographic project. Having made the proposal, the Board then faced the challenge of bringing the project to reality. Steps in this direction proved to be painstakingly slow.

To prepare for such an ambitious project, the Association established a study that collected information to plan for a large-scale preservation microfilming program of theological material. The study required nearly eighteen months to complete, and interim findings were presented to the membership in 1980.[35]

In time, information from the completed study (1981) was turned over to the Steering Committee on the Preservation of Theological Materials, which offered a comprehensive three-part program with the largest component being a theological monographs preservation microfilming project that might require as much as ten years to complete.[36] To begin the process of setting such a large project in motion, the Association approved the creation of an Interim Board for the Preservation of Religious Monographs. Now there was both this new body and the established Board of Microtext, and in 1984, the two united to form the ATLA Preservation Board.[37]

During the period when new organizational structures were planning for an Association-wide monograph preservation program, the existing preservation microfilming program encountered serious problems, the most critical of which was financial—annual deficits were more frequent than surpluses. In fact, by 1982, the capital account created by the original Sealantic grant had been virtually eliminated.[38] Organizations that have had success in a chosen endeavor sometimes must face the unpleasant fact that what was managed well by part-time, voluntary labor now requires full-time attention. So it was with ATLA's preservation microfilming work. Program and fiscal demands now required dedicated, full-time management and a centralized administration.

The changeover occurred in 1985, with the appointment of the Preservation Program Director, Robert Markham. With his appointment, the ATLA Preservation Program took shape. While perhaps giving too little attention here, there are Association records, including the *Proceedings*, which contain a rich documentation of the steps taken during the more recent years to create the organization that has produced one of the largest collections of theological literature in high-quality microform. In 1988, Markham was succeeded by Albert Hurd, who was named Executive Director of Index and Preservation Programs.

Because of the increased program size, one necessary change came about: financial resources—rather than coming directly from member institutions—now had to be obtained from outside the Association. Help with funding came from the Lilly Endowment, the Pew Charitable Trusts, Henry Luce Foundation, and the National Endowment for the Humanities.[39]

But other assistance came from within the Association and from many individuals, who recognized the valuable work that ATLA had accomplished from the early days of its preservation microfilming efforts. They continued the tradition of joining in a common Association endeavor for the benefit of theological scholarship. Some of these individuals are mentioned above, but there have been others. This writer hesitates to list names, knowing that some who have provided valuable service may be overlooked, and so apologizes in advance for any omissions. Nevertheless, it is clear that the record would be incomplete if no attempt was made to cite the assistance of John Bollier, Jerry Campbell, Robert Dvorak, Doralyn Hickey, Robert Allenson, Florence Baker, and Andrew Scrimgeour. Others, although not members, worked on behalf of ATLA's Preservation Program, including Pamela Darling and Tamara Swora; this writer also has had the privilege in recent years to assist in this important work.

Summary

For the ATLA Preservation Microfilming Program, a summary is inappropriate, because a summary may suggest a conclusion, and the need for preserving library materials in religion and theology has, by no means, come to an end. Based on surveys compiled at least fifteen years ago, more than 200,000 volumes of theological materials remain at risk. Thus the work started by the ATLA program needs to continue.

As ATLA plans additional preservation work, its members should recall the values and contributions of the Association's program. There has not been a program of similar scale or scope; the program has engendered faithful participation and cooperation by member institutions—whether by financial investment, donated collections, or labor; program directors and staff members have operated from high ethical concerns and an adherence to high standards; and high quality has been a hallmark of its product in terms of both material and bibliographic utility. In these ways and over the many years, the program has come to define Association values and to provide a sense of our mission and our work.

Endnotes

1. Raymond P. Morris, "ATLA Board of Microtext," *Summary of Proceedings* 20 (1966): 16.
2. Listings, catalogs, and promotional literature available from ATLA Director of Marketing.
3. John A. Bollier, "History of ATLA Preservation Grant Proposals," *Summary of Proceedings* 48 (1994): 165.
4. L. Charles Willard, "An Analysis of Paper Stability and Circulation Patterns of the Monographic Collection of Speer Library, Princeton Theological Seminary," in *Essays on Theological Librarianship, Presented to Calvin Henry Schmitt*, ed. Peter De Klerk and Earle Hilgert (Philadelphia: ATLA, 1980), 163-73.
5. Ronald F. Deering, Albert Hurd, and Andrew D. Scrimgeour, "Collection Analysis Project Final Report: Ad Hoc Committee for the Preservation of Theological Materials," *Summary of Proceedings* 35 (1981): 162-206.
6. For an example, see "Developing Denominational Bibliographies for Preservation Filming," in *Summary of Proceedings* 43 (1989): 180-83.
7. Robert Markham, "Religion Converted to Microformat," *Microform Review* (1987): 217-23.
8. Ibid., 217.
9. Charles E. Batten, "Cooperative Procedures of Libraries," *Summary of Proceedings* 1 (1947): 60-62.
10. Robert F. Beach, "Publications and Out-of-Print Religious Book Survey," *Summary of Proceedings* 2 (1948): 13-17.
11. Herman H. Fussler, "Microphotography—Present and Future," *Summary of Proceedings* 3 (1949), 3-9.
12. Ibid., 7.
13. Marjorie C. Keenleyside, "Microcards," *Summary of Proceedings* 3 (1949): 10-13.
14. *Summary of Proceedings* 3 (1949): Appendix A.
15. "Report of the Committee on Microphotography," *Summary of Proceedings* 4 (1950): 2-3.
16. "Report...on Microphotography," *Summary of Proceedings* 5 (1951): 19. As an aside, it is interesting to note that discussions about the

desirability of microcards over roll microfilm unknowingly foretell later debates within the Association about producing microfiche or microfilm. Cf. L. Charles Willard, "An ATLA Board of Microtext and Microfiche," *Summary of Proceedings* 27 (1973): 91-93.

17. "Committee on Microphotography," *ATLA Newsletter* (1953): 3.

18. "Report...on Microphotography," *Summary of Proceedings Proceedings* 8 (1954): 5-6.

19. Robert F. Beach, "Report of the Committee on Sealantic Fund, Inc.," *Summary of Proceedings* 10 (1956): 18-20.

20. Ibid., 19-20.

21. "Report of the ATLA Board of Microtext," *Summary of Proceedings* 12 (1958): 47.

22. Ibid., 49-50.

23. Ibid., 51.

24. Board of Microtext, "Current Recollections of Jean Morris," *Summary of Proceedings* 36 (1982): 147-48.

25. Ibid., 146.

26. Raymond P. Morris, "Recollection of Cosby Brinkley," *Summary of Proceedings* 36 (1982): 151.

27. "Board of Microtext Report," *Summary of Proceedings* 25 (1971): 32.

28. "Board of Microtext," *Summary of Proceedings* 26 (1972): 22.

29. L. Charles Willard, "Statement of Concerns of the Board of Microtext," *Summary of Proceedings* 27 (1973): 93-95.

30. Ibid., 91-93.

31. "Board of Microtext," *Summary of Proceedings* 31 (1977): 23.

32. "Board of Microtext," *Summary of Proceedings* 30 (1976): 20.

33. "Board of Microtext," *Summary of Proceedings* 31 (1977): 23.

34. "Board of Microtext," *Summary of Proceedings* 32 (1978): 23.

35. "Ad Hoc Committee for the Storage and Preservation of Theological Library Material," *Summary of Proceedings* 34 (1980): 53-54.

36. "Report of the Steering Committee on the Preservation of Theological Materials," *Summary of Proceedings* 36 (1982): 55-63.

37. *Summary of Proceedings* 38 (1984): 2-4.

38. "Report of the Board of Microtext," *Summary of Proceedings* 36 (1982): 21.

39. Bollier, "History of ATLA Grant Proposals," 165.

A Giant Step Forward: The Sealantic Fund and the American Theological Library Association Library Development Project

Paul F. Stuehrenberg

On June 16, 1961, at the banquet that marked the conclusion of the annual meeting of the American Theological Library Association, held that year in Washington, D.C., the incoming President of the Association, Connolly C. Gamble, Jr., of Union Theological Seminary in Richmond, Va., announced that the Sealantic Fund[1] had committed up to $875,000 to help build the collections of member institutions over the next three years. The announcement was greeted by a moment of total silence, as if those present could not believe what they had heard. Then the room was swept by a wave of exultation. The world of American Protestant theological librarianship would never be the same again.[2]

Over the next five years (the program was to be extended for two additional years), support for the libraries participating in the ATLA Library Development Program increased from a base of $2.5 million to $4.8 million, while expenditures for books and periodicals increased from $612,877 to $1,713,701. Over the life of the program, the Sealantic Fund provided $1,311,750 to participating libraries; they in turn raised an additional $5.6 million in support. In the process, institutional awareness of the library's role in theological education was greatly enhanced, and the librarian was increasingly recognized as a key partner in the enterprise.

From the context of the individual library, these changes were enormous. While our perspective today is clouded by the impact of more than three decades of inflation, in 1961 it was considered reasonable to assume that the average book would cost four dollars, that an additional three dollars would pay for classification, cataloging and other processing, and that one more dollar would suffice to house it—for a total per-volume cost of eight dollars.[3] Of the seventy-seven theological schools covered in the American Association of Theological Schools biennial report for 1956/57, twenty reported acquisition budgets of less than $3,000 per year; thirty-three had budgets ranging between $3,000 and $6,000; and only twenty-six spent more. The average expenditure that year was $5,960.[4] For 1961/62, the first year of the Program, the expenditures on books and periodicals of the twelve top participating libraries averaged $16,857; by 1964/65 that average had increased to $39,710.[5] How this Program came to be, what it entailed, and what theological librarians might learn from it today, are the subject of this account of the ATLA Library Development Program.

Background

The ATLA Library Development Program grew out of two earlier Sealantic Fund initiatives: support for ATLA programs to index periodicals and create microtexts, and for the Theological Education Fund, an international effort to help "younger churches." In 1955 the Sealantic Fund approached Robert F. Beach, Librarian at Union Theological Seminary in New York and President of the ATLA, about how it might help support theological libraries. Beach, in consultation with Raymond P. Morris, Yale Divinity School Librarian, and Jannette Newhall, Librarian of the Boston University School of Theology, responded on behalf of the ATLA with a request for support for two programs: the indexing of theological periodicals and the microfilming of books and serials.[6] These proposals led to a grant of $30,000 to begin the indexing project and $80,000 for microfilming. Both projects were to be self-supporting, and both eventually succeeded in accomplishing that goal.[7]

Launched in January 1958 with a grant of $2 million from the Sealantic Fund together with matching funds from eight American mission boards, the Theological Education Fund was charged with supporting theological education in Africa, Asia, and Latin America.[8] One fourth of its initial resources was committed to the improvement of theological literature and the strengthening of libraries.

Raymond Morris agreed to survey the library needs of the theological schools of Southeast Asia[9] and to prepare a book list in collaboration with an international group of scholars. The classified list of nearly six thousand titles, *A Theological Book List*, produced in 1960 "by the Theological Education Fund of the International Missionary Council for theological seminaries and colleges in Africa, Asia, Latin America and the Southwest Pacific,"[10] was sent to all the eligible schools. Libraries were invited to order books of their own choice up to a specified amount. By special arrangements with Blackwell's (Oxford) and Allenson's (Naperville, IL) supplied the books at discounted prices. This method made it unnecessary to make direct financial grants to more than two hundred different institutions, while also allowing the institutions control over what materials they would add to their collections.

The Library Development Program

In the fall of 1958 Yorke Allen of the Sealantic Fund again contacted Beach and Morris for suggestions of ways the Fund might help improve seminary libraries. Over the next year they and a select group of colleagues[11] discussed proposals that the ATLA might submit to the Sealantic Fund. Among those considered were various publications projects, the training of theological librarians, and additional support for the Index Board.

In October 1959 Morris circulated the draft of a proposal for what was to become the ATLA Library Development Program. The purpose of Morris' proposal was to increase the general level of support seminaries provided for their libraries. The focus of the proposal was on the purchase of books. Morris proposed that the Fund supply up to $2,000 per year of matching funds (ultimately the amount was increased to $3,000) in support of library acquisitions for a period up to five years, with the understanding that the seminaries would continue their level of support thereafter.

Morris chose the figure of $2,000 carefully. He calculated that amount, along with matching funds, would be sufficient to purchase 1,000 volumes per year. The additional work, Morris estimated, would require the addition of a full-time staff position: if the grant were less, institutions might be tempted to get by with existing personnel; more than that, and more than one new position would have to be added—something most institutions could not reasonably be expected to do. As a consequence, each dollar contributed by the Fund would, in effect, require at least two dollars from the participating institutions. The infusion of funds would not only require that libraries carefully analyze their own operations[12] but also require that institutions analyze their library services. In this way Morris expected that the top administrative officers would become more "library minded," and thus more favorably disposed to increasing the library's share of their seminary's over-all budget over the years.[13]

Libraries participating in the Library Development Program were required to carry out a self study prepared by Calvin Schmitt and to check their holdings against Morris' *Book List*.[14] Books purchased for the program were to support the core curricular needs of the institution; the funds were not to be used to build special collections. The Library Development Program also featured teams of visitors who were available to provide advice and counsel.[15]

Morris and a group of advisors[16] originally estimated that about fifty of the eighty-two members of the AATS would participate in the program (all members of AATS except those having notations against their libraries were eligible to participate). The response far exceeded anyone's expectations. In the first year seventy-nine of eighty eligible libraries participated (fifty-nine fully, twenty on a partial basis); in the second year all eighty-two eligible libraries participated (seventy fully, twelve partially); and in the third year the number had increased to eighty-four (seventy-five fully and nine partially). The response was so overwhelming that the $875,000[17] grant that was originally expected to fund the program for five years was fully expended in three. The Sealantic Fund committed an additional $436,750 so that the program could continue for two more years. The fourth year saw ninety participants (eighty-seven full and three partial), and in the fifth year there were eighty-nine participants (Oberlin withdrew), with only one at less-than-full participation.[18]

The Library Development Program was directed by a Board consisting of Connolly C. Gamble (Union, Richmond), Calvin H. Schmitt (McCormick), Charles L. Taylor (AATS), and Morris, as chair. Morris took a half-time leave from his duties at Yale to direct the Program. Working with the Board was an Advisory Committee composed of:

William A. Clebsch (Professor, Episcopal Theological Seminary of the Southwest)

Alice M. Dagan (Librarian, Chicago Lutheran Theological Seminary)

Donn Michael Farris (Librarian, Duke Divinity School)

Herman H. Fussler (Librarian, University of Chicago)

Charles P. Johnson (Librarian, Southwestern Baptist Theological Seminary)

Arthur E. Jones, Jr. (Librarian, Drew University)

Gordon D. Kaufman (Professor, Vanderbilt Divinity School)

Jules L. Moreau (Librarian, Seabury-Western Theological Seminary)

James T. Tanis (Librarian, Andover-Harvard Divinity School)

As the Library Development Program approached the end of its fifth year, Yorke Allen asked Morris if "there might be any basis which would justify the continuation" of the Library Development Program beyond the initial five years. Morris replied that it should be terminated.[19] As Morris reported to Jesse Ziegler of the AATS: "If the Program were continued for too long, it could become detrimental to the well-being of an institution. Five years of the Program has demonstrated what improvement can be achieved through greater library support. It is for these institutions to judge whether these gains should be retained."[20] Indeed, during that five-year period the level of institutional support for theological libraries was increased dramatically; irreversibly so, as it proved to be. The Library Development Program had fulfilled several of its chief objectives: not only had the libraries been enabled to purchase several thousand volumes they otherwise would have been unable to acquire, seminaries dramatically increased their continuing commitments to their libraries, both in terms of acquisitions budgets and in overall expenditures for library support. There was no going back.

To be appreciated fully, this level of increase in support for theological libraries needs to be placed in the context of the support for other academic libraries. Over the life of the Library Development Program, while support for participating libraries was increasing by 180 per cent, support for university libraries[21] increased by approximately 150 per cent, against inflationary increases of 140 per cent.[22] For once theological libraries fared better than average!

The Sealantic Fund justifiably took great pride in its theological library programs. The grant money was put to work by able people to fill a genuine need. The benefits that followed cut across lines and boundaries so that an entire field was helped. The level of quality of seminary libraries was raised in a measurable way; libraries after the Library Development Program could hardly be compared to libraries before it. And last but not least, the Fund's resources had been leveraged. As

Genevieve Kelly, Librarian at California Baptist Theological Seminary, noted: "The leadership of the program, in providing bibliographies and self-study aids, together with funds from the grant, have helped our theological libraries take a giant step forward."[23]

Lessons to Be Learned

What, then, does this story teach, beyond being a glorious chapter in the history of the ATLA? Is the Library Development Program something that could be replicated again today? Clearly not in its details. The ATLA and the world of theological librarianship is, if anything, more diverse than it was in 1961. If nothing else, the ATLA includes not only Protestant members (as was the case then) but also Roman Catholic and Orthodox. As a consequence, it would be very difficult, for example, to arrive at the sort of core collection epitomized by Morris' *Book List*. Moreover, the successor to the Sealantic Fund is currently nowhere in sight. However that may be, I would suggest that several features of the Library Development Program can (and have) served as models for how such a program can succeed.

First, programs should strive to involve member libraries as fully as possible, and this on the basis of enlightened self-interest. Participation in the Library Development Program approached 100 per cent, if only because libraries saw that it was to their benefit to participate.

Secondly, programs should have as their goal to leverage, as far as possible, existing resources. The Library Development Program used foundation money to raise money at the local level for local priorities.

Thirdly, programs should be flexible enough to allow decentralized decision-making. In both the Theological Education Fund and the Library Development Program local libraries ultimately decided what was best for them.

Fourth, we should learn when enough is enough, and it is time to go on to other ventures. Those responsible for the Library Development Program decided to close the program after five years, rather than to seek continued funding; this decision forced institutions to consolidate their gains, rather than become dependent on the program.

With these guiding principles, it would be possible to imagine an approach to the preservation of library materials that enabled individual libraries to decide which materials are most important for their users. With seed-money distributed by ATLA and training provided under ATLA's auspices (perhaps at the Annual Conference), they would then establish their own preservation programs. Materials so preserved could then be distributed through the ATLA network. As funds for preservation become increasingly scarce, it is increasingly necessary for individual libraries to assume responsibility for this critical function.

One could also imagine a program to encourage the acquisition of materials documenting non-Western Christianity that could be designed along the lines of the Library Development Program. With all the talk about developing programs to incorporate "world Christianity" into seminary curricula, very little effort has been made to encourage seminary libraries to collect such documentation. The ATLA Annual Conference could serve as a vehicle for coordinating such collection activity (such as having particular institutions agree to collect intensively for specific regions or churches), and for training in how to handle materials in unfamiliar languages.

While Morris' *Book List* is no longer a realistic model, its cooperative approach to building library collections is something that can be emulated. Today such cooperation can be greatly facilitated by the application of electronic technologies. One can imagine, for example, a "home page" on a World Wide Web server where such things as an annotated list of vendors could be maintained—an electronic version of directories produced by such professional organizations as SALALM.[24] An ATLA "home page" could also provide other reference functions, such as indexing religion resources on the Internet.

To be sure, ATLA has already built upon the successes of the Library Development Program and the model it presents. As we face the next fifty years of the organization (not to mention a new decade, century, and millennium), the ATLA would do well to draw upon the collective memory of its past, that the library might continue to play its pre-eminent role in theological education—a role established in no small part by the Library Development Program.

Endnotes

1. The Sealantic Fund was created in 1938 as a vehicle for the Rockefeller family to contribute money to charitable causes, with a particular focus on the education of American Protestant clergy. The name "Sealantic" derives from the names of the locations of two of the

homes of John D. Rockefeller, Jr., which were also the locations of two small churches he attended: Seal Harbor, Maine, and Pocantico Hills, New York. The Sealantic Fund was absorbed into the Rockefeller Brothers Fund in 1973. For additional information, see William G. Wing, "John D. Rockefeller, Jr., and the Sealantic Fund," an unpublished history, the manuscript of which is included in Box 30, Sealantic Fund Archives, Rockefeller Foundation Archives, Rockefeller Archives Center, North Tarrytown, New York (hereafter, Sealantic Fund Archives).

2. This account is from Wing, "John D. Rockefeller, Jr., and the Sealantic Fund," ch. 10, p. 11. An official announcement of the grant award appears in the *ATLA Newsletter* 9/1 (1961): 2-3.

3. Raymond P. Morris, "Report on the ATLA Library Development Program," *Program and Reports, AATS Biennial Meeting* 24 (1964): 75.

4. "The ATLA Library Development Program," Jan. 5, 1961 draft. A copy of this paper is included in the Raymond P. Morris papers, Record Group 80, Yale Divinity School Library Special Collections, folder 5.82; hereafter the Morris papers will be cited as RG 80. There is some discrepancy about the precise figures. Robert Beach reported that for the year 1957/58 the annual average expenditure of ATLA libraries was $6,265 for books and $973 for periodicals. See Robert F. Beach, "Protestant Theological Seminaries and Their Libraries," *Library Trends* 9 (1960): 143.

5. Raymond P. Morris, "Yale Divinity School Library Annual Report," (1965/66): 3.

6. While it might seem surprising today, the impetus for the microfilming proposal was not for preservation, but for the economical distribution of core literature.

7. The indexing project took a bit longer than did the microfilming: in 1971 the index showed its first profit and began to accumulate a contingency fund.

8. For a brief account of the origins of the Theological Education Fund, see Charles W. Ranson, "How the Theological Education Fund Began," in *A Vision for Man: Essays on Faith, Theology and Society in Honor of Joshua Russell Chandran*, ed. Samuel Amirtham (Madras: Christian Literature Society, 1978), 130-42. Wing, "John D. Rockefeller, Jr., and the Sealantic Fund," also includes a chapter on the Theological Education Fund.

9. Morris' report was published as "The Place of the Library in Christian Theological Education of Southeast Asia," *Summary of Proceedings* 13 (1959): 152-58; a slightly revised version of this paper was published as "Some Impressions of the Libraries in Protestant Theological Educational Institutions in Southeast Asia and Their Implications for the Christian Church," *S.E. Asia Journal of Theology* 1

(1960): 8-16.

10. He lists his collaborators on pp. vii-viii. This work built on his *A Preliminary and Tentative Listing of Books for the Libraries of Christian Theological Institutions in South-East Asia* ([S.l.]: Compiled for the Nanking Board of Founders, 1958). Later supplements to the *Theological Book List* contained sections on English, French, German, Spanish, and Portuguese theological literature. It was assumed that schools would be aware of the theological literature available in the languages of their own regions.

11. In a letter to Yorke Allen dated Nov. 30, 1959, Morris indicated that he had consulted with Calvin Schmitt (Librarian at McCormick Seminary), Decherd Turner (Librarian at the Bridwell Library, Southern Methodist University), Herman Fussler (Librarian at the University of Chicago), other librarians at Yale, and with Yale Divinity School Professors James Gustafson, H. Richard Niebuhr, and Liston Pope. Schmitt was a former ATLA President and Turner the current ATLA President (a copy of this letter is included in RG 80, folder 5.82).

12. The potential impact of the Library Development Program on library technical services operations and the need to closely examine existing operations are the themes of Kathryn Luther Henderson's essay, "Keeping and Casting Away: Cost Implications of the Library Development Program for Technical Services," *Summary of Proceedings* 16 (1962): 136-67.

13. "ATLA Library Development Program," October 26, 1960 draft; RG 80, folder 5.82.

14. Early drafts of the proposal prepared by Yorke Allen included the provision that the Morris list be the primary basis for titles that individual libraries would purchase. Morris foresaw that this would be problematic (letter to Yorke Allen, Jan. 19, 1961; RG 80, folder 5.83). His concern was born out by reviews solicited by Allen (letters to Allen from William S. Dix, Librarian at Princeton University, dated Jan. 17, 1961; James I. McCord, President of Princeton Seminary, dated Jan. 26, 1961; and James Babb, Librarian at Yale University, dated Feb. 2, 1961; RG 80; folder 5.83). In the final draft of the proposal, the Morris list was to be used as a tool to evaluate collections, but it was not considered prescriptive. Morris was sensitive about the use of his list: "I suspect that I am not overly modest about many things, but could we omit the name Morris and use the title, *A theological book list*, in its stead? I don't want this project to become known as the Morris project and I should like to play down the name Morris about it all" (letter to Yorke Allen, Feb. 11, 1961; RG 80, folder 5.83).

15. Over the life of the Library Development Program some sixty-nine visits were carried out, with twenty-nine individuals serving as visitors. Morris continued the visitations for several years after the

termination of the Library Development Program, using residual funds for expenses (see Yorke Allen memorandum to "Sealantic Files" dated Feb. 15, 1967; Sealantic Fund Archives, Box 22, ATLA Library Development Program 3). The practice of including librarians on AATS accreditation teams grew out of this program. In 1973 Morris turned over a balance of $470 to the ATLA Board of Microtext (see Apr. 9, 1973, letter from Morris to Charles Willard; Sealantic Fund Archives, Box 22, ATLA Library Development Program 3).

16. This group included Liston Pope and H. Richard Niebuhr of Yale, and Charles Taylor and Jesse Ziegler of the AATS.

17. This figure was originally based on a five-year program of $2,000 per year, or $10,000 per institution; of the eighty-two members of AATS, eleven had notations against their libraries, leaving seventy-one eligible institutions. For the first five-year period, then, the maximum distribution would be $710,000. A second five-year grant cycle was also originally envisioned in which fifteen libraries would be awarded an additional $10,000 each, for a subtotal of $150,000. Morris estimated administrative costs at ca. $25,000. Morris was of the opinion that the actual costs would be more in the range of $450,000 to $625,000. (See Morris' letter to Yorke Allen dated April 6, 1960; RG 80.) Taylor thought even this estimate too high and that $250,000 would be more realistic. (Letter from Morris to Yorke Allen dated April 1, 1960; RG 80.)

18. These figures are derived from Morris' final report of the project, which appeared in *Summary of Proceedings* 21 (1967): 127-38. The Library Development Program archives, which include files for each of the participating institutions, are held at Yale Divinity School Library as Record Group 81.

19. July 19, 1965, letter from Morris to Allen; Sealantic Fund Archives, Box 22, ATLA Library Development Program 2.

20. Nov. 11, 1965, letter from Morris to Ziegler; Sealantic Fund Archives, Box 22, ATLA Library Development Program 2.

21. For the purposes of this paper I compiled the spending on collections of eight of the top fifty academic libraries in the country: Harvard University, Yale University, Columbia University, University of California, Berkeley, University of Chicago, Princeton University, Duke University and Northwestern University. I chose these institutions because there are theological libraries either directly affiliated with them or in close proximity to them.

22. These figures are derived from the *Bowker Annual* for 1963-1968.

23. Aug. 5, 1963 letter from Kelly to Yorke Allen; Sealantic Fund Archives, Box 22, ATLA Library Development Program 2. An additional indication of the importance attached to the Library Development Program by theological librarians at the time is the fact that in an article on the status of theological libraries Warren R. Mehl identified three

dates as having particular significance: 1918 (the founding of AATS), 1947 (the founding of ATLA), and 1961 (the beginning of the Library Development Program); see Warren R. Mehl, "The Protestant Theological Library in America: Past, Present, and Future," *Theology and Life* 7 (1964): 238- 39.

24. For an example of such a printed directory, see Howard L. Karno and Beverly Joy Karno, *Directory of Vendors of Latin American Library Materials*, 4th ed., Bibliography and Reference Series, 32 (Albuquerque: Secretariat, Seminar on the Acquisitions of Latin American Library Materials, 1993).

BIBLIOGRAPHIES, COLLECTIONS, AND ARCHIVES

Print Bibliographies in the Field of Religion[1]

M. Patrick Graham

The following essay arises from several years experience reviewing print bibliographies, developing an electronic database of print materials dealing with the biblical books of Chronicles, and offering reference service to seminary and graduate school communities. It is clear that carefully planned and executed print and electronic bibliographies constitute one of the most important resources for research. Conversely, poorly planned and executed bibliographies not only mislead researchers but also waste library resources and undermine the reputations of publishers. While the cynical may blame the production of inferior bibliographies on the vanity of compilers or the greed of publishers, others—no less realistic, but perhaps more sympathetic—attribute this sad state of affairs to other causes. While many compilers sincerely desire to make contributions to scholarship, they often lack familiarity with principles of information management, have little understanding of the range of bibliographical resources available, and after decades of work in libraries still move as novices among the Library of Congress subject headings. For their part, publishers often know little more than compilers about the foregoing, habitually trust the "experts" in academia to design bibliographies, and neglect to call upon information specialists, whose training and experience might be relevant for their work. In addition, acquisition librarians or materials selectors, whose decisions about the purchase of these bibliographies often determine their profitability, are confronted by a flood of publications that grows more overwhelming each year. Hence, they purchase materials that they never use (and in some instances, never see), relying on brief reviews[2] and what is remembered about authors, series, and publishers.

In addition to issues related to quality, it has become increasingly evident that the widespread availability of electronic bibliographic tools for accessing monographic and periodical scholarly literature raises serious questions about the advisability of creating new print bibliographies. Nevertheless, each year more of the latter appear. The electronic tools typically have the advantage of greater speed, comprehensiveness, flexibility, and ease of updating. Therefore, it appears that their print counterparts may be justified only if they offer some additional value to the user.[3] In the essay that follows an attempt will be made to (1) describe in a limited way important questions that a compiler, editor, or publisher might raise regarding a prospective bibliography and (2) suggest some additional considerations that merit the compiler's attention.[4]

The Justification of a Projected Bibliography
The primary concern in this section is to take up the matter of how a projected bibliography may be justified, i.e., what does the bibliography provide that is not already available from existing resources? Some of the researcher's bibliographic needs are met by existing print resources and others by electronic bibliographic utilities, such as OCLC with its 32,000,000+ bibliographic records and ATLA's *Religion Indexes*. In the case of OCLC the researcher has available one of the most extensive databases imaginable, updated daily by thousands of professionals, and potentially accessible from any telephone connection.[5] Its records are searchable through various access points, and as far as subject headings are concerned, the user has the advantage of the application of a controlled vocabulary that allows great precision in searching. Moreover, in some instances the local adaptation of the database allows additional advantages, such as the searching of notes and almost any term that occurs in the MARC record. Similarly, *Religion Indexes* provides the user access to articles in periodicals, collections of essays, and book reviews. Although the database has substantially covered relevant periodicals since 1949, it approximates neither the chronological nor subject coverage of OCLC. Nevertheless, it has been compiled by professional indexers over a long period of time, is frequently updated, has employed a carefully-developed, controlled vocabulary for subject headings, and is searchable by means of

powerful software. Finally, *Religion Indexes* is moving in the same direction as OCLC in terms of its widespread availability, with some institutions having it mounted on LANs.[6] In addition to the foregoing resources, the researcher has available—as tools for searching monographic literature—RLIN and a multitude of individual library systems that may be searched from remote locations, as well as the prospects of a burgeoning number of electronic databases that provide access to religious periodical literature (e.g., *Ethics Index*, *Catholic Periodical Literature Index*). Nevertheless, there are several weaknesses in these electronic tools that a well-planned print bibliography can address. Hence the matter under consideration: What does the projected print bibliography offer that the other tools do not already provide? This will be approached by means of a series of questions that may be raised in connection with projected bibliographies.

1. *Does the bibliography encompass research resources previously neglected?*

A primary consideration in the assessment of the potential value of a new bibliography is this question: Does the bibliography encompass research resources previously neglected? This may be examined first from the standpoint of the date of the materials included. Although OCLC and RLIN are comprehensive chronologically, the periodical indexes are not. *Religion Indexes*, for example, only covers materials since the late 1940s,[7] and the other, specifically religious electronic indexes are limited to materials issued even more recently. Therefore, the potential value of a print bibliography on a religious topic increases the further back that it extends its coverage before 1949. Although some disciplines place relatively little value on such "early" publications, in theological studies these materials are significant—perhaps because the piece in question may still be the finest scholarly treatment of an issue, or because of the publication's value for the study of the history of research. In any case, it is important to set specific chronological boundaries for a bibliography so that users may be confident that the period specified has been covered and then consult other tools for periods outside the compiler's stated limits.[8]

Yet another way to encompass research resources previously neglected is to cast the compiler's net more widely so as to cover a greater number of publications. In the case of bibliographies surveying periodical literature, this means extending coverage to periodical titles that have been neglected by *Religion Indexes* or the other relevant electronic tools. Indexes typically attempt to identify those journals that regularly publish research in a certain discipline and then include all relevant articles in those journals, thus providing consistent coverage with clear boundaries. As more and more peripheral serials are added to the list of those covered, however, rewards diminish with the effort expended. Consequently, there are always pertinent articles that fall outside the net that has been cast. For the bibliographer to attempt to include these materials, though, poses significant difficulties, including that of the reward-expenditure ratio just mentioned. If the challenge is accepted, it may mean that the compiler must sift through footnotes in the books and journals covered by the indexes, consult all pertinent print catalogs and bibliographies, and scan databases devoted to non-religious subjects. Whatever one's decision on this point, the conscientious bibliographer will of necessity consult the major electronic databases, a relatively simple and speedy task, and yet something that is all-too-often neglected.[9]

2. *How will the bibliography improve subject access?*

Improvement may also be made to bibliographic control of religious publications by enhancing subject access. Although the indexers of *Religion Indexes* have often attached many subject headings to each bibliographic record, the matter is often different in the case of OCLC and RLIN records, where most have relatively few subject headings. Therefore, in the course of preparation a compiler may add considerable value to a print bibliography by increasing the number of relevant subject headings that are attached to each record.[10] Conversely, it is disastrous to structure a bibliography so that subject access is severely limited,[11] something that often occurs when the entries for a bibliography are listed by subject. While the latter practice has a certain, limited advantage, it can undermine the usefulness of a work by discouraging the application of an adequate number of subject headings.[12] Furthermore, whenever subject headings are applied to entries, careful thought needs to be given to the source of those headings. Are they devised on an *ad hoc* basis or has the bibliographer examined the possible sources for a controlled vocabulary (e.g., *Library of Congress Subject Headings*[13] or *Religion Indexes: Thesaurus*)[14] and used or adapted one of them? In addition, it will probably also be necessary to employ some kind of "see also" system of references to guide the unfamiliar user to the correct headings.

3. *Would the addition of abstracts offer significant benefit to the project under consideration?*

A third means of improvement may be sought in the addition of abstracts or annotations.[15] Such are lacking, of course, in the major bibliographic utilities such as OCLC and RLIN, and while they occur in some periodical indexes, they are largely lacking in many religious indexes. The provision of abstracts, though, introduces an array of new difficulties. Most obviously, it requires an enormous investment of time to assess each article or book and then construct an appropriate summary—something that may increase the preparation time for a bibliography many times over. Second, there is the matter of defining the nature of the abstract: Is it intended, for example, only to summarize the publication in question, or is it written as a critical evaluation of the piece? Moreover, the reader will expect a certain degree of consistency in the abstracts, both with regard to type and length.[16] Finally, the abstract must be written as clearly and concisely as possible.[17]

4. *What additional features may be added to enhance the value of the bibliography?*

The compiler may also increase the value of the projected bibliography by providing enhancements that are not presently available in the indexes or other bibliographies. The provision of English translations of foreign language titles (especially those in non-Roman scripts), for example, may be particularly helpful,[18] and the citation of additional research tools, such as book reviews or entry numbers for *Old Testament Abstracts* or *Dissertation Abstracts,* makes it far easier for the researcher to lay hands on a reliable summary of a relevant publication. If one adds the names of dissertation directors, then the specialist is given information that helps situate the dissertation in its intellectual context and place in the history of the discipline. Finally, by providing multiple indexes (e.g., author, title, subject), the value of a bibliography is enhanced. If the bibliographic citations were arranged in chronological order, for example, and each assigned a unique number, then the three previously mentioned indexes require relatively little additional space, since only the unique number need be cited. An additional index to a significant genre, such as academic dissertations, may also prove helpful.

Some Additional Considerations for Print Bibliographies

In addition to the points for evaluation that have already been mentioned, there are several other items that merit the compiler's consideration. Although some appear so obvious that one would think they hardly require mention, even a cursory examination of the bibliographies that have appeared in the last five years reveals that many have been neglected.

1. *Introductions*

First of all, bibliographies typically require an introduction that explains the genesis of the work and the method of compilation, as well as its purpose and intended audience. Did it emerge from the author's doctoral research or another project?[19] Which electronic databases, library catalogs, or print resources were consulted? Is it intended primarily for specialists in the field or for others? Moreover, its scope of coverage concerning languages of materials included, chronological range of publications, and the genre of literature included (e.g., are unpublished academic theses included?) should be specified. It should also be clear whether the compiler aims at comprehensiveness or selectivity, and if the latter, what the criteria are for decisions in this regard. Furthermore, it may be necessary to define significant terms for the student or for the specialist who comes to the work from a different discipline. Finally, it is important to explain how the bibliography may be used most effectively.

2. *Abbreviations*

In order to achieve the necessary degree of compactness in the work, it will probably be useful to provide a table of abbreviations for serial titles and other information that occurs repeatedly. Spelling out titles of series or journals becomes tiresome for the user, and referring the reader to another source for a list of abbreviations is both irritating and unnecessary. Every effort should be made in the compilation of such a table to follow commonly accepted forms. For the study of theology and religion this will probably be those abbreviations used by the two primary professional organizations AAR and SBL and listed in their most recent membership directory or in the pamphlet of instructions for contributors to the *Journal of the American Academy of Religion* or the *Journal of Biblical Literature*. Other sources for abbreviations (some not included in the AAR/SBL publications) are to be found in *Theologische Realenzyklopädie* or *Elenchus of Biblica*.

3. Citation Format

It is also important to select a certain form of bibliographic citation for the various genres of materials included and adhere to it rigorously.[20] Specialists in a discipline typically have a sharp eye for details in citations and find it extremely irritating for a compiler to be undisciplined in this regard, whether it appears in the form of incomplete bibliographic citations or in the form of following first one method of citation and later another.[21] As in the case of abbreviations, the form of citation chosen should be commonly used by scholars in the relevant discipline. In the case of religion and theology, guidance may be found in the *Journal of Biblical Literature* and the *Journal of the American Academy of Religion* or the more general and widely accepted *Chicago Manual of Style*.[22] In some cases the trend has been toward brevity, even to the extent of creating additional difficulties for researchers when they turn from the bibliography to a library catalog to find the desired publication. Given the increasing amount of material published each year and the hope that one's bibliography not create additional work or frustrations for users, it may be best to give the fuller forms of authors' names, rather than simply their initials, and to supply the names of monographic series, both the place of publication and the publisher, and the names of editors (for collected volumes of essays, e.g., but not for monographic series).

Conclusions

So what is the point in all this? It is my hope that compilers, series editors, and publishers will be a bit more critical when they assess the prospects of a bibliography that is proposed, viz., that they will ask more than the question, "Has another print bibliography been issued recently on this topic?" Perhaps they will ask the more significant question, "In light of the current universe of bibliographic tools, does the proposed work make a substantial contribution?" Moreover, instead of issuing what sometimes amounts to little more than a reading list with minimal indexing, perhaps specialists with substantial familiarity with information management issues and techniques will be consulted for advice on matters such as the arrangement of entries, indexing, advisability of abstracts, etc. Finally, it is to be hoped that serious consideration will be given to the possibility of issuing the bibliography not just in print, but also in electronic form. In these ways, conscientious bibliographers may take advantage of the unprecedented technological and bibliographic resources available to them for the benefit of all those who use their tools.

Endnotes

1. Given the nature of the present *Festschrift* and my own experience and training, the observations that ensue will deal with subject bibliographies in the field of religion. At the outset I would also like to express my thanks to Mr. Eric R. Nitschke of the Woodruff Library (Emory University) for reading this paper and making a number of helpful suggestions.

2. It is often the case that (for obvious reasons) a subject specialist, rather than a subject specialist with training in information management, will be assigned a bibliography to review, and the result is often a favorable review, because a bibliography is now available for an area, where none was before, and the obvious publications were included. Consequently, the most basic issues in the design of a bibliography are ignored, everyone is reassured about the enterprise, and nothing is learned so as to improve the next product. Cf., e.g., Henry T. C. Sun's review of John W. Welch's *A Biblical Law Bibliography*, Toronto Studies in Theology, v. 51 (Lewiston, NY: Edwin Mellen, 1990) in *Religious Studies Review* 19 (1993): 252; and the following assessments of Isaac Kalimi's *The Books of Chronicles: A Classified Bibliography*, Simor Bible Bibliographies (Jerusalem: Simor, 1990): Lawrence D. McIntosh's review in *Australian Biblical Review* 39 (1991): 66-67; Michael Mach's review in *Journal for the Study of Judaism in the Persian, Hellenistic and Roman Period* 24 (1993): 100-101; Jean-Pierre Sternberger's review in *Etudes Théologiques & Religieuses* 67 (1992): 97; and Gary N. Knoppers' review in *Catholic Biblical Quarterly* 55 (1993): 119.

3. It has become increasingly difficult to defend the reluctance to make such print bibliographies also available in electronic form.

4. A helpful checklist of elements in a bibliography may be found in William A. Katz's *Introduction to Reference Work*, 5th ed., vol. 1 (New York: McGraw-Hill, 1987), 58-59.

5. It is, of course, the case that neither all libraries nor researchers have direct access to OCLC. Nevertheless, the system is available to thousands of libraries and, through them, to hundreds of thousands of students and researchers.

6. It seems likely that at some point in the future *Religion Indexes* will be accessible online directly from ATLA.

7. In the first volume of what would later become *Religion Indexes One*, there is the following explanation: "This work contains the indexing of thirty-one periodicals which are indexed in neither the Reader's Guide to Periodical Literature nor in the International Index to Periodicals, and in general covers the years from 1949 through December 1952, although at least two periodicals are indexed back through 1948." J. Stillson Judah (ed.), *Index to Religious Periodical Literature* ([Chicago]: American Theological Library Association, 1953), v.

8. John W. Welch's *A Biblical Law Bibliography* provides a fitting example of this point. It specifies no single period for coverage and then proceeds to range over two centuries of material, selecting a modern commentary here and an obscure, nineteenth-century Latin treatise there. In the end, it is clear that no period has been covered thoroughly, and so the user is left not knowing where to go next.

9. Such neglect is evident in, e.g., Watson E. Mills' *A Bibliography of the Nature and Role of the Holy Spirit in Twentieth-Century Writings* (Lewiston, NY: Edwin Mellen, 1993); Ted Daniels' *Millennialism: An International Bibliography*, Garland Reference Library of Social Science, v. 667 (Hamden, CT: Garland, 1992); and Welch's *A Biblical Law Bibliography*. See my reviews of these works in *American Reference Books Annual* (25 [1994], entry 1534; 24 [1993], entry 1399; 23 [1992], entry 1445, respectively).

10. It is possible, though, to add subject headings indiscriminately so that the researcher must then deal with the frustrations of an overwhelming number of meaningless or insignificant "hits."

11. An especially unusual instance of such limitation is to be found in D. Campbell Wyckoff and George Brown, Jr.'s *Religious Education, 1960-1993: An Annotated Bibliography*, Bibliographies and Indexes in Religious Studies, no. 33 (Westport, CT: Greenwood, 1995), in which the subject index is not keyed to the entries, as one might expect, but to the introductory essay. Hence, there is no direct subject index for the 1,100+ entries.

12. This point is illustrated in Isaac Kalimi's *The Books of Chronicles: A Classified Bibliography*. Kalimi's work is a superb collection of literature dealing with the biblical books of Chronicles, but the bibliographic citations are gathered and listed under topical headings, with the result that a number of helpful and long-established subject headings have been omitted. Another, though much worse, example occurs in Welch's *A Biblical Law Bibliography*, where only a single subject heading was assigned to each entry—a systematic disaster.

13. 18th ed. (Washington, D.C.: Library of Congress, Cataloging Distribution Service, 1995).

14. 6th ed. (Evanston, IL: American Theological Library Association, 1994).

15. Yet another possibility is the inclusion of a bibliographic essay that guides the reader through the history of research in a discipline.

16. The annotations in Ted Daniels' *Millennialism: An International Bibliography*, e.g., are unusually poor. They vary widely in length from two lines to three pages; occasionally are omitted; sometimes are merely descriptive, but elsewhere are highly critical; occasionally suggest that Daniels has misunderstood the author's point; and at times are simply confusing.

17. In lengthy series of independently written summaries, opportunities abound for descriptions to degenerate into nonsense, unintended humor, and revelations of ignorance. As an example of a recent annotated bibliography with abstracts that have been masterfully written, one should consult Wyckoff and Brown's *Religious Education, 1960-1993*.

18. The provision of English translations for at least the Hebrew language publications cited in Kalimi's *The Books of Chronicles*, e.g., would have been enormously helpful, since about fifteen percent of the scholarly literature published on Chronicles is in modern Hebrew.

19. The preface to Mills' *A Bibliography of the Nature and Role of the Holy Spirit in Twentieth-Century Writings*, e.g., sets the piece within the compiler's career, but it does not treat adequately the work's topic, scope of coverage, and criteria for selecting publications to be included.

20. Alan David Crown's *A Bibliography of the Samaritans*, 2nd ed., ATLA Bibliography Series, no. 32 (Metuchen, NJ: American Theological Library Association and Scarecrow, 1993), an otherwise commendable work, is an appropriate example. Some authors, e.g., are cited by their initials and others by their full names; publishers are only occasionally named; dissertations are cited in various ways; and volume numbers of journals are sporadically omitted.

21. In Welch's *A Biblical Law Bibliography*, e.g., there is an unusually large number of incomplete bibliographic citations, many of which are for works that are widely held by American libraries.

22. 14th edn. (Chicago: University of Chicago Press, 1993).

Religious and Theological Reference Resources: Then and Now

Diane Choquette

What were Abraham Lincoln's devotional prayers? What is the social impact of Pentecostalism in the U.S.? What is the meaning of a skull and cross-bones at the base of a cross from Germany? Real questions. Everyday, throughout the country, reference librarians working in semi-nary and university libraries are asked a wide range of questions related to religion. The element of surprise is always there: what will the next question be? Where will I find the answer? Nowadays the search often be-gins and sometimes ends with a check into a computer database, espe-cially when the question requires bibliographic verification, a selection of books or articles on a topic, or the correct spelling of a name. But the real stock in trade of the theological reference librarian's work is the refer-ence book in all its beloved manifestations—encyclopedias, dictionaries, guides, directories, etc.

As historical fields, religion and theology accumulate knowledge and information. The reference books available and useful today include the latest issues of the *Index to Book Reviews in Religion*[1] along with the venerable early tomes of the *Acta Sanctorum*[2] from the 1860s. Naturally, we have more reference books to consult than we did fifty years ago when ATLA started. What was it like then? What books were theological li-brarians using in reference work? This essay will compare and contrast the religious and theological reference books available in the formative years of ATLA with those available now through an examination of the contents of the "Religion" sections of the seventh[3] and eleventh[4] editions of the American Library Association's *Guide to Reference Books* (hereafter referred to as the *Guide*). Certainly books other than those mentioned in the *Guide* are also useful, but that standard bibliography is unique in representing reference books found to be most useful at those times in its over ninety-year history when each edition was published.

The most obvious difference between the seventh and eleventh editions of the *Guide* is length. Two hundred fifty-eight entries comprised the "Religion" section in the seventh edition, with very few additional titles mentioned in the entries. The eleventh edition, however, contains 575 entries, with over 100 additional titles mentioned in those entries. The age of books differs, also. In 1951 the bulk of the reference books listed were published prior to 1940, and only fifty-two (i.e., one-fifth) of the titles were published in the ten years preceding the volume's closing date, 1949. We can see how the publication rate has grown by noting that 226 titles, about one-third of the entire "Religion" section, were published in the ten years preceding the 1993 closing date of the eleventh edition. Along with an increase in the rate of publication we see greater specialization and the development of new subject areas. Since increases can be seen in most subject areas, this essay will focus on the most noteworthy changes. In addition to describing how the field has developed, attention will be paid to what type of works have been and are currently lacking. In 1959, Clara B. Allen, Librarian at Fuller Theological Seminary, presented a paper to the ATLA conference in which she discussed religious and theological reference books and indicated the needs she saw,[5] allowing us a backward glance into reference work in ALTA's early years. Have those needs been addressed? Do they still exist?

Encyclopedias are very important in reference work, particularly those that are authoritative, up to date, and include bibliographies. We have been blessed with many new general religion encyclopedias and those specific to Christianity. The 1980s and early 1990s were particularly productive with general encyclopedias appearing such as *The Encyclopedia of Religion*[6] and the start of the 3rd edition of *Lexikon für Theologie und Kirche.*[7] Significant specialized works such as *The Encyclopedia of African American Religions,*[8] *Encyclopedia of the American Religious Experience,*[9] and *The Coptic Encyclopedia*[10] are valuable for opening new avenues of access to their subject areas. Of particular note among the specialized encyclopedias is the scholarly and authoritative *Encyclopedia of the Early Church*.[11] For the period since 1951 it represents a culmination of the development of new works in early church history, works which include the *Reallexikon für Antike und Christentum*[12] and the *Encyclopedia of Early Christianity*,[13] intended for general readers and students.

Closely related to the early church materials are those in patrology, an area fraught with difficulties for reference librarians and researchers. New critical texts, translations, and the indexes and manuals needed to locate them have aided our work tremendously. When ATLA was formed, the Ancient Christian Writers[14] and Fathers of the Church[15] series were both in their infancy and are now of substantial size. Unfortunately, however, the indexes of the new English translation sets are not as useful for reference purposes as are the individual volume and comprehensive subject and scripture indexes in the older Ante-Nicene Fathers set.[16] In 1952 the critical texts of the Corpus Christianorum[17] series began appearing. Its digitization and presentation in CD-ROM format as the *CETEDOC Library of Christian Latin Texts*[18] and the similar production of the *Patrologia Latina Database*[19] allows for unprecedented flexibility in searching the original language texts—an immense improvement over the indexing of Henricus Kraft's *Clavis Patrum Apostolocorum*[20] (limited to sixteen works of the Apostolic Fathers) and Edgar Goodspeed's *Index Patristicus*.[21]

In 1959 Clara Allen noted the need for a "guide to all the different sets of the Fathers, similar to *Granger's Index to Poetry*."[22] In the intervening years Maurice Geerard's *Clavis Patrum Graecorum*,[23] Eligius Dekkers' *Clavis Patrum Latinorum*,[24] and Johannes Quasten's *Patrology*[25] have all helped to fill the gap, though none fulfills every need, and the *Clavis Patrum Latinorum* is now out of date. It certainly would ease the work of both librarians and researchers to have a single resource to locate original language texts and translations of early church writings.

Changes in the biblical studies field have resulted in growth in all types of reference sources, including the publication of enough dictionaries and encyclopedias in biblical archaeology to warrant a separate section in the eleventh edition of the *Guide*. In the seventh edition not a single biblical archaeology resource could be found. General Bible dictionaries are now so numerous that they fill several shelves in the Graduate

Theological Union reference collection. Many theological libraries will not need to purchase a full complement of such dictionaries, and it may be just as well, for it is difficult to keep track of the theological or denominational viewpoint of each work. Evaluating the information within each dictionary is also a challenge, consequently one finds oneself depending on a few standard titles.

Considering the growth in all types of biblical reference books—indexes, bibliographies, dictionaries, commentaries—is the Old Testament still neglected, as Clara Allen maintained it was in her day?[26] Again, the dictionaries have come to the rescue. Johannnes Botterweck's *Theological Dictionary of the Old Testament,*[27] a fine work which we wish would speed along to completion, and the less comprehensive *Theological Wordbook of the Old Testament*[28] offer new word studies. Bibliographies, however, have continued to focus on the New Testament, and none specific to the Old Testament are listed in the eleventh edition of the *Guide*, except the *Book List of the Society for Old Testament Study*.[29] Indexing of periodical and essay literature on the Old Testament has substantially improved with the arrival of *Old Testament Abstracts,*[30] the production and expanded coverage of the *Religion Indexes* on CD-ROM,[31] and the CD-ROM versions of *Religious and Theological Abstracts*[32] and *Catholic Periodical and Literature Index.*[33] Now that computerized searching offers the capability of tailoring bibliographies to individual needs it raises questions about the value of printed bibliographies comprised mainly of subject subsets of databases. This type of bibliography is of little use to the researcher whose needs are so often more limited by time period, authorship, or subject. We are better served by expanded computerized indexing coverage and fewer, more selective printed bibliographies intended to complement indexing sources.

The age and paucity of Protestant denominational resources listed in the 1995 *Guide* stands in stark contrast to the plethora of reference books in most other subject areas. The Lutherans, Mennonites, Southern Baptists, Methodists, and Mormons managed to publish encyclopedias primarily in the period from the 1950s to the mid-1970s, leaving most out of date now. *The Encyclopedia of Mormonism,*[34] published in 1992, joins several Mormon bibliographies and guides, making that church the most well-documented in recent years. Sandra Caldwell's *The History of the Episcopal Church in America, 1607-1991*[35] and Harold Parker's *Bibliography of Published Articles on American Presbyterianism, 1901-*

1980[36] are substantial examples of the few other recent denominational bibliographies. Easy access to current denominational biographies is also wanting. General religious biography sources can only include notable religious leaders; often the reference librarian searches them dutifully, but in vain. Consistent denominational attention to up-to-date biographical resources would be appreciated.

Where Protestant denominational resources have languished, Roman Catholic ones have flourished, many precipitated by the Second Vatican Council. After the publication of the *New Catholic Encyclopedia*[37] one finds here also the trend toward one-volume works such as the *New Dictionary of Catholic Spirituality*[38] and *The New Dictionary of Sacramental Worship*,[39] both of which include the type of substantial articles one sees in encyclopedias. Of great importance to the reference librarian are the books compiling English translations of papal and conciliar documents. Sister Claudia Carlen has done a great service with her *Papal Pronouncements: A Guide*[40] and the *Papal Encyclicals*[41] in translation. The period since 1740 is quite well covered; now who will help us with those pesky earlier papal documents that we are left to hunt for in disparate, mostly Latin sources?

None of the remaining works Clara Allen was calling for in 1959 has fully materialized—a general guide to Protestant theology, a revised edition of Philip Schaff's *The Creeds of Christendom*,[42] and a guide to the field of missions. Gordon Melton's *The Encyclopedia of American Religions, Religious Creeds*[43] partially updates and expands on Schaff's work by including texts of the creeds of many small American religious groups. The missions field is still a vast expanse with few guideposts. For the guide to Protestant theology Allen had envisioned a work "which is primarily to aid students to understand the meaning of the various aspects of the Christian religion, to give the latest and all phases of theological ideas, as well as the history of their development. It should include Christian education, pastoral psychology, missions, etc."[44] As it appeared to Allen then, it also seems now that theological biases stand in the way of such a publication, and we will probably need to continue to depend on dictionaries, encyclopedias, and specialized bibliographies and guides to provide piecemeal rather than overall guidance. This approach should suffice and be more useful than a major guide that would require substantial resources to prepare and would soon need updating.

Although Christian religion occupies the major portion of theological and religious reference work and reference books available in the United States and Canada, startling increases can be seen in recent years in Jewish, Buddhist, and, to a lesser degree, Islamic reference books. Overall, between 1951 and 1995 there was a five-fold growth in the sections covering those religions in the *Guide*. In particular, encyclopedias, dictionaries, and bibliographies have served to more fully document these religions and their cultures in various countries. *The Encyclopedia of Buddhism*,[45] a welcomed addition, is, however, frustratingly slow in coming out. The attempt at comprehensiveness of the first three volumes, as seen in the many brief dictionary-type entries, was wisely abandoned with the fourth volume. The new focus on concepts of doctrine, philosophy, and civilization promises to speed the publication toward completion. A valuable contribution to the study of Islam is the new *The Oxford Encyclopedia of the Modern Islamic World*,[46] published too late for inclusion in the eleventh edition of the *Guide*, but deserving of mention here. That work provides information on a complex religion and its cultural manifestations in a way that the very important, yet less-accessible *Encyclopaedia of Islam*[47] does not. With so many titles now available for religions other than Christianity, theological libraries will be able to select what they require from a rich variety.

To conclude this review of changes in religious and theological reference books, there is one more work we lack that must be mentioned, and that is a review medium. As we know, the tremendous growth in reference book publishing—though for the most part a boon to our profession—is also an occasion for costly acquisitions expenditures. Most, if not all, libraries must be carefully selective in their acquisitions and will search for the best value for stretched dollars. The communication fostered by the ATLANTIS listserv[48] has engendered critical discussion of published bibliographies and has provided a medium for some reviews. Unfortunately, all theological and religious librarians do not have Internet access now, but that situation will change and more librarians will be connected. Also, as the ALTA Internet node develops, it promises to be a logical online source for up-to-date reviews of reference sources. A printed version of such a review medium would also be appreciated. As the fields of religion and theology continue to both specialize and find greater connectedness to other fields such as medicine, psychology, and sociology, reference librarians are further challenged to exercise evaluation in selecting the resources to place on our shelves and provide for consultation. The task of sorting out the wheat from the chaff is ever more important to our work.

Endnotes

1. *Index to Book Reviews in Religion* (Chicago: American Theological Library Association, 1986-).

2. *Acta Sanctorum quotquot toto orbe coluntur* (Paris: Palmé, 1863-1940).

3. Constance M. Winchell, *Guide to Reference Books*, 7th ed. (Chicago: American Library Association, 1951).

4. Robert Balay, ed., *Guide to Reference Books*, 11th ed. (Chicago: American Library Association, 1995).

5. Clara B. Allen, "Seek and Ye Shall Find; Theological Research," *Summary of Proceedings* 13 (1959): 102-17.

6. Mircea Eliade, ed., *The Encyclopedia of Religion* (New York: Macmillan, 1987).

7. Walter Kasper, et.al. eds., *Lexikon für Theologie und Kirche*, 3rd ed. (Freiburg: Herder, 1993-).

8. Larry G. Murphy, Gordon J. Melton, and Gary L. Ward, eds., *Encyclopedia of African American Religions* (New York: Garland, 1993).

9. Charles H. Lippy and Peter W. Williams, eds., *Encyclopedia of the American Religious Experience* (New York: Scribner, 1988).

10. Aziz S. Atiya, ed., *The Coptic Encyclopedia* (New York: Macmillan, 1991).

11. Angelo DiBerardino, ed., *Encyclopedia of the Early Church* (New York: Oxford University Press, 1992).

12. Theodor Klauser, ed., *Reallexikon für Antike und Christentum* (Stuttgart: Hiersemann, 1950-).

13. Everett Ferguson, ed., *Encyclopedia of Early Christianity* (New York: Garland, 1990).

14. *Ancient Christian Writers: The Works of the Fathers in Translation* (Ramsey, NJ: Paulist Press, 1946-).

15. *The Fathers of the Church: A New Translation* (Washington, D.C.: Catholic University of America Press, 1947-).

16. Alexander Roberts and James Donaldson, eds., *The Ante-Nicene Fathers* (New York: C. Scribner's, 1899-1900).

17. *Corpus Christianorum* (Turnhout: Brepols, 1953-).

18. Turnhout: Brepols, 1991- .

19. Release 3. Alexandria, VA: Chadwyck-Healey, 1994.

20. Munich: Kosel, 1963.

21. Leipzig: J. C. Hinrichs, 1907.

22. Allen, "Seek and Ye Shall Find," 112.

23. Maurice Geerard, *Clavis Patrum Graecorum* (Turnhout: Brepols, 1974-87).

24. Eligius Dekkers, *Clavis Patrum Latinorum*, Sacris Erudiri: Jaarboek voor Godsdienst-Wetenschappen, 3 (Steenbrugis: In Abbatia Sancti Petri, 1961).

25. Johannes Quasten, *Patrology* (Utrecht: Spectrum, 1950-86).

26. Allen, "Seek and Ye Shall Find," 111.

27. Johannes G. Botterweck and Helmer Ringgren, eds., *Theological Dictionary of the Old Testament* (Grand Rapids: Eerdmans, 1977-).

28. Laird R. Harris, ed., *Theological Wordbook of the Old Testament* (Chicago: Moody Press, 1980).

29. Society for Old Testament Study, *Book List* (Sheffield: s.n.).

30. *Old Testament Abstracts* (Washington, D.C.: Catholic Biblical Association of America, 1978-).

31. *ALTA Religion Database on CD-ROM* (Evanston, IL: American Theological Library Association, 1993-).

32. *R & TA on CD-ROM* (Myerstown, PA: Religious and Theological Abstracts, 1990?-).

33. *Catholic Periodical and Literature Index* (Winona, MN: Catholic Library Association, 1968-).

34. Daniel H. Ludlow, ed., *Encyclopedia of Mormonism* (New York: Macmillan, 1992).

35. Sandra M. and Ronald J. Caldwell, *The History of the Episcopal Church in America, 1607-1991: A Bibliography* (New York: Garland, 1993).

36. Harold M. Parker, *Bibliography of Published Articles on American Presbyterianism, 1901-1980*, Bibliographies and Indexes in Religious Studies, no. 4 (Westport, CT: Greenwood, 1985).

37. *New Catholic Encyclopedia* (New York: McGraw-Hill, 1967-89).

38. Michael Downey, *The New Dictionary of Catholic Spirituality* (Collegeville, MN: Liturgical Press, 1993).

39. Peter E. Fink, *The New Dictionary of Sacramental Worship* (Collegeville, MN: Liturgical Press, 1990).

40. Claudia Carlen, *Papal Pronouncements: A Guide: 1740-1978* (Ann Arbor, MI: Pierian Press, 1990).

41. Claudia Carlen, comp., *The Papal Encyclicals* (Wilmington, NC: McGrath, 1981).

42. Philip Schaff, *Bibliotheca Symbolica Ecclesiae Universalis: The Creeds of Christendom with a History and Critical Notes*, rev. ed. (New York: Harper, 1919).

43. Gordon J. Melton, ed., *The Encyclopedia of American Religions,*

Religious Creeds (Detroit, MI: Gale, 1988).

44. Allen, "Seek and Ye Shall Find," 116.

45. G. P. Malalasekera, ed., *Encyclopaedia of Buddhism* (Colombo: Government of Ceylon, 1961-).

46. John L. Esposito, ed., *The Oxford Encyclopedia of the Modern Islamic World* (New York: Oxford University Press, 1995).

47. H.A.R. Gibb, et. al., *The Encyclopaedia of Islam*, new ed. (Leiden: Brill, 1954-).

48. ATLANTIS is the American Theological Library Discussion List that was developed at Harvard University by L. Charles Willard, Director of the Andover-Harvard Theological Library.

Special Collections: A Retrospective View, 1971-1996

Brian Carter

For fifty years, the Association has been exercizing its influence to sustain and improve the quality of theological libraries by means of its periodic meetings, special committees, and the expertise of librarians involved in the accreditation process. For almost exactly half that time, I have been in contact with many of those libraries on account of my business as a bookdealer specializing in antiquarian and out-of-print books in the fields of theology and church history. It is possible that my perceptions differ from other bookdealers from abroad, because I have visited and revisited theological libraries on some four hundred occasions during frequent trips to America over the last twenty-five years. I am not aware of any other overseas bookdealer with that level of first hand experience with these libraries. It is, I think, for this reason (and because I have been fortunate enough over the years to develop good and tested links with a number of librarians) that I have been asked to contribute a reflective article for this fiftieth-anniversary volume.

Current Religious Climate in America

Occasionally I have wondered whether there were any similarities between the religious situation and theological education in Britain, as it stood about one hundred years ago, and the American scene today. In the latter years of the nineteenth century in Britain, there was a widespread familiarity with and interest in theological matters and religious debate among the laity. This period also witnessed an extraordinary expansion of church and chapel building—especially in the cities—and the establishment of many theological colleges. To an interested observer, the country's religious life would have appeared vigorous. One century later, though, a significant number of these theological colleges and seminaries have been closed or merged with other institutions, and many of the churches are no longer in use—some lie derelict and others have been converted into homes, warehouses, or shops. There has also been a remorseless decline in theological awareness to the extent that, according to a recent writer in the London *Times*, we are "on the verge of becoming a religiously illiterate society."

Although American churches have not been immune from similar vicissitudes, it is nevertheless my impression that the contemporary scene in America reflects many of the same manifestations of the vigorous religious life found in England a century ago. Nowhere is this more evident than in the wide variety of modern churches that represent all Christian traditions, and in the case of seminaries, one finds theological libraries that offer unrivaled facilities and resources for study and research.

Growth of Theological Libraries in America

In the last twenty-five years, librarians in America have been presented with greater opportunities, as well as difficulties, than at any other time in their history, and it has generally been a period of extraordinary expansion. When I visited a library with holdings of about 90,000 volumes recently, I was reminded of another library of similar size in 1971. After twenty-five years, the latter library now contains just under a half million volumes. During the same period, I have seen many other libraries also increase dramatically in size, and much of this expansion has been based on retrospective collection development.

A quarter century ago, a small group of old and esteemed institutions were dominant among theological libraries. Alongside these was another group of theological libraries, some attached to universities, others freestanding, and many serving old institutions. With a few exceptions, this latter group tended to have excellent holdings in biblical studies and in materials relating to their own particular religious traditions, but with surprisingly little of significance outside those areas. In the intervening years a distinctive feature of many of these libraries has been the extent to which they have diversified from their own Christian religious traditions. For example, there are libraries once strong in British Methodist history, which now have outstanding holdings for doctoral-level research in Recusant and Roman Catholic history: twenty-five years ago these libraries had little to offer in that area. This example could be replicated in the experience of other libraries, where there are now collections of exceptional quality that were built from the ground up within only a few years. So now, after twenty-five years, the landscape of theological libraries is no longer dominated by just a few of the older institutions.

Obviously, collection development on such a scale is not possible without the librarian's vision and determination, the two most elements in the growth of a library. Other factors naturally play their part, such as the purely contingent matters of financial resources and availability of materials. There has always been and will continue to be a good, if diminishing, supply of pre-twentieth century imprints, but in the 1960s and 1970s in England unusual opportunities arose as many colleges and seminaries closed and some Cathedral libraries were liquidated. These events produced an unusually rich and plentiful supply of theological books and pamphlets from all religious traditions. Librarians in America had an unrivaled opportunity to transform their libraries, and some of them took advantage of that opportunity. The American librarian did not have exclusive access to this cornucopia, because, at the same time, there was a worldwide expansion of universities and the urgent need for their libraries to offer appropriate resources. Many of these universities developed programs in the field of religion, and these have had a profound impact on theological colleges and their libraries.

What at one time would have been seen as purely theological material was subject to a reassessment and change of nomenclature, as the new universities with their new courses came to this material as if to a quarry, removing works that could be accommodated under the heading of cultural studies, sociology of religion, social history, English literature, anthropology, and so on. I recollect an American state university librarian in the early 1970s considering the acquisition of a collection from me of books on what would traditionally have been understood as the history of Christian foreign missions. The librarian told me that, as a state library, they had no interest in Christian missions, nor could they justify buying such a collection. If the books were evaluated from a different perspective, however, they could be seen as satisfying the criteria for an anthropology collection. As such, they were purchased. The question of nomenclature in the library would make an interesting study.

Altered perceptions, political correctness, as well as the advent of new subjects, have all played a part. In some instances, "rare book collections" have been renamed "special collections," "rare book" sounding elitist and with more resonance of artefact than source of information. Even the designation "library" has been eschewed for terminology that better describes the variety of modern forms of information storage, and so the post of librarian has been transmogrified into "Director of the Multi-Media Center."

Collection Level Acquisitions

Returning to collections and the advantages of purchasing them: buying a collection of a thousand books requires one decision, as opposed to one thousand—even supposing that the opportunity exists to buy them individually over a long period of time. A collection, once cataloged, also makes a substantial amount of material immediately available to the reader. The same principle applies whether the collection comprises 100 items or 50,000.

During the past two decades, I have bought complete collections from institutions and scholars, but more often I have assembled them myself, sometimes over several years. Themes of some of these have included, for example, Jansenism, the Oxford Tractarian Movement, Anglican sisterhoods of the nineteenth century, Cambridge Platonists, women and religion, and deism. The size of these collections has ranged from 100 to 8,000 volumes, and over the years, some 140,000 books and pamphlets have passed from me, directly or indirectly, to American theological libraries, a very substantial proportion of which having been as collections. In retrospect, I know how difficult it would be to reassemble some of those collections.

Although it was not possible at the time to determine when the major contraction of institutional libraries in England was over, it is clear that by the early 1980s it had come to an end, and with it ceased an apparently unending supply of large quantities of books printed from the seventeenth to the nineteenth century. We have returned to more normal times in Britain, and I have observed over the last three or four years some limited strategic reductions in holdings coming from institutions that have altered their entire admissions policy, as they evolve from having been predominantly theological colleges into more secular, liberal arts colleges. New subjects and curricula require library space, and theological collections have to give way to alternative subjects. Fortunately, some of the most interesting works, from a scholarly point of view, have been disposed of as not being required for undergraduate study.

If the purchase of entire collections has assisted rapid expansion, the time arrives when they become less attractive to an institution as the percentage of duplicates rises. For many librarians, however, the traditional custom of selecting item by item has always been the preferred method of acquisition. It is my impression that those librarians who maintain personal control of collection development are the ones who create the most dynamic libraries. There is an extraordinarily wide variety of methods of selection from library to library. Recently, I visited a library where the faculty had full control of the book budget; in another, there was a committee that made the decisions; in still another, any book over a certain value had to be discussed in committee; and in yet another, the onus was placed mostly on bibliographers. I have never been overly-impressed with the way that some of these schemes work: they may convince some as theoretical models, but at times they ensure that nothing much happens rather slowly. (Some librarians discover to their dismay that they have inherited these schemes, which may have arisen at a time when a faculty member accepted temporary responsibility for acquisitions in the time between the appointment of one librarian and another or during the prolonged absence of the librarian.) Moreover, while some of the schemes may work well with books in print, they are less useful in the case of out-of-print material listed in catalogues, where speed is of the essence.

Obviously, any good librarian will consult with others whenever they wish and oblige faculty with all reasonable requests. In the case of those outstanding American theological librarians whom I have known over the last twenty-five years, not one has allowed his or her independence to be fettered by conceding any formal or informal rights of consultation to others on the expenditure of the normal library budget. The one area where consultation is essential, however, is in major acquisitions outside the normal budget: then, obviously, the agreement and support of the faculty and administration is vital.

Collection Development Policies
In the last decade, the library world has seen the advent of written collection development policies as well as mission statements and other

types of management documents. Although collection policies have benefited libraries by clarifying their priorities and generating systems for measuring the quality of their special collections, they can also become defensive tools and restrict a librarian if they are too detailed. It can be difficult to write a realistic collection development policy with regard to out-of-print material, since the librarian is absolutely dependent on what becomes available.

The Virtual Library

The question of availability takes us to the very heart of the issues that have arisen in the library world with the ever-increasing dominance of the computer and modern forms of information storage and transmission. The 1960s saw the establishment of a number of companies that reprinted essential texts to meet the demand of the new universities, and these were supplemented by the filming of important multi-volume works. Many of the reprint houses had several successful years, but some were overtaken subsequently by a worldwide recession, and others failed through grossly overpricing their products. They have all been affected by the constant refinement of modern systems of information technology that have lead to the feasibility of a "virtual library" with fulltext online facilities. This development has profound implications for all libraries.

Should the "virtual library" become a reality, what will be the role of the traditional library? Historically, most libraries have been confronted continually with space problems. Libraries have responded with a combination of compact shelving, off-site storage facilities, the exchange of print periodicals for microform copies, and new library buildings—all providing only temporary relief. As we know, the library of the future could hold in modern format all the works that have ever been printed in the field of theology and require little physical space for storage. Will there emerge new types of institutions that, unencumbered by the costs of maintaining traditional libraries, will be able to offer access to library materials at a fraction of the present cost? Perhaps all their students will be enrolled in "distance learning" programs. Just as the decline of many British theological colleges was in part due to a decline in the number of students available and the relentless increase in costs, it may be that the aggressive development of distance learning programs by some American institutions—even without access to the "virtual library"—will erode the financial viability of institutions with more traditional educational programs, and so there will be a further reduction of theological colleges.

Should the "virtual library" become a reality, the availability of out-of-print books for sale would no longer be a problem, nor would collection development policies be necessary. Theoretically, all material would be equally available to everyone with the electronic means of access. How would a library make itself distinctive? What could the librarian contribute by way of a personal impress on the library? What could the directors of a library look back on after twenty years and identify as their particular achievements, and ones which could not also be replicated elsewhere?

The Place of Archives and Manuscripts

These kinds of questions are with us already. Some university libraries have already shifted their resources away from the purchase of older print materials to the acquisition of archives and manuscripts. Part of the rationale for this shift is the conviction that unique materials offer the greatest promise of distinguishing their collections from others. There is always the temptation, though, that the importance of such acquisitions will be inflated in order to justify their substantial purchase and processing costs. Since important manuscript and archival collections become available even more infrequently than out-of-print books, it becomes the more difficult to formulate a collection development policy to accommodate their purchase.

It is important that manuscripts and archives should take their place alongside books, but not as a substitute for books, for they in turn will be stored in electronic format and be made widely available. It has struck me over recent years that despite the formidable quantity of material now available in microform, this has had less effect on the acquisition of special collections than one might have imagined. I have seen no diminishing of interest on the part of librarians in adding to their special collections.

Development of Endowments

One of the problems that arises as a library becomes very large is that it contains within it many subsidiary special collections, and each in turn requires supplementation. With a standard budget covering all acquisitions, it becomes extremely difficult to support these collections, especially with the increasing costs of early printed books. Some librarians have overcome this difficulty by raising endowments for specific collections—by no means a quick or easy achievement. This insures, however, resources for uninterrupted purchases in a particular area and releases budgeted funds for other materials. I have never ceased to be impressed by the level of benefactions enjoyed by various libraries, but these gifts rarely come without a considerable effort by the librarian. Although some development officers may have misgivings about the involvement of librarians in fundraising, the involvement of the librarian in such development contacts is often crucial, and the ideal situation is for the development officer to work closely with the librarian who, in some cases, should take the lead.

It is by no means the case that the largest libraries have all the best special collections. Among my visits to various libraries, I have come across some with relatively small holdings and very modest budgets where the individual librarian has built an outstanding special collection. These fine collections stand as a testimony to the concentrated focus of the librarian over a number of years—such a long term, consistent pattern of acquisition is one of the keys to building a special collection of note. Conversely, years of neglect may erode the excellence of once great collections.

Coordinated Collection Development
There have been various schemes for coordinated responses to problems common to all members of ATLA, the preservation project being a good example of a positive approach to resolving one of these. It may not turn out to be the ideal solution, but it was thoroughly researched and has made a valuable contribution. A topic about which there has been a great deal of discussion is globalization. Everyone stresses its importance, but does anything happen? Consciousness has been raised, but I am not aware of any changes in strategy or practical response to the issue. Some libraries were addressing the question of globalization years before it became fashionable, but who has followed them as a result of all the subsequent discussions? Two schemes were operating in British universities and public libraries for several years in an attempt to ensure that there was comprehensive coverage of books in two quite separate areas. Universities apportioned among themselves years in the sixteenth and seventeenth centuries so that, as well as their normal acquisitions, a

particular university would also try to purchase books published in certain years allocated to them. Another scheme, shared among most public libraries, attempted to collect all fiction titles and so divided letters of the alphabet among various libraries so that, again, in addition to their normal acquisitions, they would endeavor to acquire any works by authors whose names began with the letter of the alphabet assigned to them. It seems to me that there ought to be an opportunity among American theological libraries to devise a plan to diversify their holdings on a geographical basis: each participating library assumes responsibility for a certain country or region and attempts to gather as much as possible of the theological material published there, so that no part of the globe would escape attention. One or two libraries have been outstandingly successful in pursuing a policy of gathering publications from other continents, but there are very few others that have taken up the challenge. I imagine that there would be scarcely any part of the world where alumni of the many theological colleges and seminaries were not to be found working in some capacity, as teachers, missionaries, doctors, etc., and these alone could provide an extraordinarily fruitful first point for contact and source of information.

Realistically, however, coordinated joint ventures have always been difficult to devise and maintain, largely because each participant in the program must perceive some direct benefit. No matter how attractive an utopian vision they bring, it is one unlikely to be realized for the present. It is the application of modern technology that will ultimately lead to the realization of these aspirations.

The Future of the Book

The future of special collection development is difficult to predict—whether for twenty-five years or a hundred. The romantic view of scholars traveling from library to library to examine scarce books in pursuit of scholarship is still with us, and this is one of the reasons that libraries continue to build special collections. Nevertheless, we all know that a substantial portion of the corpus of important western literature and theology is available in reprint or microform. From the 1930s onwards, University Microfilms International has been filming all early books printed in England, and over the decades an ever-increasing wealth of other sources has been made available in even more sophisticated forms. The result is that in many areas of research no scholars need travel beyond their desks, where they can now read texts that were once virtually unobtainable.

Why do librarians continue to purchase the original books for their special collections, when in so many cases, the reader can call up the text on a screen? Historically, a library's quality has been judged in part by the size and the richness of its holdings. To acquire, display, and make available these materials has been a source of pride, and it has traditionally been part of the librarian's duty to act as the custodian of a scarce and valuable resource.

Some of the natural enjoyment and professional satisfaction most librarians derive from collection development is in the tangible objects—the books—that can be seen, handled, read, or displayed, as against the "invisible" book, viewed only in its fleeting presence on the screen, the perfect palimset. (The "invisible book" would seem more in harmony with the "Invisible College" referred to by Robert Boyle in the mid-1640s.)

Therefore, it is with extreme difficulty now that we contemplate breaking with books as we have known them for the last half millennium. The importance of the book as a symbol of culture, wealth, power, and knowledge is historically well represented in many Renaissance and post-Renaissance paintings and portraits. Invariably, the (often richly bound) book—a tactile object, desirable and also symbolizing a civilized way of life—is depicted in the hand of the subject of the portrait. In some paintings where several figures are depicted, a number may be seen carrying a book. As direct heirs of this long tradition, we do not yet know how this break with the book and its symbolic significance will evolve. The librarian has the professional responsibility of facing this question and finding a solution. For the moment most librarians continue to exercise part of this responsibility by standing firmly in the tradition that has evolved by continuing to acquire earlier material, while managing a period of radical change, unparalleled since the invention of printing. The considerable reluctance felt by most librarians to drop their interest in earlier printed books would, I think, be supported by most of the users of their libraries, who often prefer the original copy over a microfilm or an electronic version. There are also prudential reasons for retaining an active interest in the acquisition of older materials for special collections. The printed book has stood the test of time; many of even the earliest are still in fine condition. What do we know of modern formats? How long will the technology last? How long will the servicing companies survive and sustain their support? What will be the cost to a library over the next fifty years, let alone five hundred?

A Final Word

I mentioned earlier the apparent vigour of the religious situation in Britain in the last decade of the nineteenth century and compared it with evidence of similar vigour in America in this last decade of the twentieth century. In Britain there was a gradual erosion among all the churches in the early part of this century, and in the subsequent decades they were overtaken by challenges that they failed to appreciate and address. If the wider church in America reflects what I have observed in the theological libraries and in the leadership and foresight of their librarians, then it need fear no similar fate. As for theological libraries, I would expect to see them offering an even more sophisticated level of service to an ever-increasing readership.

A Major Library Acquisition of 1838:
Three Vignettes and a Reflection

Milton M^cC. Gatch

In 1838, during the first year of its operation, the New-York Theological Seminary (which after January 1840 would be known as Union Theological Seminary in the City of New York) purchased a library of some 13,000 volumes from Leander van Ess, a German ex-Benedictine, sometime Catholic professor in the Protestant University of Marburg, and author of a translation of the Bible into German that circulated more widely than any besides Luther's.[1] At the time, the seller was living in Alzey, near Worms. The transaction has been described several times in greater or less detail.[2] Archival resources—some of them hitherto unavailable, others neglected—enable some amplification of earlier accounts and lead to reflection on the place of this event in the history of American academic libraries.

Edward Robinson and the Purchase of the Library of Leander van Ess

Edward Robinson (1794-1863) was one of America's first great research scholars.[3] His connection with the purchase of the library of Leander van Ess has been reported, but it has never been rehearsed in the detail that the record will allow. Robinson had begun his career in biblical studies as a student of Moses Stuart at Andover Theological Seminary and had studied at Halle and Berlin from 1826 to 1830. He had established a journal of biblical studies and published Greek and Hebrew grammars and lexicons and, by the time he was invited to a chair at the New-York Theological Seminary in 1837 (having already refused a post at New York University), was recognized as a very bright star of American scholarship. In 1838, a young Swiss woman living in New York gathered information for a correspondent at home about theological education in America; she was told by the president of the new seminary, Thomas McAuley, that "Dr. Robinson is undoubtedly one of the greatest scholars in the world."[4] Although his appointment to Union was not uncontested,[5] he was invited to take up the biblical professorship early in 1837 and given permission to go on leave from July of that year to Germany and the biblical sites to work on the biblical geography that would be the keystone of his scholarly achievement. He would return (after the grant of extensions) only in the autumn of 1840.[6]

In his letter accepting the post at the new seminary, Robinson outlined his broad agenda for biblical studies:

> A base examination of the particulars, that fall within the department of Biblical Literature will shew that it covers a wider field, than is usually supposed. To it, properly belong full courses of instruction in the Hebrew, Greek, and Chaldee languages and also as auxiliaries in the Syriac, Arabic, and other minor dialects, in Biblical introduction, or the History of the Bible as a whole and its various parts, its writers, its manuscripts, editions, versions &c in Biblical criticism, on the history and condition of the text, in Biblical hermeneutics or the theory and principles of Interpretation—in Biblical Exegesis or the practical application of those principles to the study and interpretation of the Sacred books—in Biblical Geography—in Biblical Antiquities, and further, a separate consideration of the version of the Seventy, as a chief source of illustration for both the Old and New Testaments.[7]

To support the teaching mission of biblical studies, Robinson felt that a large library was necessary:

> On the general subject of a Library, it is here only proper to remark that a full apparatus of books in every department of Theology, is of course indispensable to the prosperity of the Institution. In particular, the Library should also contain, a complete series of the works of the <u>Fathers</u> so called, in the best editions and with proper apparatus and likewise the best editions of every Greek and Roman writer, with the necessary aids for their eluci-

dation. There is not a page of any Greek writer, which does not in some way, yield illustration to the sacred text, and the same is true also in a modified sense of all the Roman writers.[8]

Robinson offered to be of any service possible to the board during his sojourn abroad, and his examination of the library of Professor Leander van Ess was to be the chief service he performed. He had, in fact, already served as a procurer of books for Andover Seminary during his years as a student in Germany in 1836-1840.[9]

In President McAuley's account of the purchase of the library, he refers obliquely to the fact that the availability of Leander van Ess's library was brought to the attention of the New-York Theological Seminary by Calvin Stowe,[10] who had been an acquaintance and colleague of Robinson's at Andover. Stowe, then a professor at the Lane Seminary in Cincinnati and recently married to Harriet Beecher, the daughter of the president of Lane, had been sent abroad to buy books for his institution in 1836, returning via New York in February of 1837.[11] The Board minutes for April 26, 1837, state that a letter from Stowe "was read and referred to the Library committee," and a later minute (5 July) makes it clear that the first communication was addressed not to Stowe's former colleague, Robinson, but to Richard Townley Haines, a merchant and supporter of the Bible society, and a founder of the seminary, who was from 1840 to become president of the seminary Board. The library committee, however, had put the matter into Robinson's hands, and at the meeting on July 5, they reported to the Board that Stowe had responded "very satisfactorily" to a letter from Robinson. Resolutions were passed that the library be acquired "at any reasonable price" and "That the Revd Dr Robinson be requested to examine said Library, and make a full response to the Board of Directors as soon as may be, of the state of the Library, its value as a selection of books for the N-Y Theological Seminary, the price at which it may be purchased, and the terms of payments and if practicable to secure the refusal of it until he can receive the answer of the Board."[12] Although he was not given funds for further purchases, Robinson was not restricted to the Leander van Ess transaction in acquiring books for the new seminary. He was authorized at the same session of the board "to solicit and accept of donations of Books suitable for the Library, from any individual or public bodies who may be in possession of such and disposed by such donations to patronize the Seminary."

In his account of the purchase of the van Ess library, McAuley states that Stowe forwarded information about its availability to the New-York Theological Seminary, because he had acquired all the books needed for Lane. Other commentators, assuming perhaps that Stowe had communicated with New York from Europe rather than after his return, have suggested that the funds available for purchase of books for Cincinnati had been exhausted.[13] The chronology of events in the minutes, however, shows that Stowe wrote Mr. Haines about the books after his return to the United States. As we shall see anon, it is likely that, having acquired enough books in Europe to bring the collection at Lane to approximately 10,000 volumes—the largest library in the West—Stowe and his colleagues thought their collection completed.[14] McAuley's estimate of the motivation for Stowe's apparently generous gesture is, thus, the more plausible.

None of the correspondence between Robinson and the officers of the seminary in New York concerning his examination of the books survives, but the minute-books of the Board allow a reconstruction of the approximate chronology of Robinson's visit to examine the books. Robinson sailed for England in July 1837, at the end of his first term of teaching in New York. He is said to have traveled up the Rhine to "Frankfort" and to have proceeded to Berlin, whence he departed at the end of November for his travels in the Levant, sailing from Trieste to Athens on December 1, 1837, and afterwards, going up the Nile to Thebes, he left Cairo on March 12, 1838, for the biblical sites, returning to Berlin in October to request an extension of his leave through August of 1840 in order to work on the manuscript of his three-volume *Biblical Researches in Palestine, Mount Sinai and Arabia Petraea*.[15] Robinson's wife, Therese Albertine Louise von Jakob, a woman of very great literary accomplishment, who sometimes published under the acronymous pseudonym Talvj, was the daughter of a professor of philosophy at Halle. She is said to have "moved in the literary circles of Hamburg, Leipzig, and Dresden" during the European sojourn of 1838-1840,[16] and Robinson may have traveled some with her after his return from the East. The visit to Leander van Ess can only have taken place while the Robinsons were en route to Halle or Berlin, perhaps while they were at Frankfurt am Main in late summer or early autumn. After Robinson was already in Athens, on December 22, 1837, the minutes of the board recorded receipt of a letter from him concerning the library. The matter was referred to the Library Committee for action, and preliminary steps were taken by the board to finance the purchase. By the June

1838 meeting of the board, it is clear that the purchase had been authorized. Minutes for November 20 imply that the books were already in New York. At this meeting of the Board, a committee was appointed to consider the possibility of compensation for a Mr. Wolf, who had packed the library, and thanks were conveyed to "Caspar Meier & Co[17] for their kindness in attending to the importation of the library without charges." President McAuley's account of the purchase, part of an address at the dedication of the seminary's building on December 12, 1838, states that the library was in hand and available for use.

Robinson, then, must have paid a single visit to the household of Leander van Ess at the end of the summer or in the early autumn of 1837. He could not have returned personally to consummate the arrangement, because he had left Germany before his report to the board in New York had been received. Perhaps the final negotiations with Leander van Ess were carried out by his wife or other agents of the seminary in New York; but it is more likely that the letter from Robinson recommended the purchase and conveyed information that the seminary had been offered first refusal, so that the purchase could be completed by a letter of acceptance. Although Leander van Ess did not know English, his housekeeper-companion Elisabeth von Elliot knew English and acted as his secretary when necessary.[18] It is clear from other sources that Professor van Ess's household was still awaiting final word on consummation of the sale in early April.[19]

One yearns for details of the meeting of the distinguished American professor of Scripture and the famous and controversial German translator of the Bible. Such particulars would come, if they are ever to be found, from the Robinson *Nachlass*.

Deficit Financing in 1838

The library of Professor van Ess was purchased at a difficult time in the life of the new seminary in New York City, in the midst of the Panic of 1837.[20] In New York City, the financial crisis had been exacerbated by great losses incurred in the "Great Fire" of December 16, 1835.[21] The school was at the time erecting a permanent building in University Place and four faculty residences in the back of the lot, on Greene Street. A subscription of funds had secured pledges of nearly $70,000, but payments on the first installment had yielded only $10,000. This sum was adequate to secure the land, but not to proceed with the building project or to meet current expenses for professors, books, and so forth. The second installment was due in June 1837, but the financial climate was extremely unpromising, and funds could only be found to continue the building project and to meet current expenses by taking loans. So it is that the Minutes of the board for December 22, 1837, immediately after the reference to receipt of Robinson's report on the German library, instructs the finance committee to secure loans for the completion of the buildings and also to find resources for "the current expenses of the Seminary & also to purchase a Library." The professors were unpaid, and the theologian White is said to have borrowed heavily and made his home a boarding house. At times it was wondered whether the institution could continue, and the board in May of 1840 spoke with some relief of having funds to remain in operation for the next year.[22]

Against this backdrop, the institution (with little apparent nay-saying or doubt about the propriety of its action) purchased a German library of 13,000 volumes for $5,070.08, or 10,000 florins.[23] It seems curious that only Gillett in his unpublished "Detailed History" noted the source of the funds to make payment to the German scholar, although the facts were recorded in the minutes of the Board.[24] On December 26, 1838, it is recorded that "The Treasurer was authorized to borrow five thousand dollars from D^r McAuley to pay for the Library and to execute his bond as Treasurer for the same, also to mortgage the Library as security, the Library to be insured, & the policy to be transferred to D^r McAuley." Efforts to secure gifts or commercial loans to finance the purchase had evidently failed, and the president had come to the rescue at an extraordinary session of the board on the day after Christmas with an offer that saved the institution the embarrassment of failure to pay for the books on its library shelves.[25]

Little is known about McAuley save that he undertook his role at the seminary, while retaining the pastorship of the Murray Street Church. To some extent, therefore, his involvement with the struggling new seminary must have been a labor of love. Gillett takes the loan as indicating that McAuley was a person of means.[26] This may be so, but he was not a person of so great means that he could turn the loan into a gift. McAuley in February 1840 presented his resignation from the presidency of Union Theological Seminary, and with it he presented a bill for expenditures made "in behalf of the Seminary and the house now occupied by him."[27] The library mortgage came due at the beginning of September, 1843—a fact that McAuley drew to the board's attention.[28] The matter is mentioned in minutes for May 31; but the debt could not be settled, and on October 11 the board resolved to turn to the alumni, asking each to raise at least fifty dollars towards retirement of the debt. A circular letter dated in November was sent to the alumni, explaining that "the circumstances of the holder [of the mortgage] render it necessary for him to call for its payment" and raising the specter of having to liquidate the library, worth easily twice the amount of the loan, which would be an irreparable blow to the institution. The matter dragged on with increasing acrimony, however, and McAuley did not receive full satisfaction until August 2, 1847.

The purchase of the library of Professor van Ess was a bold move for a struggling seminary in times of great financial distress. The inability of the institution to meet its obligation for the library for nearly four years after the loan from McAuley fell due casts only a momentary shadow on the achievement. The new school's leadership, which seems hardly to have flinched at undertaking a large expense without visible resources, displayed visionary courage; and the president who came forward to cover the expense by making a loan from his personal resources displayed his qualities as a leader.

A Little Help from a Friend

When Leander van Ess resigned his professorship at Marburg in 1822, he moved to Darmstadt, where his household, managed by Elisabeth von Elliot,[29] included her son Leo and two nephews of the scholar-priest, Leander and Andreas August Heidenreich. Andreas became a medical doctor in Darmstadt, and Leander, with Leo von Elliot, was farming at Alzey between Mainz and Worms in Hesse from 1835 to 1840. Later, Leander Heidenreich had a farm at the village of Affolterbach in the Odenwald, near Wald-Michelbach.[30] The professor made his home with his nephew and namesake for the rest of his life. He died and was buried at Affolterbach, and a number of his papers are presently there in the Heidenreich family archive.

Among the papers at Affolterbach is a letter written on March 22-23, 1837, by a young Swiss woman in New York to her brother in Geneva.[31] The preceding year, Henriette Wolff had married an American surgeon, Gurdon Buck, who had been studying in France and was to become one of the preeminent "American surgeons of the pre-Lister era."[32] The letter in question is a long one, whose contents are not directly relevant to our interests here. Philippe Wolff, the brother, had evidently asked about the possibility of continuing his theological education in America, and his sister, apparently homesick and longing to lure her brother to New York, had inquired of Dr. McAuley and others, whose information enabled her to prepare an interesting description of Princeton and New-York seminaries. There are also fascinating descriptions of life and events in New York and of a harrowing surgical procedure at which Gurdon Buck had assisted. Our interest, however, is in the reason for the presence of the letter among the papers of the family of Leander van Ess.

In the accounts of the purchase of the library of Leander van Ess, there are several references to Philippe Wolff ("Mr Wolf") as having volunteered to pack the books for shipment to New York. It has already been reported that the possibility of compensation for him had been referred to a subcommittee of the board on November 20, 1838. In President McAuley's account of the purchase, which he delivered at the dedication of the seminary building on December 12, he reported that

> through the disinterested kindness of a lady of this city, we obtained the invaluable aid of her brother, Mr. Philip Wolff, of the University of Erlingen [*sic*], who not only travelled several hundred miles for us, but also spent fourteen weeks in examining the library, and in so packing every volume with his own hands, that, perfectly free from injury, it was transported from Alzey, in Germany, to our Seminary in this city. And to his praise be it spoken, he gave all this time and labor without *fee* or *reward*, his only motive being a desire to promote the interests of the kingdom of the Redeemer. Let this sacrifice on the altar of God be held in remembrance; yes, let it be imitated by every one who names the name of Christ.[33]

A little more can now be said concerning this student from Geneva, who had evidently migrated to Erlangen rather than to New York. The Wolffs were followers of César Malan, the center of a community of evangelicals within the Genevan church. Malan was a witness to the marriage of Henriette and Gurdon Buck.[34] Henriette's letter to her brother implies that Philippe was leaving studies at Geneva because of some controversy, doubtless related to the rigorism of the group with whom they were associated, who were influenced by Scottish Presbyterian evangelicals and by the British evangelical and Bible societies. Several persons who can be identified as students contemporary with Philippe are mentioned by name in his sister's missive. Philippe, who migrated to the

University of Erlangen in 1837 but returned to Geneva in 1838-39, was later to emigrate to a pastorate in Canada and to marry in Boston.[35]

Philippe must have been contacted by Henriette in behalf of the New-York Theological Seminary sometime in the winter or spring of 1838, when Professor Robinson had departed on his travels and Union needed an intermediary to help complete the purchase and transfer of the books. He had been to Alzey sometime before April and must have left behind him the long epistle of his sister with its description of reformed theological schools in the vicinity of New York for the information of his host about the place to which his books might go. On April 6, he sent a thank-you note from Landau to Frau von Elliot. He had, he reports, so agreeable a visit in the household of Leander van Ess that his emotions on leaving were comparable to his feelings when he left his family to study in Germany, and his report of his visit in Alzey has prompted his own mother to write a note of thanks to Frau von Elliot. After leaving Alzey, he had been entertained by the Drs.Heidenreich—Andreas and his wife[36]—in Darmstadt, whence he had returned to Geneva for a visit. But he hopes to return to Alzey shortly to help to pack the books for shipment to New York:

> I received a letter yesterday from Mr. Meier who told me that he would be very pleased for me to direct the packing of the library, if he can arrange it with Dr. Van Ess. I would like very much to have that opportunity to see you again. But it is doubtful that I will remain in Landau until Easter and I believe that if in 5 or 6 days I do not receive a second letter that tells me that the negotiations are completed, I will make my way towards my prison, the monotonous Erlangen. On the advice of Dr. Van Ess, I will work hard there on Hebrew and Arabic during the summer, and in September I will return home through Munich. Goodbye, Madame, Goodbye to Dr. Van Ess, Goodbye to Mr. Baron, Goodbye to Mr. Cappellan. Give my greetings to Mr. and Mrs. Heidenreich and thank them.
>
> Philippe Wolff
>
> P.S. If Dr. Van Ess writes to Bremen, I would appreciate his letting Mr. Meier know that I received the letter he wrote me. If it happens that in a few days the sale of the library is concluded, please advise me about it because then I will come immediately to Alzey.[37]

Easter fell on April 15 in 1838, the week after Wolff's letter was written. The Meier company, which seems to have taken charge of the final negotiations between the seminary and the Professor, must have concluded arrangements within that span. If the packing began at Easter, Wolff's fourteen weeks of work on the books would have extended to the middle of July. The checkmarks against entries in the catalogue of the collection in the hand of Leander van Ess must be Wolff's, a testimony to the care he exercised.

This was a difficult time for the Alzey household, for Elisabeth von Elliot died in mid-May, probably on the twenty-fourth.[38] The packing and shipment of the books seems to have continued, none the less, and to have been completed on June 18, as Leander van Ess reported in a letter of the seventeenth to the shippers, Meyer & Co, in which he also mentions Wolff.[39] The professor was evidently so deeply stricken with grief that it was then necessary for him to rest at a *Bad* or spa.[40] Philippe Wolff, it seems, stayed almost a month beyond the completion of his chore to comfort and assist his host. It is not impossible to imagine that Leander Heidenreich enlisted Wolff to accompany his grieving uncle for the cure at a spa and to assist with his correspondence.

One wonders whether the seminary had any direct contact with Leander van Ess. There is a fragmentary draft of a letter from him to McAuley dated June 20:

> Most honored sir: A grievous death in my family, which had very detrimental consequences for my health, caused me to leave Alzei for a considerable time, and hence the routine of my work was completely disrupted. We want, therefore, to extend profoundest apologies that only now does a communication come to your hands after the completion of our transaction.[41]

Perhaps the letter was completed elsewhere, or Wolff assumed the task of communicating the grieving van Ess's gratitude to the seminary. Before President McAuley's account of the purchase of the library, there seems to have been no knowledge among the New Yorkers of Leander van Ess and the history of his collection. McAuley's remarks, delivered at the dedication of the seminary's new building, however, contain considerable anecdotal information, and Hatfield's early account of the seminary contains much of the same information. It is not impossible that the reports about Leander van Ess came from Robinson or Stowe, but it is more likely that they came to New York in a communication from Philippe Wolff, whose "careful examination of the books"[42] kept him so long at Alzey.

Wolff's contribution to the transaction was a remarkable and generous one. The letters that have recently come to light in the house where Leander van Ess spent his last years add both detail and a human context to his gift.

Reflections

The collection that was brought to New York in 1838 was said to contain between 13,000 and 14,000 volumes. The three parts of it listed in van Ess's "Catalogus" had 4,209 books printed between the sixteenth and the nineteenth centuries, 430 incunabula and 37 manuscripts.[43] It made Union's by far the largest collection of incunabula in America at the time.[44] The purchase was the largest single acquisition of the time[45] and instantly put the Union library with Andover's at the forefront of American theological library collections—and this despite the fact that the institution's financial viability was seriously in doubt. The collection continued to grow so that by 1876 it held 34,000 volumes;[46] and in 1889, the end of its first half-century, it claimed 55,000 books, 47,000 pamphlets and 183 manuscripts.[47] Thus from the moment of the purchase it remained the first or second largest theological library in America,[48] and to the final decades of the century few (if any) college libraries could match it.

The connection of the acquisition of van Ess's library with Calvin Stowe and the history of the library of the Lane Seminary in Cincinnati invites comparison of their subsequent histories. Stowe clearly wanted a library that rivaled Andover's, which at the time numbered around 10,000 volumes. He achieved that goal, but Lane's library did not continue to grow. Having assembled "the premier academic library of the West," Lane was "beset by a static view of [the] collection" and "showed little sense of need for new acquisitions."[49] The Panic of 1837 affected Lane, as New-York,[50] but the attitude toward the library—including hours of opening "for the delivery of books and consultation" only from one to two o'clock on Saturday afternoons[51]—were not conducive to active use of the collection.

What in the ethos of the new institution led it to the financial risk of the acquisition of the library of Leander van Ess and to a commitment to building upon that foundation? Why under the librarianship of Robinson (1841-1850) and Henry B. Smith (1850-1876) had Union attracted further and special collections[52] well in advance of the growth of research libraries and special collections in American institutions of higher education at the end of the century?[53] Why was the New-York Seminary's library open for two hours each weekday morning and afternoon[54] at a time when seminary libraries were commonly open only a few hours each week?

Answers to such questions may be pondered and debated. Surely the acquisitiveness of new-rich New Yorkers cannot entirely explain the growth of Union's library, which (in any case) antedates the great age of acquisitiveness. For the moment, I can think of no better answers than those suggested by Edward Robinson in two articles, in which he compared American and German education.[55] Robinson, already thirty-two years old when he first went to study at Halle in 1826, drank deeply at the well of European learning. He knew that American colleges were little more than advanced secondary schools for the rounding of young gentlemen and that professional education was not coordinated in universities but isolated in special-purpose schools, such as theological seminaries. He recognized that American resources were so limited that a native genius like Franklin could hardly have been expected to blossom more fully without advantages comparable to those enjoyed by Newton and Laplace.[56] But Robinson was profoundly and decidedly an American. He felt that European education suffered from a lack of rootedness in practical issues and experience and that professors isolated from the world compelled their students "to build their speculations without any foundation of experience and practical common sense."[57] He believed that German education was bound by examinations, by licenses, and by control of the civil service (which—most alarming to Americans—included church appointments) to governments that (however benevolent) were, in fact, despotic. Robinson understood that such a system could and should never be emulated in America. At present, the roads to success in America were too easy to spur the young to undertake the rigors of an education comparable with what was available in Germany, and Robinson saw little support for advanced education from the government.

> In this land of civil freedom, we can use no legal force to compel young men to obtain an education. We can bring only a moral influence to bear; and when this shall have been long enough employed; when the moral wants of the community shall demand other institutions; they will no doubt spring into existence, of a

The founders of Union wanted to build a seminary that would combine good learning and the inculcation of piety with the resources of the urban church and community, making experience a vital part of their enterprise, in the American mode.[59] Robinson and his colleagues in New York believed they were responding in the fullness of time to the desire of theologians for an education as fine and as deep as could be had in the universities of Germany and were nurturing a seminary and library "of a rank and nature adapted to the exigencies of the case."

Endnotes

1. Wilhelm Fischer: "Leander van Eß: Ein Leben im Dienst der Bibel," *Jahrbuch der Hessischen kirchengeschichtlichen Vereinigung* 4 (1953): 74-100, is the most comprehensive attempt at a biography of Leander van Ess now available. A brief survey is Milton McC. Gatch, "Leander van Ess: Enlightened German Catholic Ecumenist," *The Unbounded Community: Papers in Christian Ecumenism in Honor of Jaroslav Pelikan*, ed. William Caferro and Duncan Fisher (Garland, forthcoming). Johannes Altenberend is preparing a full new biography.

2. In addition to the Minutes of the Directors, existing in both rough and fair copies (Archives, The Burke Library, Union Theological Seminary, New York), cited below as Minutes, accounts of the purchase of the Ess library include Thomas McAuley, "Extracts from a Speech Delivered at the Dedication of the Edifice Belonging to the New-York Theological Seminary, 12th Dec. 1838" (New York: for the Seminary, n.d. [1839]) (the only extant copy of which is bound in a volume of pamphlets following the inaugural lecture of Edward Robinson); and Edwin F. Hatfield, *The Early Annals of Union Theological Seminary in the City of New-York* (New York: for the Seminary, 1876), 14-15; George Lewis Prentiss, *The Union Theological Seminary in the City of New York: Historical and Biographical Sketches of its First Fifty Years* (New York: Anson D. F. Randolph and Co, 1889), 27, 73-104. There is also a brief account by Charles Ripley Gillett in G. L. Prentiss, *The Union Theological Seminary in the City of New York: Its Design and Another Decade of its History* (Asbury Park, N.J.: M. W. & C. Pennypacker, 1899), 352-53; Henry Sloane Coffin, *A Half Century of Union Theological Seminary 1896-1945: An Informal History* (New York: Charles Scribner's Sons, 1954), 202-5; and Robert T. Handy, *A History of Union Theological*

Seminary in New York (New York: Columbia University Press, 1987), 17-18. Biographical information on the founders and early officers will be found in Prentiss, *Union*, 113ff., and *Alumni Catalogue of the Union Theological Seminary in the City of New York, 1836-1926*, comp. Charles Ripley Gillett (New York: for the Seminary, 1926). The fullest attempt at a history of Union's Library is Thomas P. Slavens, *A Great Library Through Gifts* (New York: G. K. Saur, 1986), which treats the van Ess purchase on pp. 23-31. A typescript summary of all the archival materials on seminary history (some no longer extant) is Charles Ripley Gillett, "Detailed History of the Union Theological Seminary in the City of New York, Containing all of the Items of Importance Found in the Archives...," 1937, TMs, Archives, The Burke Library, Union Theological Seminary.

3. There is no full biography. The most complete resources are the notice in *The Dictionary of American Biography* by William F. Albright; Henry B. Smith and Roswell D. Hitchcock, *The Life, Writings and Character of Edward Robinson* (New York: Anson D. F. Randolph, 1863; reprint, America and the Holy Land, ed. Moshe Davis et al. [New York: Arno Press, 1977]); and Julius A. Brewer, "Edward Robinson as a Biblical Scholar," *Journal of Biblical Literature* 58 (1939): 355-63. Professor Jay Williams is working on a study of Robinson based on newly available resources at Hamilton College, Robinson's *alma mater*; a preliminary account of his work is to be published as Friends of the Burke Library, Occasional Paper No. 4 in 1996.

4. "Le docteur Robinson est sans doute un des premiers savants du monde." Henriette Wolff Buck to Philippe Wolff, ALS March 22, 1837 (Heidenreich Family Archive, Affolterbach, Germnay). I am grateful to Dr. Magda Heidenreich for bringing this letter to my attention and allowing me to bring the original to New York for transcription by Ann Anderson. See further below on this letter.

5. According to the Board's Minutes, on September 30, 1836, the Committee on Professors nominated two slates for two professorships. On the first slate, The Rev. George How (i.e., Howe, a Professor at Columbia Theological Seminary in Columbia, South Carolina) was nominated for Professor of Theology and Robinson for Biblical Literature; on the second, the Rev. Henry White was nominated for the post in Theology and Howe for Biblical Literature. White was elected to Theology by a vote of fifteen to five; Howe won the post in Biblical Literature by 15 to 4 with one abstention. Obviously the board was significantly divided, and one senses some deep conflict. Howe asked for time to consider and, although the board members wanted a quick decision so that the new seminary could begin classes, his continuing indecision was reported on November 24. Finally on December 20, Howe's declension was in hand and a vote

was taken, which resulted in Robinson's unanimous election.

6.   Minutes, January 20, 1837, and November 20, 1838.

7.   Minutes, Jaunary 20, 1837.

8.   Robinson also recommended that the new institution consider founding a press, pointing out that texts in the biblical languages "can be printed only at a single press in the whole land and that connected with a sister Seminary." He refers to Andover, where his own earlier works had been published under the imprint of Flagg & Gould and where Moses Stuart had imported the first fonts of Hebrew and other Oriental types in America in 1821 (cf. the article on Stuart by W. F. Albright in *Dictionary of American Biography*). Stuart was truly the creator and nurturer of the earliest American biblical scholarship.

9.   Earle Hilgert, "Calvin Ellis Stowe: Pioneer Librarian of the Old West," *Library Quarterly* 50 (1980): 329.

10.   "Extracts from a Speech . . . ."

11.   Hilgert, "Stowe," 338-41.

12.   The minutes here and elsewhere refer to the acquisition as "the Hamburgh Library"—a confusion that is difficult to explain. Since Stowe had returned from Europe in January after a very long passage, his communication was not sent from Hamburg, although he may have heard about van Ess's library from someone there. By the time McAuley wrote his account of the purchase, something was known about Leander van Ess, and the location of the library at Alzey was correctly stated.

13.   Slavens, *Great Library*, 24.

14.   Hilgert, "Stowe," 341, 348.

15.   The sources of the chronology are Robinson's "A Brieft Report of Travels in Palestine and the Adjacent Regions in 1838..." *The American Biblical Repository* 33 (n.s. 1) (1839): 400-27 at 400-401, and Smith and Hitchcock, *Robinson*, pp. 67-69. According to Gillettt ("Detailed History," 1044), the New York *Evangelist* reported on October 14, 1837, that the Robinsons had reached Europe. *Biblical Researches*, published simultaneously in German and English in 1841, must have been completed or nearly completed by the time that Robinson returned to America.

16.   Earnest A. Kubler, "Therese Albertine Louise von Jakob Robinson," *Dictionary of American Biography*.

17.   According to the New York directory for 1838, Caspar Meier & Co. was a firm of merchants at 42 Broad Street. As appears below, they also had offices in Bremen, Germany.

18.   For letters translated by Elisabeth von Elliot, see correspondence concerning the sale of manuscripts and incunabula by van Ess to Sir Thomas Phillipps in 1824 (e.g., Oxford, Bodleian, MS Phillipps-Robinson b.120, fols. 185-87 [January 24(?), 1826]).

19. Philippe Wolff to Mme. von Elliot, ALS Landau, April 6, 1838 (Heidenreich Family Archive, Affolterbach). See further below.

20. The following account is based on the earliest review of the matter by Hatfield (*Early Annals*, 12-13), which is repeated by Prentiss, *Union Theological Seminary*, 25-27 (photo from engraving of the building facing title page). See also the Minutes of the Board and Gillett, "Detailed History," 38, 205.

21. Gillett, "Detailed History," 23, 205ff.

22. The difficulties were, of course, national. Lane Seminary in Cincinnati, for example, experienced similar vicissitudes at this same time (see Hilgert, "Stowe," 344).

23. McAuley, "Extracts from a Speech . . .," quoted extensively by Prentiss, *Union Theological Seminary*, 75.

24. At 455-56.

25. Such an event would not have been new for Leander van Ess, for he had struggled for several years to secure final payment for the manuscripts and books sold in 1824 to Sir Thomas Phillipps (A.N.L. Munby, *Phillipps Studies*, 5 vols. [Cambridge: University Press, 1951-60] 3: 29-33). Remembering this, perhaps van Ess had insisted that the shipping company pay him in full upon dispatch of the books for New York.

26. "Detailed History," 455-56.

27. Ibid.

28. The following account is based on Gillett, "Detailed History," 1098-1101, and on the minutes.

29. Frau von Elliot was customarily introduced by Leander van Ess as his sister. His relationship with her had been the cause of rumor in the British and Foreign Bible Society, which had supported his biblical translations financially. Perhaps more than controversy over the inclusion of the Apocrypha in the translation, this was the cause of the severance of van Ess's ties with BFBS. Defending himself, he admitted privately that the "Vorsteherin meines Hauses" was called his sister "aus zarter Rücksicht vor der Welt" (Private letter to A. Brandram, attached to a letter to a committee of the BFBS, ALS, Darmstadt, September 1, 1829 [Archives of the British and Foreign Bible Society, FC 1 1829/3/90, Cambridge University Library]).

30. Magda Heidenreich, *Wesentliches und Unwesentliches aus einer weltoffenen südhessischen Familie* (Darmstadt: Eduard Roether, 1980), 10-11. My knowledge of the family history is immeasurably enriched by conversations with Dr. Heidenreich.

31. Cited above, note 4. Mrs. Buck had some continuing interest in the seminary, for in 1881 she presented a manuscript sermon written in 1782 by the Swiss ecclesiastic, Johannes Kaspar Lavater, now Burke

Library MS 100. Some of Lavater's printed work had been collected by Leander van Ess.

32. Article by John F. Fulton *Dictionary of American Biography*. Buck's first name is invariably misspelled in the Union records; he was named for Gurdon Saltonstall, Governor of Connecticut, his great-grandfather on both sides.

33. "Extracts," 2.

34. July 27, 1836: Commune d'Eaux-Vives, Actes de Mariage et divorce 1836, No. 8 Archives d'État, État Civil, Canton de Genève. On Malan, see *Encyclopédie de Genève*, ed. Catherine Santschi, et al., vol. 5 "Les religions," ed. Catherine Santschi and Jean de Senarclens (Geneva: Association de l'Encyclopédie de Genève, 1986), 172. Théodore Huilier, another evangelical minister who was the second witness to the marriage, is mentioned in the letter from Henriette to Philippe at Affolterbach.

35. *Le Livre du Recteur de l'Académie de Genève (1559-1878)*, ed. Suzanne Stelling-Michaud, 6 vols., Travaux d'Humanisme et Renaissance, 33.6 (Geneva: Librairie Droz, 1959-1980), 256. See also the Livre du Recteur of the École de Théologie, Société Évangelique, Cp Past. 360, Archives d'État, Geneva.

36. Older than her husband, Marianne Theodore Charlotte Heiland von Siebold was the second woman admitted to medical practice in Germany. A midwife, she assisted at the births of the future Queen Victoria and of her future consort, Albert (Heidenreich, *Wesentliches*, 9).

37. "J'ai reçu hier une lettre de M. Meier où il me dit qu'il serait bien aise que je dirige l'emballage de la bibliothèque, s'il peut tomber d'accord avec M. Van Ess. Il me serait bien agréable d'avoir cette occasion de vous revoir. Mais il est douteux que je reste à Landau jusqu'à Pâques, et je crois bien que si dans 5 ou 6 jours je ne reçois pas une seconde lettre qui m'annonce que les négotiations sont terminées, je m'acheminerai vers ma prison, le monotone Erlangen. D'après les conseils de Dr. Van Ess, j'y travaillerai bien l'Hébreu et l'Arabe pendant cet été et en Septembre je retournerai par Munich à la maison paternelle. Adieu, Madame, Adieu au Dr. Van Ess, Adieu à *Herrn Baron*, Adieu à *Herrn Cappellan*. Saluez de ma part M. et Mme Heidenreich et les remerciez.

Philippe Wolff

P.S. Si le Dr. Van Ess écrit à Bremen, il me fera plaisir d'accuser reception à M. Meier de la lettre qu'il m'a écrite. S'il arrivait que d'ici quelque jours la vente de la bibliothèque fut conclue, vous me feriez plaisir de m'en avertir parce qu'alors je me rendrai de suite à Alzey." Philippe Wolff to Elisabeth von Elliot, ALS, Landau, April 6, 1838 (Heidenreich Family Archive), transcribed and translated by Ann Anderson.

38. Dr. Heidenreich's sources record this date, but Johannes Altenberend tells me that van Ess recorded the date of Elisabeth von Elliot's death in the Catholic register at Alzei as May 24 and in the Protestant record as May 19.

39. This and other letters from the summer of 1838 mentioned in this paragraph are cited from a letter copy book in the Heidenreich Family Archive. On June 18, van Ess acknowledged receipt of payment in full from Meyer & Co of 10,224½ florins (or Gulden), indicating that the price was prepaid by the shipper for the seminary. In the June 17 letter, he indicates that the purchase price was 10,024½ f. and that Wolff had expended 200 f. for "Kisten und Verpackung."

40. Copy of letter to Lucas Howard in London June 20/July 4, 1838. (The Professor did not tell his London friends of the sale to New York until letters of December 1, when he described the sale as an example of divine help in time of need.) Several letters written in mid-July imply a return to routine. The letter to McAuley (next note) implies that this sojourn took place in late June-early July.

41. "Wohlgeborener
    hochzuverehender Herr!
ein schmerzlicher Todesfall in meiner Familie, der eine sehr nachtheilige Wirkung auf meinen Gesundheitszustand äußerte, bewog mich, Allzei auf eine geraume Zeit zu verlassen, wodurch der Geschäftsgang meiner Arbeiten gänzlich unterbrochen wurde. Wir wollen daher gütigst entschuldigen, daß erst jetzt nach Abschluß des Geschäftes ein Schreiben in Ihre Hände gelangt." This draft is dated "Allzei den 20ten Junij 1836." Obviously "1838" is the correct year. It may have been written at the spa, as also two letters to London, drafted on June 20, whose date was later altered to July 4.

42. Hatfield, "Early Annals," 15.

43. I am preparing a study of the collection and its sources.

44. In a lecture on February 3, 1995 at the Library Company of Philadelphia, Paul Needham posited that the history of incunabular collections in America begins with collection of William Mackenzie at the Loganian Library (now the Library Company) since 1828 and continues with Union's van Ess collection. The Library of Congress had, however, been prevented from obtaining a collection of nearly 1,000 incunabula in 1836 (Peter M. van Wingen, "The Incunabula Collections at the Library of Congress," *Rare Books and Manuscripts Librarianship* 4 [1989]: 85-86).

45. See Norman J. Kansfield, "'Study the Most Approved Authors:' The Role of the Seminary Library in Nineteenth-Century American Ministerial Education" (Ph.D. diss., University of Chicago, 1981), 198-200, on *en bloc* acquisitions.

46. Department of the Interior, Bureau of Education, *Public Libraries in the United States of America: Their History, Condition and Management: Special Report*, Part I (Washington: Government Printing Office, 1876), 153.

47. Prentiss, *Union*, 73. Pamphlets may not have been counted in the official reports.

48. Tables summarizing the official reports are given by Kansfield, "'Study,'" 171, 173, 175, 177, 179, 182 (1829-31, 1850, 1856, 1876, 1884, 1889). From 1850 to 1876, Union's and Andover's were the largest collections. By 1884, Andover had slipped, and in 1889, Hartford Theological Seminary had the largest library.

49. Hilgert, "Stowe," 348.

50. Ibid., 344, 346.

51. Ibid., 335, citing rules of 1834, in which Stowe probably had a hand.

52. C. R. Gillett's note in Prentiss, *Union*, 353-54 and 358, speaks of Robinson's own bequest of 1863, the McAlpin Collection of British Theology and History (endowed by David H. McAlpin but first collected by Gillett's father, Professor Ezra H. Gillett of New York University), E. H. Gillett's Collection of American Theology and History, and the McAlpin purchase of a large collection of Greek testaments from the estate of Isaac H. Hall, the important New York lay orientalist.

53. William L. Joyce, "The Evolution of the Concept of Special Collections in American Research Libraries," *Rare Book & Manuscripts Librarianship* 3 (1988): 19-29 at 22-24.

54. "Catalogue of the New-York Theological Seminary, January, 1940," 13-14; the issue of 1841 is a virtual reprint, save that Robinson has returned to assume the librarianship, held temporarily in the preceding year, when the books arrived from Germany by a middler, Hermann Bokum, born in Königsberg.

55. "Theological Education in Germany," *The Biblical Repository*, 1 (1831): 1-51; and "The Aspect of Literature and Science in the United States, as Compared with Europe," *Biblia Sacra and Theological Review* 1 (1844): 1-39.

56. "The Aspect," 2.

57. "Theological Education," 50.

58. Ibid., 51.

59. Preamble to the Consitution, quoted in full by Handy, *A History of Union*, 7-9.

Archives and Manuscript Collections in Theological Libraries

Martha Lund Smalley

Archives and manuscript collections were not uppermost in the minds of the theological librarians who gathered fifty years ago to form the American Theological Library Association. A. F. Kuhlman's view of the role of theological libraries, stated at the 1947 Louisville conference, is echoed at various times in the early years of the ATLA: "The theological library is not an end in itself. Its primary purpose is to serve as a means of instruction. Secondary or other purposes that it should seek to serve are research, and general or cultural education with reference to our religious heritage and spiritual values. The instructional purposes are primary and they should be met first . . . ."[1] Few theological libraries had the resources necessary to create research collections, and even these libraries focused on acquiring specialized works and early imprints to undergird their research base, rather than manuscript materials.

The past few decades have seen a burgeoning interest in the raw research materials contained in archives and manuscript collections, not only in theological libraries but in the academic world as a whole. During this period the Society of American Archivists, the professional organization of the archival field, has increased its membership dramatically, and the perception of archivists as clerk-like custodians of dusty records has been replaced by an appreciation of their important role in the research process. In part, the increased value placed on papers and archives generated in North America has been tied to growing recognition of the value of studying American history. It is interesting to note that a paper presented by Richard D. Pierce at the Fourth Annual Conference of the ATLA in 1950 lamented the "studied neglect of American Church History," stating that "American History, in general, and American Church History, in particular, have been tardily recognized by the historians as worthy areas of investigation."[2] Pierce alerted his audience of theological librarians to the "mines of information" represented by primary source materials and called upon them to create "union lists and catalogues of available resources—particularly manuscript sources."[3]

The history of treatment of archives and manuscript collections at the Yale Divinity School Library is perhaps representative of the wider picture. Raymond Morris, librarian at Yale from 1932 to 1972, had the vision to see that archives of organizations such as the Student Volunteer Movement or personal papers of figures such as John R. Mott ought to be preserved. From the 1940s onward, such records were received by the library and maintained more or less intact, but with minimal description or access provided. If anyone worked with these archival resources, it was untrained student workers who made internal file lists. There was only the most sketchy conception of a collecting scope or policy.

It is to the ATLA's credit that its annual conferences have periodically provided direction regarding the treatment of archival material. At the Tenth Annual Conference in 1956, for example, Mrs. Julia H. Macleod of the Manuscripts Division of the Bancroft Library presented a session on "Problems in Manuscript Cataloguing." Macleod's presentation emphasized the basics of archival practice, such as "keeping together material from a single source" and "that the material itself determines the arrangement."[4] Surely there were some librarians in the audience who squirmed when she said, "I would also like to point out that the sorting and arrangement of a group of papers should be undertaken by the most highly trained and experienced staff members and not the casual help." Her detailed discussions of proper techniques of arrangement, description, and storage of manuscript material show that many of the issues facing today's archivist are much the same as those faced in the past.

Macleod's presentation must have been eagerly soaked up by some in the audience who had manuscript holdings, for there was a genuine dearth of "how to" literature in the field. Others in the audience probably listened most closely when she spoke phrases like "our work with manuscripts is largely a 'playing by ear' technique" or "each repository has to solve such problems in its own fashion." This was the era before standardization became a clear goal of the archival profession. The casual accumulation of archival materials, with no subsequent pressure to conform a set of standards for arrangement, description, or storage, was the norm for theological libraries.

At the Annual Conference in Boston two years later, Lester J. Cappon, Director of Early American History and Culture at Williamsburg, VA, addressed the issue of archival records at theological schools:

> During the nineteenth century, in every denomination certain seminary libraries became centers for its historical collections, varying from official minute books of the highest administrative bodies in the ecclesiastical organization to records of local churches. These national, regional, and local archives, though seldom designated as such, received usually from relatives and descendants, the correspondence of clergy and laymen who had played influential roles in the life of the church. Thus almost imperceptibly at first, seminaries acquired research materials; by steady accretion their holdings became notable, attracting scholars and stimulating further research. Before the twentieth century, however, since these repositories did little or nothing to publicize their holdings, many a scholar overlooked them.[5]

While in 1958 Cappon was still pointing to William Allison's *Inventory of Unpublished Material for American Religious History in Protestant Church Archives and Other Repositories*[6] as the primary general tool of access to archival records in theological libraries, by 1961 Nelson R. Burr was addressing the ATLA Annual Conference in Washington to recruit entries for the National Union Catalog of Manuscript Collections. The National Union Catalog, begun by the Library of Congress in 1959, has remained the primary overall tool of access to manuscript collections until the present day. Now its printed form is rendered increasingly obsolete by the advantages of national electronic bibliographic databases, and before long it will be reformatted using the new technology.

The 1961 Annual Conference in Washington, D.C. was also the appropriate setting for another detailed presentation of the principles of archival work, this time by Mabel Deutrich of the National Archives. Deutrich began her workshop with a wise disclaimer—"Description, accessioning, arrangement, disposal, microfilming of documents—a thorough discussion of any one of these would take more than the time allotted for this session."[7] She went on to give a masterful presentation that could serve as a basis for archival training even now, more than thirty years later. Deutrich reiterated the basic principles of archival arrangement: "The first principle that must be kept in mind in the arrangement of archives is that the records of a given unit (school, church, family) must be kept together. The second companion principle is the preservation or reconstruction of the order in which the records were originally arranged."[8] After some discussion of arrangement and description, she got down to "brass tacks" for the theological librarians (as she phrased it), posing the question "What kind of archives do I think you should have?" and going on to emphasize both the need for creating finding aids for archival collections and the need for a "definite plan" for archival collecting.

One wonders if librarians such as Yale's Raymond Morris were sitting in the audience, hearing Deutrich's admonitions, yet wondering where on earth they would find the staff and money to deal appropriately with their manuscript holdings. Many of the same librarians must have said a silent "Amen" two years later in California when Julia H. Macleod opened her session on "The Care and Treatment of Manuscripts" with the statement: "Manuscripts are the chief 'problems' of all libraries housing them, and we, the librarians, are all seeking ways and means of dealing with them cheaply and expeditiously."[9]

Macleod proceeded to reiterate much that she had presented seven years earlier in Berkeley, emphasizing the principles of archival arrangement and description, document care and storage, and the creation of finding aids. At the same Annual Conference, the theological librarians heard from historian Clifford Drury, who left them with three recommendations: (1) "Get in touch with the descendants of...individuals who have been important in the work of your denomination...and ask whether or not they have diaries, journals, correspondence, pictures, or other items of historical importance which they would give to your library . . . . (2) Be alert to the importance of collecting original church records of your area . . . . (3) Do not overlook contemporary movements within the life of Protestantism today and/or of your own denomination . . . ."[10]

The theological librarians no doubt returned home from the 1963 conference once more eager and encouraged to have their staffs tackle the boxes of manuscript material occupying the dark corners of their libraries. But perhaps the situation at the Yale Divinity School Library was not atypical—several years passed without any permanent staff or funds being devoted to an archival program. The inertia was understandable. Establishing an archival program requires a long-term commitment. The work of organizing and describing collections is labor intensive; the physical materials needed to house and preserve records properly are relatively expensive; and the necessary space for storage, and acceptable temperature and humidity controls must be assured. The administration of an institution must be committed to ongoing staff and financial support.

The break for the Yale Divinity School Library came in 1968 when the National Council of Churches of Christ in the U.S.A. approached the library about becoming a central player in the Council's China Records Project. Fearing that the papers of Protestant missionaries who had served in China would be lost, the Council set about to contact more than 3,000 former China missionaries or their families and inquire about the status of their personal papers. The missionaries were encouraged to deposit their papers in a denominational repository, or at the designated central repository, Yale Divinity School Library. The Yale Divinity Library obtained a grant from the National Endowment for the Humanities that enabled it to hire and train staff, purchase document storage cases, and in general, to jump-start a full-fledged archival program. By the end of the grant sequence in 1975, the Yale Divinity Library had made a commitment to continue staff support for its archival program. It began the process of defining the program's parameters and clearing up its "problems."

It was a full fourteen years after the 1963 Annual Conference before another archives workshop for theological librarians was noted in the ATLA Proceedings. The workshop presenter in this case, Richard Bernard, did not begin with encouraging words for the librarians. "If avoidable, do not get into the archival business. It is a disservice both to scholarship and the materials themselves if they are not handled properly," he suggested.[11] This 1977 workshop and another in 1985 addressed the archival basics of arrangement, description, retrieval, conservation, and planning. A new feature in the 1985 workshop was discussion of the "wheres and hows" of securing grant support.

Meanwhile, the archival profession was picking up steam. "How to" literature was becoming readily available even to "lone arrangers" in distant outposts. Terms like "record group," "series," and "finding aid" were no longer esoteric. A series of basic manuals published by the Society of American Archivists included August R. Suelflow's *Religious Archives: An Introduction*,[12] which spelled out in detail policies and techniques appropriate for a first class archives program. In 1986 the Society of American Archivists published *Planning for the Archival Profession: A Report of the SAA Task Force on Goals and Priorities*,[13] a document that, for the first time, attempted to define the overall archival mission. Rather than just being passive receptacles, archival repositories began to take a more intentional approach to the collection of records by using "documentation strategies." One archivist described this approach as seeking "to consider the total universe of documentation on a given topic or field, to anticipate likely future as well as present needs, to involve creators and users of records as partners in documentation planning, and to consider advocating creation of records where needed to assure adequate documentation."[14]

The advent of computer technology has revolutionized the archival scene. Archivists quickly recognized the opportunity for enhanced access that national bibliographic databases provided. Increasing standardization in arrangement and description techniques was a corollary to participation in national networks; the MARC AMC format became a widespread guide for collection level description. Escalating levels of access to finding aids for archival collections are now available through the Gopher and Internet. Digital scanning of the entire contents of collections may someday be commonplace.

In this brave new computer-assisted environment, many of the thorny issues that have always confronted archivists remain, and they have been joined by new conundrums. When shelf space and staff time are at a premium, the questions of "what to get" and "what to keep" take on new urgency. Paper continues to deteriorate, while archivists seek to demonstrate the value of their programs by attracting increasing numbers of researchers. As more and more bibliographic records flood the national bibliographic databases, the importance of providing appropriate points of access increases. Helen R. Tibbo wrote recently in the *American Archivist*:

> In this day of information gluttony and those surfeited years that surely lie ahead, responsible appraisal and provision of access to significant materials are central to the archivist's function. We

know we cannot save everything. Now we must learn that only a portion of what we do save will merit specialized avenues of access. If we do not practice such restraint and temperance, the national bibliographic databases will grow to useless proportions and our processing backlogs will overwhelm us. We need to represent those materials deemed worthy with as much specificity as possible to stem the tide against the meaninglessness of massive retrievals from electronic systems.[15]

Raw computer technology is not a panacea for the difficulties of identifying and accessing archival material. Archival methods of organizing material by categories, with finding aids that provide context and valuation, will have increasing rather than diminishing value in a context of information overload. There will be a continued need for guides such as Robert Benedetto's *Guide to the Manuscript Collections of the Presbyterian Church, U.S.*, which aims, not simply to list manuscript materials, but also "to make these diverse files, diaries, sermons, minutes, letters, and other materials more intelligible to both the university and the church."[16]

If all the archival and manuscript collections related to a particular denomination or topic had both collection-level records in a national bibliographic database and full finding aids mounted on the Internet, it would certainly be possible for an experienced and expert researcher to identify all pertinent materials, but the archivist's role of making materials "more intelligible" should not be pushed aside in the rush to make materials electronically accessible. Just as archivists are no longer just "custodians" of records but rather "documentation strategists," so they should not be just "distributors" of bits of information about the holdings of their institutions but rather "map makers," creating intelligible overviews and pathways through the mass of electronic records.

Where should ATLA libraries go from here in creating and maintaining archives and manuscript collections? Each library's situation will be different. Some seminary libraries are the repositories for their schools' records; some collect only for research purposes; but many combine these two functions. Libraries that are serious about maintaining archival programs should build a strong foundation by having a written mission statement defining the parameters of the program.[17] Collection development policies should be formulated and perhaps circulated among other member libraries in order to avoid undue competition or duplication of effort. Libraries should enable their archivists to keep abreast of the rapidly changing technology that now dominates the archival field. The ATLA will do well to continue providing workshops and sessions at annual conferences that allow archivists and librarians from smaller repositories to keep in touch with advances in technology, preservation techniques, etc. Archivists in theological libraries should work together to create guides and pathfinders to help researchers through the jungle of primary source materials documenting religious and denominational history.

In his *Theological Libraries for the Twenty-First Century: Project 2000 Final Report*, Stephen Peterson stated that the true benefit of technology should be "to marshal constructively the particularity and imagination of our several theological institutions."[18] In an environment where print resources are increasingly shared and accessible, the archival and manuscript collections of theological libraries provide significant "particularity." Archivists can revel in the particularities of their tasks, but as "map makers," they should also cooperate with their colleagues who are exploring adjacent territories, joining together to make maps that aid and encourage further exploration.

Endnotes

1. A. F. Kuhlman, "The Library and Instruction," *Summary of Proceedings* 1 (1947): 12.

2. Richard D. Pierce, "Bibliography in the Field of American Church History," *Summary of Proceedings* 4 (1950): 13.

3. Ibid., 18.

4. Julia H. Macleod, "Problems in Manuscript Cataloguing," *Summary of Proceedings* 10 (1956): 44-45.

5. Lester J. Cappon, "Archival Good Works for Theologians," *Summary of Proceedings* 12 (1958): 83.

6. Carnegie Institution of Washington Publication, 137 (Washington, D.C.: Carnegie Institution of Washington, 1910).

7. Mabel E. Deutrich, "Workshop on the Administration of Archives and Manuscript Collections," *Summary of the Proceedings* 15 (1961): 84.

8. Ibid., 85.

9. Julia H. Macleod, "The Care and Treatment of Manuscripts," *Summary of Proceedings* 17 (1963): 155.

10. Clifford M. Drury, "Adventures in Historical Research,"

Summary of Proceedings 17 (1963): 113.

11. Richard Bernard, "Archives Workshop for Librarians," *Summary of Proceedings* 31 (1977): 173.

12. Chicago: Society of American Archivists, 1980.

13. Chicago: Society of American Archivists, 1986.

14. Bruce W. Dearstyne, "American Archives: Challenge and Change," *CSSR Bulletin* 17 (1988): 67-68.

15. Helen R. Tibbo, "The Epic Struggle: Subject Retrieval from Large Bibliographic Databases," *American Archivist* 57 (1994): 311.

16. Robert Benedetto, *Guide to the Manuscript Collections of the Presbyterian Church, U.S.,* Bibliographies and Indexes in Religious Studies, 17 (New York: Greenwood, 1990), Preface.

17. For detailed information about starting and maintaining an archives program, see Martha Lund Smalley, *An Archival Primer: A Practical Guide for Building and Maintaining an Archival Program* (New Haven: Yale Divinity School Library, 1994).

18. Stephen L. Peterson, "Theological Libraries for the Twenty-First Century: Project 2000 Final Report," *Theological Education* 20 (1984): 36.

THE THEORY AND PRACTICE
OF
THEOLOGICAL LIBRARIANSHIP

Theological Librarianship and Theological Education

Paul Schrodt

When one joins the profession of theological librarianship, it is tempting to think of oneself as somehow now being called upon to follow the traditions of some of the famous theological librarians of the past. St. Jerome is recalled for his efforts in seeking out the best biblical manuscripts available anywhere. Cassiodorus is credited with the founding of one of the most important libraries in the early Middle Ages, and through the efforts of his copyists, of shaping the extant biblical text. Caesar Baronius, as custodian of the Vatican library, collected an enormous number of sources—some twelve folio volumes—for the history of the church until the year 1198. Ludovico Muratori, as librarian of the Ambrosian Library in Milan in the eighteenth century, discovered among the manuscripts in his charge the earliest fragment detailing the canon of the books of the New Testament. Adolf von Harnack, appointed towards the end of his scholarly career to direct the Prussian State Library, demonstrated that a church historian could be impartial enough to promote and inspire the spirit of research in all the sciences. Librarian scholars such as these, each of whom helped shape our common intellectual history, suggest something of the seriousness with which one might undertake the work of theological librarianship today.

What is the image of the librarian today? Probably the most traditional of all is simply that of the keeper of books. Yet there are others that surface from time to time: information manager, database technician, bibliographer, or professor of bibliography. The recent film, *Pagemaster*, designates one exercising this role as, "Pagemaster, keeper of the books, guardian of the written word." One of the more creative descriptions was coined by the author of a short article in a recent issue of *Glamour* magazine.[1] In the course of describing the profession of library and information management as an attractive career option, it dubbed the late twentieth century professional in this area an "info-surfer." As attractive as this term may be, we could suggest "infonaut," as possibly more to the point. It suggests traveling through space at incredible speeds towards the active exploration of some unknown or partially-known planet of human experience and endeavor. And as a metaphor it adds a dash of professionalism to the overworked comparison of the information science professional as someone who can "surf the Internet," with its suggestion of purely recreational leisure activity.

One of the most attractive images of the librarian as professional is the one described by Francis Bacon in his sketch of the ideal future city, New Atlantis. In Solomon's house, the research institute of this visionary tale (does not the name "Solomon's house" suggest that what is being described would be the fruit of the richest endowments imaginable, and therefore worthy of Solomon himself?), Bacon describes those employed in information management and procurement thus: "For the several employments and offices of our fellows, we have twelve. . . who bring us the books and abstracts, and patterns of experiments of all other parts. These we call Merchants of Light."[2] Indeed, this metaphor suggests that knowledge itself has an angelic character.

Infonauting or the purveying of light may be what we think we are doing, but the term "librarian" is still historically correct, if not completely technically so. For as a term it obviously derives from the Latin *liber* ("book"). Yet what we do today in information management certainly transcends the collecting and accessing of the traditional codex, and it includes other media such as microfiche or microfilm, video and audio tapes, CD-ROM files, and the almost daily manipulation of online databases. It is true then that what is done in the library can no longer be described as the keeping of books, or of simply the keeping of books and associated materials, or of the activities associated with a generalized description of the librarian's function such as ordering, subscribing, cataloging, shelving, etc. of books .

In addition to all of these, there are more significant aspects of librarianship that need to be brought into perspective. Nearly twenty-five years ago Jesse H. Shera stated, "The object of the library is to bring together human beings and recorded knowledge in as fruitful relationship as it is humanly possible to be."[3] When Shera made that statement, which expressed something of the humanistic foundations and aspirations of librarianship, he in no way anticipated the modern-day exponential changes bought about by the electronic revolution in information storage, management, and retrieval. Yet their cumulative effect has been to make the role of librarianship much more opaque. No longer is the ideal of the so-called "compleat" librarian anything like the renaissance inspired humanist able to lead each and every inquirer through the fonts of printed knowledge. Today one must also approach being an electronic maven able by the manipulation of a keyboard to summon up prodigiously complete databases which practically write someone's term paper, complete with properly formatted APA or MLA style Endnotes. For the wizardry expected of the information professional today absolutely requires him or her constantly to conjure the modern crystal ball in the form of a 486 or Pentium with attached CD-ROM databases and online capabilities through gophers, web clients, and WAIS, that is, "wide area information server," the web of circuitous circuitry that opens the only semi-arcane world of cyberspace, where one can cruise at nearly the speed of light through business, educational, commercial, organizational, and governmental nodes of knowledge on the Internet.

I am reminded of a quote from the *Charleston Courier* of December 29, 1831, now displayed with an antique steam engine on a platform fitted with steel wheels in the State Museum of South Carolina at Columbia. When this first steam locomotive reached Charleston on Christmas day of 1830, one rider was quoted as saying, "We flew on the wings of the wind at the varied speed of fifteen to twenty-five miles an hour, annihilating time and space . . . leaving all the world behind . . . like a live rocket, scattering sparks and flames on either side." Today we laugh at the "varied speed of fifteen to twenty-five miles an hour." Yet the difference between travel in the early nineteenth century and today is equally paralleled, and perhaps surpassed, by the realities of information storage and retrieval. In successive moments while seated at my office computer I can read a fax just received from a colleague in Europe without it being at either end printed out on paper, read the text of yesterday's *San Francisco*

Chronicle online, and do research in the University of Nuremberg's library to see if it has recorded any new publications on the pamphlet literature of the Reformation. Truly the modern library annihilates many of the limitations formerly imposed by space and time.

Despite the wizardry of information retrieval in the electronic library of today there is something, I believe, that is much more important than the wizardry itself: that elements of wisdom, understanding, and intellectual comportment can never be furnished through a screen or a handy printout. Real learning is not simply the joining of human capacity with raw fact, but something uniquely personal and personally constructive. If education is the vitalization of data with the human spirit, then the function of the library may not be reduced to the repetition of isolated bits and bytes of information. Although I compose this essay on my word processor, the essence of the thing can never be isolated electronic impulses resident on my hard disk, nor the sheets of paper on which the characters they represent are printed, nor even the garnering of isolated facts. As John Henry Newman said, while contrasting the elements of a liberal education with the mere garnering of mechanical facts, ". . . knowledge [philosophical knowledge] is not a mere extrinsic or accidental advantage, which is ours today and another's tomorrow, which may be got up from a book, and easily forgotten again, which we can command or communicate at our pleasure, which we can borrow for the occasion, carry about in our hand, and take into the market; it is an acquired illumination, it is a habit, a personal possession, and an inward endowment . . . . [For] education is a higher word; it implies an action upon our mental nature, and the formation of a character; it is something individual and permanent, and is commonly spoken of in connection with religion and virtue."[4] Education may not be reduced to the mere communication of brute facts, although it seldom takes place without them.

To continue with Newman's thoughts: ". . . the communication of knowledge certainly is either a condition or the means of that sense of enlargement or enlightenment," which he so aptly described as the hallmark of a liberally educated person. ". . . it is equally plain, that such communication is not the whole of the process. The enlargement consists, not merely in the passive reception into the mind of a number of ideas hitherto unknown to it, but in the mind's energetic and simultaneous action upon and towards and among those new ideas, which are rushing in upon it. It is the action of a formative power, reducing to order and meaning the matter of our acquirements; it is a making the objects of our knowledge subjectively our own, or, to use a familiar word, it is a digestion of what we receive, into the substance of our previous state of thought; and without this no enlargement is said to follow."[5]

Although the classroom may serve for a certain enlargement of mind through the animation of lively and meaningful discussion, when the lecture method descends to the mere droning of facts and their mechanical applications, it is much less the midwife of education than an hour or two of self-directed study in the library. For there one can make converse with the greatest conversationalists of story and history, and there the mind can be supremely active, as it seeks out at its own unhurried pace the personal enlargement of spirit that true education is. For all the foregoing reasons, the library may never be relegated to the status of simply an adjunct or storeroom for the sole use of the classroom. It has a right to be, in and of itself, as an educator in its own right.

The function of theological librarian is that of an educator, but with particular responsibilities for maintaining and providing information resources for the institution and its individual members. As an educator/librarian one knows that while it is essential to understand and to build virtual electronic libraries around our physical libraries, ". . . the real challenges are in dealing with the person and the group in their relation to information, knowledge, problem-solving, and societal actions . . . . It is certainly true that the library, although an intellectual phenomenon, has happened to occur in the concrete space of a place." Yet we share these thoughts of D. Kaye Gapen that the library is "a social phenomenon . . . (and) the perception that the library is librarians rather than books—that the library is 'communication' rather than routines or a store house, and that the 'mission' of the library is actually the social and intellectual responsibility of the librarian to participate with our publics in the solution of problems and the creation of new knowledge. Libraries are about communication. As well, libraries are about knowledge."[6]

The theological library is about religious knowledge and about communication in a theologically informed context. And the role of the librarian here is not unlike that of other faculty members with full-time teaching responsibilities. Yet her/his role as administrator of a particular department requires that one direct a substantial part of most work days to the purchasing of resources and thereby helping to spend the annual budget. This in itself is a highly professional activity, for it assumes that one through previous experience and education is able to purchase, and to reject possible purchases, with an eye to their educational and/or research value for a specialized clientele. For libraries are much more than simply collections of books and other information sources related to a specific subject. They are intelligently directed and purposefully collected information resources that fill out the historical, diversified, and foundational reaches of knowledge surrounding a discipline or disciplines that have a natural linkage.

Why is the role of the theological librarian akin then to the role of other educators of the institution? It is because education is about empowerment. Education is the empowerment to act and to think maturely and independently. Professors empower students for learning through lectures, discussions, and other classroom and learning arena techniques. Yet since learning is primarily an active process that the student must undertake for her or himself, the classroom is only one of the avenues towards learning. Alongside the classroom is the library, a parallel educational arena.

Theological Libraries: an Historical Note

If libraries are about education, then it seems not to be amiss if we spend some time looking at the history of seminary libraries in this country, as well as at the development of the role of the theological librarian. I am indebted at this point to the historical work on the development of the library in Protestant seminaries of Norman J. Kansfield, now President of New Brunswick Theological Seminary and formerly Librarian of the Colgate Rochester Divinity School.[7]

It seems that Eliphalet Pearson (1752-1826) was the first on these shores to express the ideal of a library dedicated to the training of students for ministry. Pearson, a Congregationalist, was in the course of his career both a professor of Hebrew at Harvard College and for a time its president. Later he helped found the Andover Seminary, where he served as professor of sacred literature, and later as trustee.

Pearson expresses a view of the world as the battlefield between the forces of good and those of evil. Since the forces of evil and infidelity use ". . . books of many kinds, and in various other ways, their deadly poison is extensively, though in some respects secretly diffused throughout our country. In proportion as these enemies of God and man increase in number, learning, and activity, will be the necessity of an able and learned clergy, to expose their wiles, refute their sophistry, and counteract the misapplication of their science, literature and talents. . . . We must then defend ourselves by soldiers and weapons of our own. On such an emergence, what can be more necessary or happy, than to have a vigorous band of young men, already trained for this holy war, armed with the whole armour of God, and ready for the attack? Of what unspeakable importance then must an institution be, in which may be formed such a phalanx for the defense of the Christian cause! Students in divinity may there enjoy a public library, which in addition to treasures of common science, will be furnished with rich variety of books in the several branches of sacred literature; many of which, through of primary importance, such as are seldom, if ever, found in the libraries of clergymen."[8]

The ideal of a seminary library is then much different than that of an ordinary pastor's library. It should include works not normally found there. Kansfield comments, "This has implications for more than just the composition of the book collection. It further implies that this seminary collection of books was to be consciously and actively acquired. The inheritance of deceased pastors' libraries would not be enough, for many of the books most needed were 'seldom, if ever, found in the libraries of clergymen.'"[9]

Samuel Miller, who was a member of a committee of the General Assembly of the Presbyterian Church in 1810, which formulated a "Plan of a Theological Seminary," elaborated the intended direction of collection development which would eventually lead to the library of the Princeton Seminary. There should be, he said, "a library of sufficient extent to furnish every standard work which may be quoted or recommended on every subject which may become matter of discussion in the Institution."[10]

This ideal for collection development certainly implies the careful attention of one trained in the disciplines represented by the seminary curriculum. For to build up a collection meaningfully, one must somehow participate in the "discussions" in the institution. However, the ideal was not always something to be easily realized. Some twenty-seven years later the General Assembly of the Presbyterian Church had still not accepted Miller and the committee's plan, and he was given to complain of the Princeton library: "Instead of one hundred thousand volumes, which the Institution ought to possess, it has less than a twelfth part of that number."[11]

Pearson, however, had gone on to forge the necessary link between the classroom and the library. "No small benefit also will be derived to students in divinity from the recommendation and character of books incidentally and formally given in . . . lectures."[12] The professors have then a bibliographic function, inasmuch as it is assumed that they will explain and direct their students to works in the library for personal recourse and study. There is then an inextricable link between the classroom and the library. The assumption of this is that education does not nor can not take place in the classroom alone. The library provides an essential context where the work of education, begun in the classroom, is completed.

Pearson elaborates on the role of the library, ". . . here it will be recollected that this necessary information is not to be found collected and arranged in one huge volume; but lies scattered in a multitude of books in various languages, and difficult to be procured, the expense of which alone places them at an inaccessible distance from the young student of theology. But were they collected in one place, still without the means of residence there, and even with those means, they would be in great part useless to him, without the assistance of an able guide to direct the course of his researches and to regulate his studies."[13] This first ideal of a seminary library provides then for a complementary relationship between classroom and library, neither of which is complete in and of itself. Pearson clearly saw that the professors had a bibliographic function which went beyond the mere factual presentation of a subject. The library was to have the function of illustrating and confirming what was explained in lectures. In one sense, it provided the laboratory where the theory of the classroom could be tested and confirmed against the approved authors. Dare one add at this point that the library also served the function of stimulating active and personal research which, because of active personal involvement, is the highest type of learning?

In the nineteenth century, seminary libraries were often open for only a few hours a week and, in many locations only for an hour or two a day. Although a faculty member was normally given the title of librarian, the actual running of the library was usually entrusted to students. In some, books could be used only on the premises; in others students were limited to borrowing only two or three at a time.

Nevertheless, in these varied statements from the early nineteenth century one can discern something of the development of strategic planning for theological libraries. They must be formed with the philosophy of providing a collection of sources that go far beyond the expectations of a pastor's library; they must be able to explain and confirm what is presented in the classroom; and they must outfit one for apologetic battle with the intellectual aspects of secularism. And through a process of purposeful acquisition, every "standard work" referring to all topics that might be a topic of discussion at the institution are to be sought out. To these we have added our own understanding of the library as being a locus of education, especially self-directed education, parallel to the classroom—an element lacking in earlier formulations of library philosophy.

For the library of the theological school can not and may not be relegated simply to the ancillary role of serving the classroom. It has a reason for being within itself. "For there is a richness deep down things," to paraphrase the poet, Gerard Manly Hopkins. There is a richness to books that is rooted in their physical nature and has little to do with any monetary value.[14] One of the reasons that libraries, as physical collections of books, continue to be important is the scholarly need to stimulate the imaginative mind. To peruse a list of bibliographic entries on a computer screen, whether with or without abstracts, is simply not the same as to wander through stacks of physical volumes, scanning titles and subjects relating to a current or enduring research interest. For as one wanders, a volume will be pulled down here and there, tables of contents or indexes scanned, paragraphs or a couple of pages consulted from time to time, and here or there an as yet unknown tome will be selected for further inspection.

The point is that none of this would have taken place if access to physical volumes were replaced by electronic bibliographic records alone or by a full-text, electronic database. The cost in resources and time to call up everything that is revealed electronically as available, or even as just tangential, is too great. And many items that prove themselves useful, if only marginally, may never have suggested themselves through Boolean searching and computer logic. This is not meant to impugn the skills of professional indexers, or even of those who employ hypertext logic and keyword searching, but to assert that the imaginary and visionary intellect is often served best by serendipity, which is by definition a non-logical approach to a subject or phase of reality.

Nothing serves serendipity better than a collection of books, indeed a very large collection of books, in all their physicality, differences of bindings, illustration, conception, prefaces, execution, indexing, and even juxtaposition—the larger and more variegated, the better. Therefore, the seminary library must continue to build its physical collection of books and other materials, because scholars and students will continue to require them. And a serious look at the history of communication reveals that new types of communication do not obliterate older ones, but simply add a variety and richness to what the older modes were able to offer. Marconi's wireless did not replace the telegraph, and television has not made radio obsolete. And even if, impossible dream that it is, the whole of recorded knowledge were available on the screen of a scholar's workstation, many of us, computer literate though we may be, would still prefer to pick up a book.

For all these reasons, I should like then emphatically to make the point that the library is not dependent on the classroom: it has an educational function in its own right. For inasmuch as true education of the human spirit can never be reduced to a type of spoon feeding, but is ultimately a self-directed and immanent activity of absorption, reconceptualization, and of personal expression, the library is the best environment imaginable for this most eminent of human activities.

Theological Librarianship: the Growth of Professionalism

The role of professionalism in theological librarianship was also something slow in accomplishment, although the need was recognized early on. A subcommittee of the prudential Committee of the Hartford Theological Seminary was appointed "to examine certain claims presented to . . . [the] chairman by the librarian: and to consider the needs of the library." In examining the claims of the librarian about the needs of the library the members wrote,

> The fact, that the librarian is a professor in the institution, points toward the scope of his duties: but they are more fully indicated by the position occupied by the library in the educational system proposed by the present administration. The librarian at East Windsor Hill, half a century ago, did not need much brain, nor a large salary. Now, the library of the Hartford Theological Seminary comes well to the front among the theological libraries of the country. To put 45,000 little packages of blank paper upon shelves would be to any of us quite a formidable undertaking. But, when we think of the 20,000,000 pages, (more or less) of these 45,000 Vols., as thought-bearing records; requiring a thorough classification, we are forced to confess our need for a master in bibliography to master them for best service in our seminary curriculum . . . .

Take a few items.

> He must be a master of prices—a practical book-buyer. He must be
> an accurate examiner of books delivered, that the library be not
> loaded with the many frauds, and inaccuracies of publishers. He
> must be a master of classification, not simply that the book may be
> found when wanted, but that the library as the great literary or-
> ganism of the institution, may reveal its merits in the presence of
> other librarians. Then, he must be a master of administration.
> The books must be furnished to users in a systematic way. He
> must know what is in the library, and be alert for consultation re-
> specting the merits of books. He ought to know what the professors
> in the seminary are doing and be able to guide the students in their
> investigations.

Then comes the scholastic side of the librarian's work.

> Bibliography must be at his tongue's end, and if he has not some
> knowledge of many languages, he will be a cheap 19th century li-
> brarian . . . .
> Furthermore—the library takes its place as a striking literary
> exponent and advertisement of the institution. Its manuscripts,
> its antiquarian tomes, its records of research in bible lands, and
> in all lands where are left special records of God's doings among
> the nations, are weighty items in its furnishing, and for the pur-
> chase and handling of which, only a bibliographical specialist is
> fit. It is not to be wondered as therefore, that a man who has en-
> tered this vast field for life, having a fairly rounded talent for the
> service, should, in consideration of the exacting duties of the posi-
> tion ask for himself a professor's seat, and a professor's compen-
> sation; shoulder to shoulder with other titled educators.[15]

So comprehensive a statement of the role of the theological librarian in the
seminary or theological school exists, to my knowledge, nowhere else,
even in the professional literature of our own century. And although the
Hartford Seminary could boast that the expressed ideal was well realized
in the person of Ernest Cushing Richardson, whose lifelong career was as
seminary librarian at that institution, the situation elsewhere was usually far from the ideal.

A case in point is the noteworthy example provided by John Charles
Van Dyke, who became librarian at the New Brunswick Seminary in
1878. Although neither a librarian nor a theologian by profession—Mr.

Van Dyke was an art historian—he was quick to seize the opportunity of a proffered sinecure. Years later he wrote of the opportunity:

> One day an unexpected offer came to me. Would I take temporarily the acting librarianship of the Sage Library? I went to see it. The library building was the gift of Colonel Gardner A. Sage of New York to the Seminary of the Reformed Church in America at New Brunswick. It had been built only about five years and then held about 30,000 volumes .... It was not for the public but for the seminary students, biblical scholars, and others engaged in research work. The duties of administration were not too exacting nor the salary too high. I should have leisure for my own work and several months each summer to go to Europe if I chose.
>
> I said "yes" without hesitation, and to myself under my breath: This shall be the resting place for the sole of my foot! And so it has proved."[16]

Well, some fifty-three years later Mr. Van Dyke was still in office. The point in narrating this sad tale is to call attention to the 53,000 opportunities, at a minimum, which were lost to the faculty and students of the New Brunswick Seminary during all those years by the administrative blunder of hiring someone not educated properly for the role of theological librarianship. For would one expect knowledgeable advice in, say, studying the mysticism of Gregory of Nyssa, or on early formulations of the Trinitarian doctrine before the great Council of Constantinople in 381 from an art historian? Or would the taste of the dilettante be a responsible source of library augmentation when it came to purchasing works in Old Testament theology? Would a sense of the aesthetic in its historical manifestations be a decent background for choosing works to support the practice of pastoral counseling?

This is a profession that requires at least a twofold professionalism. One needs to move confidently in the world of librarianship, that is to say, be conversant with both the theory and the practice of classification systems and subject analysis, to be familiar with the policies of various publishers, to know theological bibliography, and to be able to carry out online searching as basic skills. In addition, one needs ideally to be educated not simply to the level of ministerial ability, but to the level of instructional capacity in the ministerial and theological sciences. Remember, the ideal of the seminary library is to be something decidedly better than the libraries of deceased pastors.

One must have an eye for theological trends, read the professional journals, study the reviews, and attend and participate in scholarly and professional conferences. The ideal is, once again, not education simply to ministerial level, but to the level of an educator in ministerial and theological studies, and perhaps even to the level of an educator's educator— one who can also stimulate the faculty to reflection and to further research. For if one of the principles of collection development already foreseen in the nineteenth century was to further the level of discussion in the seminary by the introduction of appropriate materials into the library, this needs to be accomplished on all three of those levels. It is for all of these reasons that the role of the theological librarian can never be reduced to simply that of an administrator of resources, both personal and financial, without grave harm to the entire educational process.

Yet the bifold education of a theological librarian, as fundamentally necessary as it may be, does not quite say it all. There is one more ingredient that should ideally be there but was indeed sadly lacking in our beloved whipping boy, Mr. Van Dyke. It is that final ingredient that makes all the difference between a line of work, a livelihood perhaps, and a real vocation. I speak, of course, of a person's deeper affections—what excites and gives momentum to one's life. One of my students once said, "I want to get to know you. Tell me what your passions are." In the last analysis it is our passions that define us, just as it is our truly human or volitional acts that define us as ethical and moral beings.

If life is defined philosophically as immanent activity, then what one does when in a state of rest or of leisure most nearly defines the excitement of his or her being in the world. Above and beyond education and opportunity, the personal *Dasein* of the theological librarian is characterized by a fondness for perusing antiquarian book shops while vacationing in the great capitals of the world, by using up available weekends in attending professional conferences, by scheduling study stops at miniature Bodleians wherever they might be, and by filling up every available alcove in the home with bibliographic projects in some remote stage of progress. An old adage says, "Tell me what you read and I shall tell you what you are." Tell me something of what you do in your off time, and I shall know better who you really are. It is emotion recollected and expressed in tranquillity that defines the ultimately personal quality of existence.

The Theological Librarian as Teacher

Today in the circles emanating from the Association of Theological Schools there is much reason for what is spoken of as, "the good theological school." Since in the accrediting process superintended by that organization there is in recent years less concern with simply setting standards than there is a sense of allowing individual institutions to define their goals and then to demonstrate how they are fulfilling them, I should like to describe how I envision the role of theological librarian as teacher and educator.

In many theological schools the librarian is designated "professor of bibliography." In mentioning this fact one may well ask, "Is this nomenclature simply in order to give the incumbent person faculty status and recognition, or does the librarian really teach something?" It is my contention that the sense of this title is that the librarian really does by profession teach something. He or she may also be an administrator of corporate resources and responsible for personnel, but if she or he is not also a teacher by inclination, by education, and by choice, then I would maintain that the title professor of bibliography or of anything else, for that matter, is improper.

What is theological bibliography? And how is it taught? Bibliography must be bibliography of something, since it is assumed that the subject at hand is not the purely technical study of book production, format and collation, such as has been classically treated by Fredson Bowers in his *Principles of Bibliographical Description,*[17] or by Ronald B. McKerrow in his *An Introduction to Bibliography for Literary Students.*[18] These scholars study the formats used in book production, the signs of various states within an edition, and the collation of individual pages or signatures in examples of a printed text.

Theological bibliography is not this. It is indeed more than this. It is the study of something. In the widest sense it is the study of theological encyclopedia. For theological bibliography, like all bibliography that is not simply a study of principles, must be subject specific. The subject of theological bibliography is the written records, the forms of classic expression, and the varieties of scholarship that relate to all the disciplines of the theological curriculum. Yet since this is done in the context of bibliographic instruction, a library activity that is rarely a credit bearing course, it is not uncommon to downplay its importance.

However, the importance of bibliographic instruction becomes poignant when the librarian becomes the research consultant on location, who can offer meaningful aid to a student at a near complete loss about how to begin a research paper in a new subject. As any librarian knows, this type of bibliographic instruction often overflows into helping the student in conceiving or, more often, in reconceiving the theme of the intended paper. Bibliographic instruction becomes the excuse for engaging the inquirer in a dialogue that was somehow missed in the classroom, or that one was simply not able to carry on alone.

Librarians do not simply extend the instructional curriculum of the classroom. They often provide the personal help that is difficult or impossible in the classroom situation. But their ability to do this is ordinarily conditioned by their personal and professional acquaintance with the subject. Having been there and run the course—in a Master of Divinity program or in a pastoral situation or perhaps in a doctoral program—all of these provide the authority of experience, which needs to be mediated at various opportune moments, to every incoming class of neophytes. As the single person most able to pinpoint the resources necessary to complement and to complete the work in the classroom, we might designate this function of the librarian as "research consultant."

It is also pertinent for the librarian to be engaged, albeit on a limited basis, in classroom teaching. Sometimes this will be a session or two on the library resources pertinent to a particular course of study being taught by another professor. Often, however, it can take the form of a course on research methods and resources. For the past five years I have been engaged in designing and in teaching such a course. The title of this course, which was offered for academic credit, was: "Bibliographic Resources for Theology and Ministry." Despite the title, a good deal of time was spent on the modes of accessing available electronic resources. Yet the focus of the course was to integrate a knowledgeable approach to the available resources with the traditional mechanics of writing the research paper. Students who come to ministerial studies from a variety of professional backgrounds and courses of study in college need to be (re-)introduced to the structure of the research paper and to be able to know how it differs from a reflection paper or from homiletic material.

Although no research paper was required for this exercise in theological bibliography, the students were required to work through the writing of a paper required for another class, using the steps outlined in a carefully structured and sequential way, and with personal help at every turn.

All of the functions so far mentioned—collection development, research assistance, and instruction in theological bibliography—help delineate the role of the theological librarian as an educator, and the library as a partner in the educational process on a par with the classroom. It would seem not to be especially fruitful to try and rank them in some sort of hierarchical schema in conjunction with the more usual thinking about the function of the librarian as a keeper and maintainer of material resources as well as a personnel manager. They are, and will remain, the hallmarks of the vocation of theological librarianship in its integrity and, I submit, formative elements of the good theological school.

Endnotes

1. Laural Tonby, "The New Librarian as an Info-Surfer," *Glamour* 92 (April 1994): 126.
2. *The Harvard Classics*, vol. 3 (New York: P. F. Collier & Son Company, 1909), 179.
3. *Sociological Foundations of Librarianship* (New York: Asia Publishing House, 1970), 30.
4. *The Idea of a University* (London: Longmans, Green and Co., 1919), 113-14.
5. Ibid., 133-44.
6. *The Virtual Library: Visions and Realities*, ed. by Laverna M. Saunders (Westport: Meckler, 1993), 5-6.
7. "'Study the Most Approved Authors:' The Role of the Seminary Library In Nineteenth-Century American Protestant Ministerial Education," (Ph.D. diss., University of Chicago, 1981).
8. "Importance . . . ," 312-13, quoted from Kansfield, ibid., 104-105.
9. Kansfield, idem, 105-106.
10. *A Brief History of the Seminary of the Presbyterian Church at Princeton, New Jersey* (Princeton: John Bogart, 1838), 41-42; quoted from Kansfield, idem, 108.
11. Ibid., 42.
12. Pearson, idem, 310; quoted from Kansfield, idem, 106.
13. Pearson, idem, 308; quoted from Kansfield, idem, 106.
14. Cf. Hopkin's line, "There lives the dearest freshness deep down things," from "God's Grandeur," in *Gerard Manley Hopkins: Poems and Prose*, ed. W. H. Gardner, (New York: Penguin Books, 1963), 27.
15. Samuel B. Forbes and Charles A. Jewell, "To the Prudential Committee of the Hartford Theological Seminary," Hartford Seminary

Foundation, Archives; 2-4; quoted from Kansfield, idem, 156-57.

16. John C. Van Dyke, "My Golden Age: A Personal Narrative of American Life from 1861 to 1931," (New York, 1931, typescript), 63-64; quoted from Kansfield, idem, 217.

17. Princeton: Princeton University Press, 1949.

18. Oxford: Clarendon Press, 1927.

What Does a Professor of Bibliography Do? Reflections on a Common Title

Stephen D. Crocco

Why is a librarian called a "professor of bibliography?" Asking students, faculty, administrators, and board members (not to mention parents, spouses, and children) is likely to elicit puzzled looks and shrugged shoulders. "I don't know—I guess it has something to do with books." Could most librarians give a better answer? How important or meaningful is the title "professor of bibliography?" Will it survive the present or will it give way to something like "professor of information?" That there has been little discussion of titles in the literature may indicate that the whole question is uninteresting and unimportant. However, in this essay I suggest that for the sake of the profession, there are reasons for busy and satisfied librarians to consider titles. Precision in this area may support librarians where issues of status and standing are nebulous or have eroded from former levels. Titles may also be used to reflect or clarify standards that the American Theological Library Association and the Association of Theological Schools can use to prepare, shape, and discipline its members. This essay is a contribution to such discussions for librarians with faculty rank. I begin by commenting on the proliferation of academic titles generally and librarians' titles in particular. Then I consider whether "bibliography" and "research" are feasible as subject areas. Answering that question in the negative, I contend that bibliography and research are included in a title to signify or demonstrate the

150

teaching nature of the librarian's position. A discussion of parallels between titles for librarians and academic deans helps to make this clear. The essay concludes with a proposal for understanding the relationship between a librarian's subject specialty, titles with bibliography or research in them, and the task of a librarian as teacher.

Proliferation of Titles

Head librarians in ATLA institutions have a variety of titles. "Librarian" seems to have given ground to other titles or combinations of titles, such as "librarian and professor of bibliography," "director of the library and professor of research," and "director of library services and professor of bibliography and research." Some librarians embraced new titles, hoping they would give fresh visibility and status to their positions. Others accepted new titles simply as one more round of administrative reorganization. A few resisted change because they prefer the simple, traditional title, "librarian," or because they were content with titles that reflected a more traditional theological subject specialty (e.g., "professor of New Testament") and so followed a widespread pattern of the nineteenth century in which a member of the theological faculty served as librarian.

The variety of titles for librarians is an illustration of the proliferation of academic administration. In earlier times, faculty members would serve their institutions by taking a turn as president, dean, registrar, dean of students, business manager, and librarian. Growing institutions added personnel to support classroom faculty—some as clericals, some as professionals, and some as faculty. As libraries grew in size and complexity, they added clerical workers and librarians with an M.L.S. to do technical processing and cataloging. The duties of selecting books and shaping the direction of the library remained in the hands of faculty members. Later, faculty were appointed to be full-time librarians. Changes in titles both reflected and created an organizational structure in the institution.

Fine-tuning an institution's administration over the years was also a response to different organizational schemes foisted on or coveted by academia in the post-World War II era. Today, business models are in place at many ATS schools. A president is also a chief executive officer, a dean is a vice president of academic affairs, and a business manager is a vice president of finance. How many librarians are vice presidents in schools with a corporate administrative structure? Some librarians breathed a sigh of relief at not having been made vice president, lest they be consumed by more meetings and administrative work. But this relief should not be enjoyed until a series of questions are answered to the librarian's satisfaction. If not a vice president or dean, where is the librarian in the structure of the institution? To whom does the librarian report? Does this relationship serve the best interests of the librarian and the library that he or she serves? Is the librarian comfortably ensconced in the faculty and/or the administration, or is the librarian's status unique and therefore unclear? Does the librarian have meaningful access to decision making that affects his or her work? Is the librarian eligible for promotion, tenure, and other faculty privileges? If not, are the reasons relevant and nondiscriminatory? To which group does the librarian submit work for evaluation? Different institutions answer these questions differently. However, the unique character of most librarians' positions within their institutions make these questions pertinent, if not for the incumbent librarian, then certainly for successors. [1]

"Bibliography" and "Research" as Subject Areas

What did administrators and librarians have in mind when they gave the name "professor of bibliography" to theological librarians? It is relatively clear what professors of theology or Christian education do. But what do professors of bibliography or research do? Is the librarian a professor of bibliography in the same way that someone is a professor of pastoral theology? Some expect librarians to teach in bibliography or research but few schools offer full courses in these areas. Are professors of bibliography given the title because they are specialists in one of the many forms of bibliographic study? A brief sketch of these of these forms will illustrate why I answer the question in the negative.[2] A systematic or critical bibliographer compiles as complete a list as possible of books, tapes, etc. by a particular author or subject area. Systematic bibliography tries to order titles in a way that reflects the internal or natural structure of the body of material being compiled. As a more general form of systematic bibliography, enumerative bibliography emphasizes the listing done and stresses thoroughness in completing the task. Today, anyone with access to electronic bibliographic utilities can become a decent enumerative bibliographer by downloading author or subject records! In systematic and enumerative bibliography, value judgments about the quality of materials are put aside. Unless the bibliographer is grounded in the subject area, he or she is not qualified to prepare selective bibliographies, except on objective criteria such as date, language, or place of publication. Selection by a judgment of quality (i.e., good or important books) is necessarily left to the subject specialist.

Are professors of bibliography named so because they study books as physical objects? Those who aspire to be critical or analytical bibliographers must know the history of printing and publishing. They must scrutinize bindings, paper, water marks, illustrations, ink, and fonts. They must give their days and nights to the study of Stokes's *Esdaile's Manual of Bibliography*, Gaskell's *A New Introduction to Bibliography*, Carter's *ABC for Book Collectors* and *Taste & Technique in Book Collecting*, *Bookman's Price Index*, and the major national bibliographies. Specialists in early printed books will also study works such as Briquet's *Les Filigranes: Dictionaire Historique des Marques du Papier* and Panzer's *Annales Typographici.*[3]

Critical bibliographers may specialize in historical bibliography. This sub-discipline emphasizes the history of printing and publishing, as well as technological developments in paper, ink, type, fonts, etc. The historical bibliographer is an historian with a specialty in the history of written communication. Mastery of Boorstin's *The Discoverers*, Levarie's *The Art & History of Books*, Feather's *A Dictionary of Book History*, and McArthur's *Worlds of Reference: Lexicography, Learning and Language from the Clay Tablet to the Computer* are entrees into the extensive and highly specialized literature of historical bibliography.[4] Descriptive bibliography is yet another sub-discipline of critical bibliography. A practitioner describes the production of the book by identifying its content, its edition, and any imperfections or irregularities. Descriptive bibliographers follow carefully established formats to collate (i.e., do a critical analysis of) the book. Some of the best descriptive catalogers are booksellers and exhibitors, and their catalogs deserve to be collected and studied.

Most librarians do not specialize in preparing lists of books or dealing with bibliographic minutiae, rare and antiquarian books, first editions, and other primary concerns of systematic or critical bibliography. Are librarians professors of bibliography simply because they need to answer questions about the value of family Bibles and "old" books given to the library? Is it because they select new books for the collection? Is it because they are expected to recommend books for patrons or point to a good, new, or interesting book in a field? Are they professors of bibliography because they are knowledgeable about theological literature in a general sense? These bibliographic tasks are important but none gets to the heart of the matter. Even librarians who prepare lists of books do so not primarily because they are professors of bibliography. They are not specialists in preparing lists of books as much as they are specialists in the subject areas in which they work. To suggest that most librarians are specialists in the area of preparing bibliographies is like suggesting that James D. G. Dunn, Bonnie B. Thurston, and Abraham J. Malherbe are specialists in the area of writing books about the New Testament. This is surely an odd way to put things!

The same questions can be raised about librarians with the title "professor of research." Reference or public service librarians focus on teaching patrons how to do research. Their goal is to teach patrons how to do research for their subject interests and not to teach them how to do research in the literature about research. Are professors of research supposed to write books like Beasley's *How to Use a Research Library*?[5] A few searching tips from a librarian can be a great help to a patron. But tips do not replace the patron's subject knowledge or a skilled researcher with a subject specialty. Librarians are not called "professors of research" primarily because they can direct patrons to the ATLA's *Ethics Index* on CD-ROM, the *Elenchus Bibliographicus Biblicus*, or Bollier's *The Literature of Theology*.[6] In this sense, any faculty member who does research is a professor of research. The question remains: Why is a librarian called a "professor of bibliography" or "professor of research?"

Titles for Librarians and Academic Deans

The titles and position of an academic dean may shed some light on the question of titles for librarians. A dean may have a number of titles including, "dean of the faculty," "vice president of academic affairs," and one that indicates his or her subject specialty such as "professor of Old Testament." Using so many titles is awkward; so all but the most pretentious simply use "dean." I suggest that "librarian" is the shorthand equivalent of the title "dean." The librarian is the professor of bibliography and the director of the library. The title "professor of bibliography" is not parallel to the dean's title, "professor of Old Testament." Bibliography and research are not subject areas for the librarian in the way that Old Testament studies is for the dean. If anything, the titles "dean of the faculty" or "academic dean" are parallel to the titles "professor of bibliography" or "professor of research." The title "vice president of academic affairs" is parallel to the title "director of the library." The faculty title refers to the qualifications of the librarian as the teacher who runs the library. The administrative title refers to what the librarian does and how he or she fits in the institution's organizational chart. "Dean of the faculty," "academic dean," "professor of bibliography," and "professor of research" all speak to the teaching (i.e., the faculty nature) of their positions. Librarians who want to be called "director of the library" are like deans who want to be called "vice president of academic affairs." Those who named librarians "professors of bibliography" did not expect that librarians would be specialists in bibliography as much as they expected that librarians at this level needed a title that reflected the teaching or faculty dimension of their positions. Librarians are specialists in bibliography and research in the same way that deans are specialists in dean's duties that require faculty rank. Librarians, like deans, are not half-faculty and half-administration in terms of their person or position. To borrow a classic christological formulation, librarians and deans are fully-faculty and fully-administration. Any attempt to assign percentages results in academic heresy. Faculty qualifications are necessary for both, because both function primarily as teachers, although neither teaches in a classroom as much as classroom faculty.[7]

To expect bibliography and research to be primary teaching and publishing areas for librarians is like expecting deans to offer courses and publish primarily in the areas he or she needs to know when deaning (i.e., evaluating transcripts, being conversant with tenure policies, learning and teaching theories, evaluating proposals for sabbaticals, reviewing applications for teaching positions, etc.). Of course, deans do teach when they instruct committees, advise young colleagues and write for publications such as *Theological Education*, but most do not do so at the expense of their primary subject area. (Would we call a dean who did, a "professor of deaning?") The intensive "dean schools" for new deans offered by universities such as Carnegie Mellon and Harvard have a number of parallels to the librarian's M.L.S. degree.[8] Both speak of the need for additional training but not at the expense of a subject specialty. There are now doctoral programs in academic administration, but these degrees have not caught on in theological institutions. For that matter, neither have librarians with Ph.D.s in library science. I suspect that both are few and far between, because institutions continue to value the subject area in those they call to be librarian and dean.

A dean needs a subject specialty as a faculty member to be a dean of the faculty. Similarly, a librarian needs a subject specialty to be a professor. Viewing bibliography and research as subject areas minimizes the librarian's true subject specialty, whether it is Old Testament, systematic theology, or church history. This subject specialty is the foundation of the librarian's approach to bibliography and research. It is also the basis for the librarian to be embraced by his or her peers on the faculty. While many, if not most, librarians have subject specialities and teach in those areas, they are rarely reflected in their titles. Thus, librarians's titles, to be complete, should be something like this: "professor of research, director of the library, and professor of New Testament." Or, if I am right that the professor of bibliography and the director of the library is the librarian, "librarian and professor of New Testament" will do nicely. In this case, any other titles used for the sake of the organizational chart, such as "director of the library," "dean of library services," or "vice-president of information services," are there, but implicit.

Conclusions

The professor of bibliography is first and foremost a teacher, whether that teaching takes place in a classroom, over a reference question, while selecting materials for the library, doing research, or when advising the staff. Schools that require librarians to have a Ph.D. or a second masters degree presumably acknowledge that to teach in these ways requires a subject specialty in theology or a related field. But this degree is not just a credential. The librarian's own subject specialty is the basis and model for teaching as the professor who runs the library. If the librarian has a Ph.D. in liturgics, for example, he or she knows the depth and breadth of that field and what it takes to be a responsible liturgics scholar. By studying catalogs, reviews, bibliographies, and the shelf list, the librarian also knows that all theological subjects have a similar depth and breadth. The librarian's approach to his or her own discipline becomes the way of approaching other disciplines. Librarians, like other faculty with wide-ranging interests, build on their subject specialty to become generalists in other areas. As such, librarians become familiar with the topics and literature of theology. The librarian is a generalist, a dilettante (in the best sense of the word), and an encyclopaedist. He or she is well poised to teach students and faculty that a theological education requires breadth as well as depth and a continuing commitment to study in all the disciplines of theology.

Endnotes

1. See Stephen D. Crocco and Sara J. Myers "Standards for Innovation: The Case for Theological Librarians." *Theological Education* 31/2 (1995): 51-62.

2. The following descriptions of analytical and critical bibliography are gleaned from Roy Stoke's *Esdaile's Manual of Bibliography*, 5th rev. ed. (Metuchen, NJ: Scarecrow, 1981).

3. Stokes, *Esdaile's Manual of Bibliography*; Philip Gaskell, *A New Introduction to Bibliography* (New York: Oxford University Press, 1972); John Carter, *ABC for Book Collectors*, 7th ed., with corrections, additions and an introduction by Nicolas Barker (New Castle, DE: Oak Knoll, 1995); *idem, Taste & Technique in Book Collecting* (London: Private Libraries Association, 1972); *Bookman's Price Index* (Detroit: Gale Research, 1964-); C. M. Briquet, *Les Filigranes: Dictionaire Historique des Marques du Papier*, 4 vols. (New York: Hacker Art Books, 1985); Georg Wolfgang Franz Panzer, *Annales Typographici*, 11 vols. (Hildesheim: Georg Olms, 1963).

4. Daniel J. Boorstin. *The Discoverers* (New York: Random House, 1983); Norma Levarie. *The Art & History of Books* (New York: Da Capo, 1982); John Feather, *A Dictionary of Book History* (New York: Oxford University Press, 1986); Tom McArthur, *Worlds of Reference* (Cambridge: Cambridge University Press, 1986).

5. David R. Beasley, *How to Use a Research Library* (New York: Oxford University Press, 1988).

6. *Ethics Index* on CD-ROM (Evanston, IL: American Theological Library Association, 1994); *Elenchus Bibliographicus Biblicus* (Rome: Biblical Institute Press, 1920-); John A. Bollier, *The Literature of Theology: A Guide for Students and Pastors* (Philadelphia: Westminster, 1979).

7. One difference between deans and librarians is that deans are frequently called from the faculty to serve one or more terms and then return to full-time teaching. Librarians are usually hired as librarians and remain so for the duration of their association with the institution. Some drive a wedge between deans and librarians at this point and argue librarians ought not to be eligible for tenure and other privileges enjoyed by the rest of the faculty. Some argue this on the grounds that librarians are not truly faculty, or they take the view that the position is too important

for tenure or sabbaticals. These arguments are flawed, but they deserve more attention than can be given to them here.

8. It may be heresy to some to suggest this, but four to six week intensive courses in various aspects of librarianship may be an alternative to the M.L.S. for some librarians.

Chicago Area Theological Libraries and the Elusive Goal of Regional Library Resource Sharing

Newland F. Smith

When administrators think of cooperation among seminaries, they inevitably turn to their libraries as the area most likely to be fruitful for resource sharing. Although this seems to be a reasonable course of action, the following analysis of the past thirty years of cooperative efforts by the Chicago area libraries will attempt to document some of the pitfalls that librarians have encountered in their search for successful resource sharing. I will argue that even with daily or three times a week courier service among a group of libraries with reciprocal borrowing privileges for the faculty and students of the participating schools and with check lists of currently received periodicals and monograph series, it is extremely difficult to engage in constructive resource sharing until users and staff have easy bibliographic access to the holdings of the libraries. This paper is not so much a history of the three Chicago theological library area organizations, two of which continue to exist, as it is an attempt to document the crucial importance for resource sharing among the Chicago area theological libraries for users to be able to access the holdings of the member libraries and for collection development librarians to be able to access the order files of the other libraries.

The three library organizations are the Chicago Area Theological Library Association (CATLA; est. 1965), the Librarians' Council of the Chicago Cluster of Theological Schools (CCTS; 1970-1985), and the Library

Council of the Association of Chicago Theological Schools (ACTS; est. 1983). The Chicago Theological Institute, whose members consisted of the North Side schools, was founded in 1969. Although provisions made for a library committee, it ceased to function after several years because of the work of CATLA and the Librarians' Council of the CCTS.

It can be said that the impetus for formal library cooperation in the Chicago area was a letter dated October 14, 1965, from Paul H. Eller, then President of the Interseminary Faculties Union, an organization to which faculty members of any of the Chicago area seminaries were eligible to join, to the presidents of the member schools. Eller asked the presidents to urge, if necessary, their librarians to attend a meeting on November 4, at Chicago Theological Seminary in order "to gather in professional conversation." Twenty-four librarians, not only from the Chicago area but also from Grand Rapids in Michigan and Goshen in Indiana, attended that meeting, which was hosted by Robert Gordon Collier, the Librarian at Chicago Theological Seminary. According to the minutes a number of proposals were made. Charles Harvey Arnold, the Librarian at the University of Chicago Divinity School Library, suggested a "coop card catalog" and "an information network between librarians." John David Batsel, Librarian of Garrett Theological Seminary, proposed that the "Union List" be brought up to date and that "an inventory of major collections" be made.[1] Batsel went on to say that "concrete proposals needed . . . enough talk done already . . . time to act . . . area cooperation requires planning . . . we need a) concrete proposal and b) backing of our administrations and (possibly) foundations to insure financial support." Batsel concluded his comments with the question, "Should we reach out to R. C., Jewish, and Orthodox institutions?" Marlin Heckman, Library Director at Bethany Theological Seminary, also mentioned the Union List of Serials and "a union catalog and/or coop acquisitions recorded . . . in connection with subject control, to avoid unnecessary duplication, as well as access to required materials." Finally, Calvin Schmitt, Librarian of McCormick Theological Seminary, also stressed the necessity of concrete proposals: "Institutions should commit themselves to a monthly meeting . . . for only the institutions can effectively act in concert . . . librarians alone cannot and librarians change."

Each library was invited to bring to the next meeting on December 3 a one-page summary that listed resources and priorities of needs. The statement from Chicago Theological Seminary was the most ambitious and far reaching and began with the following recommendation:

> We recommend that the theological seminaries of the Chicago-area establish an organization with responsibility for such cooperative library programs as shall be desirable, that each cooperative program be so designed that only those seminaries that desire to do so need take part, and that as many seminaries as possible be included that all may profit from broader cooperation.

First priority was to be given "to research in the following areas of activity: 1. Cooperative ordering and cataloging; 2. Union catalog; 3. Union list of serials; 4. Deposit library; and 5. Technical advances (microreproduction, machine retrieval, electronics, etc.)." The statement ended with this admonition: "Full support by the administrations of each seminary involved is the price of support in cooperative activities." The staff of McCormick Theological Seminary's library added a directory, collaborative collection development, and a list of theological monograph series.

At these initial meetings, according to Patricia Bush Dominquez and Luke Swindler, most of the essential factors for successful library cooperation were named: a cooperative card catalog, a current union list of serials, a cooperative acquisitions program, institutional support, frequent meetings of the librarians, and outside financial support. One factor not mentioned was a delivery system, although one was in place for some of the libraries by the early 1970s. Dominquez and Swindler's article about the Research Triangle University Libraries in North Carolina points out the importance of "shared bibliographic information" for the success of cooperation. "Indeed," they wrote, "until faculties and librarians knew what both libraries held cooperation could not work."[2] Daily delivery service was in place by 1935 between the Duke University Library and the University of North Carolina Library. Copies were made of the card catalogs to form a union catalog at each of the libraries. An outside grant of $12,500 was made from the General Education Board to the two schools "for a joint catalog that facilitates the interchange of books and makes possible a co-ordinated development of future book collections."[3]

By 1965, the seminary librarians had organized themselves as the Chicago Area Theological Librarians Association. CATLA differs from the Librarians' Council of the CCTS and the Library Council of ACTS in that each of these two library councils were or are part of a consortium of seminaries accredited by the Association of Theological Schools. Institutional membership according to the Constitution of CATLA (adopted October 20, 1972) was open to "theological libraries and other libraries involved in or associated with theological concerns." Membership was not limited to the Chicago area but included schools in southeastern Wisconsin, western Michigan, and northern Indiana. The association was to hold meetings three times a year. The following three purposes as stated in Article II of the Constitution have been the most important for the work of CATLA:

> To sponsor bibliographic and related projects for the betterment of theological and ministerial education and information; to promote possibilities of cooperation in acquisition, technical services, and personnel, and to give mutual help and development to each other as professional, theological librarians.

Already by 1972 the initial proposals for a union catalog and cooperative ordering and cataloging were abandoned, as it became apparent that CATLA's membership extended far beyond the Chicago area. Yet, CATLA undertook a number of projects in order to provide information about the holdings and services of its libraries. A monograph series list was completed in 1969, a handbook with brief description of each library was compiled, and a union list of serials was issued in 1974.

The union list of serials was an early foray into computer technology. At the December 1967 meeting CATLA voted that "John Batsel, together with the officers of our group investigate the costs of producing the Union List of Serials and report at our next meeting." Funding for this project and for the monograph series list was to be raised by assessing each participating library one percent of its annual budget for books, periodicals, binding, supplies and equipment. Two years later the minutes of the December 12, 1970, meeting indicate that $750.00 would be available for this project from the Association of Chicago Theological Schools, which was established with fourteen seminaries in 1968. At the same meeting the Committee on a New Union List of Periodicals presented a full proposal, which was adopted. The total estimated cost was $6,725, $5,000 of which was for key-punching and verification of some 5,000 titles and 60,000 records. It would not be until 1974 that this union list would appear, and even at that it had to be produced manually. Although on November 14, 1971, CATLA had signed a contract with a Mr. Ed LeShea to produce a computerized union list and had advanced him over $3,000, LeShea was unable to fulfill the contract. As reported in the minutes of CATLA's October 19, 1973, meeting, consultation with McCormick Theological Seminary's legal counsel and a meeting with the State's Attorney's Offices revealed that although CATLA did not have a criminal case, the situation was in the State Attorney's words, "a clear case of breach of contract." Because to bring a civil suit would have cost from $500 to $700, with no assurance of recovery even if CATLA should win the suit, CATLA's Executive Committee decided on September 19, 1973, "that, because of unresolved problems with Mr. Ed LeShea, and since the most feasible way to produce the Union List at this time is to do it manually, the Editorial Committee be authorized to proceed accordingly." The 673 page union list of the serial holdings of the twenty-two member libraries was ready for distribution by 1974. But it was not produced without controversy. The librarians in Hyde Park and at Bethany and Northern-Baptist seminaries, who in 1970 had formed the Librarians' Council of the Chicago Cluster of Theological Schools, adopted a motion at their October 22, 1973, meeting, which ends with this sentence: "We strongly urge that the manual production be halted and a special meeting of CATLA be called to decide in a constitutional manner whether a manually produced list should be generated, what its form should be, including methods of additions, updating and funding." These librarians questioned whether CATLA's Executive Committee had the authority to make the decision to produce a manual list instead of a computered-generated list. But at the January meeting of CATLA the members affirmed the decision of the Executive Committee.

Although CATLA was not organized to create a union catalog and to sustain a collaborative collection development program, the participation of the Chicago area seminary librarians in the meetings and projects of those early years gave them the experiences on which to build both as part of CCTS and of ACTS. CATLA continues to function by holding fall and spring meetings for the professional development of its members.

The CCTS, which consisted of the six seminaries in Hyde Park (Bellarmine School of Theology, Catholic Theological Union, Chicago Theological Seminary, Lutheran School of Theology in Chicago, McCormick Theological Seminary, and Meadville/Lombard Theological School) and the three seminaries in Oak Brook, Lombard, and Lemont (Bethany Theological Seminary, Northern Baptist Theological Seminary, and De Andreis Institute of Theology, respectively) emerged at a time of lively ferment in ecumenical theological education. As early as May of 1970, the organizational structure was established with provision for a Common Council consisting of Deans and Presidents, a full-time, paid Executive Director, and a number of working committees, including a Librarians' Council, which began meeting as early as 1969. By 1972, a Long Range Planning Committee had prepared "A Picture of the Chicago Cluster Five Years Hence."

> This document envisioned a southside and a westside focus with common scheduling in each, a unified library system, an academic council, at least five full-time staff, library and student exchange privileges with the University of Chicago, and such cooperative programs as an academic doctorate, continuing education and summer school.[4]

The Librarians' Council consisted of the library directors and other members of their staffs so designated by the directors. A Library Program Director served on a paid, half-time basis and served as an ex-officio member of the Common Council. In its fifteen years of work the Librarians' Council made significant progress in its collaborative efforts. Couriers made the route four times weekly during the school year among the Hyde Park libraries and twice a week to the libraries in the Western suburbs. In the summer, though, service was suspended. Telecopying machines at the libraries of Bethany/Northern Baptist, Catholic Theological Union, Chicago Theological Seminary, De Andreis, Jesuit-Krauss-McCormick, and Meadville Theological Seminary made possible the rapid transmission of book requests, proposals for book orders, and copies of periodical articles among these libraries. A union list of currently received periodicals was first issued in 1972, with revised editions in 1973, 1975, and 1979. As a result of a major grant from the Lilly Foundation, a microfiche *Chicago Union Catalog of Religion and Theology*, consisting of 460,000 entries arranged by title, appeared in 1981. In addition to the pre-1978 holdings of the Cluster libraries, the list included the religion holdings of the University of Chicago Library and the Newberry Library. The Acquisitions and Collection Development Committee undertook a major analysis of the collections of the Cluster libraries and prepared a "Collection Development Profile" in 1974. This committee met frequently to discuss titles being considered for purchase. The librarians had agreed that before a given library would order a book costing more than $25.00, that library would check with the other libraries to determine if another Cluster library had already placed an order for it. Duplication of new titles, according to Kenneth O'Malley's undated (1982?) "Outline of CCTS Library Cooperation," was reduced from 34% in 1972 to 17% in 1974. In the chapter on the libraries of the CCTS in the 1981 Self-Study of the CCTS, Hedda Durnbaugh (then the Library Project Director) reported that "the Cluster libraries cooperatively save approximately $30,000/year in the area of periodical subscriptions.[5] After the libraries (with the exception of De Andreis) became members of OCLC in 1978, the computer generated catalog cards became the basis of a union catalog, which was housed at the Jesuit-Krauss-McCormick Library.

The work of the Librarians' Council was reviewed during a consultation in 1978 and the Self-Study in 1981. In the fall of 1978, Maria Grossmann and Paul Mosher were invited by the CCTS to come to Chicago for a two-day consultation on library cooperation with particular focus on collaborative collection development. In the final four-page report (written by Paul Mosher) a number of observations were made about the Librarians' Council. In particular, he noted the lack of clarity about

> the mission and goals of the institutions, the Cluster, and the University of Chicago . . . Library policies, goals and programs should be developed in support thereof . . . . In the absence of clear understanding of institutional priorities, missions or goals, librarians seem individually and collectively to be trying to piece together rational programs of cooperation. Yet at the same time, they seem somewhat at sea in terms of institutional priorities, or institutional commitment to desired ends or goals.

Mosher and Grossmann were critical of the title-entry union catalog. Mosher observed that it ". . . is of minimal benefit to users, and is of little use to processes of collection analysis or evaluation." Mosher urged the librarians to make an author-entry union catalog "the highest priority as a useful tool for users and librarians to use in gaining access to resources and as a possible tool for collection analysis or evaluation." A program of coordinated collection development and resource sharing must be "sensitive to the goals, missions, and priorities of the various institutions." Although the consultation was held under the sponsorship of the Lilly Endowment and auspices of the CCTS, a number of seminary librarians from the North Side seminaries participated.

In 1980, the CCTS agreed to embark upon a self-study in preparation for an ATS accreditation visit of all the schools in 1981. Unfortunately, the chapter on the Cluster libraries was essentially a description of the libraries and of the Librarians' Council and its committees. The only concerns raised in this self-study emerged from a questionnaire filled out by the librarians: (1) the need to develop better circulation procedures "to ensure faster response to inter-library loan requests"[6] and (2) better communication with faculties about procedures for requesting reserve materials from other Cluster libraries.

In light of the report by Maria Grossmann and Paul Mosher, it seemed that the projects of the Librarians' Council were not understood by the Cluster presidents and deans as supportive of the educational programs of the schools. Dominquez and Swindler's observation that "the experience of TRLN and other cooperative consortia demonstrates that librarians must provide information about the holdings of cooperating libraries and maximize the availability of their collections"[7] was most appropriate for the work of the Librarians' Council, because its failure to provide such information limited the effectiveness of this cooperative effort. The title-entry union catalog was not the answer.

In 1981, the Jesuit School of Theology (formerly Bellarmine School of Theology) closed. This loss combined with inflation, growing budget constraints, and "the movement of the seminaries toward their constituencies"[8] meant that these seminaries were no longer willing to fund a central CCTS office with a full-time director.

The December 2, 1977, revision of the "Structure and Operation of Librarians' Council" reads in part, "Cluster associates have the privilege of participating in the work of the Joint Acquisitions and Collection Development Committee."[9] Between this time and 1983, eight associate institutions (Billy Graham Center, Garrett and Seabury-Western Seminaries, Loyola University, Moody Bible Institute, North Park Seminary, St. Mary's of the Lake Seminary, Trinity Evangelical Divinity School, and the University of Chicago) participated on a regular basis in the work of this CCTS committee. Each library prepared a profile of its institution and library, and these served as background material for three sub-committees formed in 1981 to address collaborative collection development in the areas of Evangelicalism, "Mainline" Protestantism, and Roman Catholicism. Although the enlarged Acquisitions and Collection Development Committee continued to meet in the seven years before the formation of the Library Council of ACTS in 1983, its work was limited, because it could not be done in the context of institutional cooperation.

But the work of this enlarged committee was to bear fruit. At its October 22, 1982, meeting, the Librarians' Council of the CCTS decided to "embark on a planning process to assess the present level of cooperation among theological libraries in the metropolitan area and to suggest options for the future." William Lesher, President of Lutheran School of Theology in Chicago, served as chair of this planning committee. At the third meeting after each of the seminary librarians had presented his or her goals for future cooperation, according to William Lesher's "Report on Metro-Cluster Library Committee (dated December 30, 1982), the following four points were made:

> 1. There is a great deal to be learned from the experience of cooperation to date in two areas. Library cooperation is a process that requires both administrative support and encouragement in the development of policy arrangements between schools as well as high motivation on the part of professional librarians.
> 2. Verbal contracts and good intentions result in little cooperative action between libraries. It is when written agreements are formed that actions result.
> 3. There are some immediate low budget areas of metro cooperation that would make a big difference both as actual facilitators of library cooperation as well as symbols of a closer relationship (e.g., daily reliable courier service.)
> 4. There is a variety of other more complex forms of cooperation that could be pursued if there is the will, leadership, and financial support. One could envision a metro-wide theological library system, fully computerized with all holdings listed, with full access to all collections and with acquisitions relations and policies integrated for each library for each area as well as for the metropolitan system as a whole.

At a meeting of the Metro-Cluster presidents and librarians from the thirteen seminaries on January 9, 1983, Neil Gerdes listed the following five options for future library cooperation: (1) metro-wide document delivery system, (2) coordinated acquisitions and collection development, (3) machine readable database, (4) storage problems, and (5) retrospective conversion possibilities. These initial conversations among the Metro-Cluster presidents and librarians identified many of the same basic factors for effective library cooperation, as did the Chicago area librarians during their first meetings in 1964 and 1965.

By 1984, the Metro-Cluster presidents had agreed to form the Chicago Area Theological Schools, which in 1985 was renamed the Association of Chicago Theological Schools. The annual budget of its Library Council was funded completely by the member schools. From its inception the Library Council was clear that collaborative collection development would not be effective until faculty and students had full and easy access to the holdings of the libraries. The Library Council, in addition to agreeing to reciprocal borrowing privileges among the libraries, provided faculty and students of the ACTS schools access to the collections in the following three ways: courier service, Serials of Illinois Online (SILO), and OCLC. The courier made a stop at each school three times a week during the regular academic year and twice a week for most of the summer. In May of 1984, the Library Council decided to participate in the SILO project. Each school entered its serial holdings into OCLC and agreed to update these records as needed and to continue to enter new titles. In 1988, a paper copy of the SILO list for ACTS was purchased and copies made for the libraries. This list with holdings for each of the libraries has been of great assistance for users in locating journals. OCLC provides a way of locating material, but it is of limited value, because the records of many titles are still found only in the card catalogs of the ACTS libraries. In 1986 and 1987, the Task Force on Acquisitions labored with great diligence in completing its slightly revised version of the ATLA Conspectus as part of the North American Theological Inventory Process, compiled a checklist of currently received periodicals in order to analyze existing duplication, and began a review of a check list of standing orders for monograph series. Except for periodical subscriptions, the ACTS librarians have found it very difficult to convince one's faculty and students of the validity of resource sharing when they do not have easy access to the holdings of the other libraries.

In the past nine years, however, the Library Council has been taking steps to provide better access to the holdings of its libraries. By the fall of 1986, the Library Council concluded that new technology would be required to raise cooperation to new levels. In the spring the Library Council applied to the Association of Theological Schools for a grant of $2,000 to cover part of the cost of a consultation to examine issues of space, preservation, bibliographical access, and collection development. When ATS informed the Library Council that it would make a grant of $1,800, the Library Council decided to retain Ronald Diener as a consultant to prepare a "Plan of Action for Cooperative Efforts." Mr. Diener worked from July 1987 until January 1988 and presented his report at a meeting of the ACTS presidents, deans, and librarians in March. Diener concluded that further cooperative efforts would come to naught until appropriate administrative procedures were in place in each of the ACTS libraries. Diener was especially concerned that "there is no understanding within the institutions as whole what the library's policies and procedures are, particularly in collection development... There is no reporting procedure that reviews frequently an agreed body of statistical and financial information to test whether the library is meeting agreed goals and objectives."[10] Although Diener made specific recommendations to address the issues of space, preservations, bibliographical access, and collection development, the presidents and librarians did not find his report to be of much assistance.

In spite of the Diener report, William Lesher invited the Library Council to submit a proposal for retrospective conversion and automation to the Common Council, whose members are the presidents of the ACTS schools, at its 1989 winter meeting. As a result of that presentation and discussion, a revised proposal was prepared under the direction of the ACTS Development Committee for submission to two foundations, both of which rejected this proposal.

A year later the ACTS Library Council submitted a proposal to the Lilly Foundation for $60,000 for a planning grant in order to develop a program of resource sharing. The summary of this proposal, dated December 12, 1990, from the Library Council to David Ramage, Chair of the ACTS Development Committee, reads as follows:

> The nine ACTS libraries want to make their present holdings of 1.2 million volumes and their new acquisitions readily accessible to the faculties and students of the thirteen member schools as well as to the broader theological community in North America. To develop this program of resource sharing the following steps need to be taken:
> 1) The creation of a database of our collections; 2) the use of computer technology to enable users to have ready bibliographical access to these collections; and 3) a coordinated collection development program.

When ACTS received word that the Lilly Foundation had approved their request, the Library Council selected RMG Consultants, Inc., to submit a report that would document costs for an ACTS resource sharing project, an ACTS database, and the administrative structure needed to maintain the system and the programs.

The Plans and Recommendation for an ACTS Library Resource Sharing and Recon Project was presented by Robert McGee of RMG Consultants to the presidents, deans, development officers, business managers, and librarians in January of 1993. The report called for the creation of an integrated library system to support a single online catalog and other functions such as cataloging, acquisitions, and circulation. This centralized system would have made it possible for faculty and students in their own libraries to make one search in the ACTS database for any desired item held by any of the ACTS libraries in order to locate and borrow it. Another major part of the project was the retrospective conversion of 866,000 titles. The total cost of the project was estimated to be $5.3 million, $2.8 million of which was for retrospective conversion. Because of issues of governance and the annual cost of maintaining the database, the ACTS Common Council decided against the centralized system. Instead it was decided that each school—with the exception of Catholic Theological Union, Garrett-Evangelical, Seabury-Western, and Wheaton College (an associate member), whose libraries had already installed automation systems—should find funding for the cost of automating their libraries. Given developments in computer technology and telecommunications, the ACTS librarians expected that it would be eventually possible to provide access from any one of the ACTS libraries to the online catalogs of the other ACTS libraries.

Since December 1994, a volunteer project director for fund raising has been at work to draft a case study for what is now called the ACTS Online Project. The case study calls for the conversion of all the remaining catalog cards into machine readable records, the installation of automated library systems for those ACTS libraries that do not already have them, and the production of a joint catalog of ACTS library resources on CD-ROM or other reproducible mass storage medium.

In the fall of 1991, the Library Council identified eight goals in order to carry out its mission. The first goal is "to provide ready access for the academic communities of the member institutions to information about the resources for theological education and research available in the

ACTS libraries." I have argued in this paper that after thirty years of cooperative library efforts, a program of effective resource sharing among the Chicago area theological libraries has yet to succeed because of the inability to provide easy bibliographic access to the holdings of the libraries. Patricia Bush Dominquez and Luke Swindler in their analysis of cooperative collection development among the North Carolina Research Triangle libraries wrote of the early years of cooperative efforts between the libraries of Duke University and the University of North Carolina, "Indeed, until faculty and librarians knew what both libraries held, cooperation could not work."[11] Although providing bibliographic information about the resources of the member libraries in a consortium is not the only factor essential for effective cooperation, it is an important one and for the Chicago area theological libraries it has been the main factor that has hindered effective resource sharing.

Endnotes

1. John Warwick Montgomery, Arnold's predecessor had edited the *Union List of Serial Publications in Chicago Area Protestant Theological Libraries* in 1960.

2. Patricia Buck Dominquez and Luke Swindler, "Cooperative Collection Development at the Research Triangle University Libraries: A Model for the Nation," *College & Research Libraries* 54 (1993): 472.

3. Ibid., 422.

4. Donald E. Miller, *A Self Study of the Chicago Cluster of Theological Schools* (Chicago, June 1981) v.I; a Report, 12.

5. Ibid., 86.

6. Ibid., 85.

7. Dominquez and Swindler, "Cooperative Collection Development," 488.

8. Miller, *Self Study*, 130.

9. Ibid., 81.

10. Ronald E. Diener, *P A C E : a Plan of Action for Cooperative Efforts*, (Columbus, OH, 1988), 3.

11. Dominquez and Swindler, "Cooperative Collection Development," 472.

Information or Divine Access: Theological Librarianship Within the Context of a Ministry

Andrew J. Keck

"**W**hen you come, bring the cloak that I left with Carpus at Troas, also the books, and above all the parchments" (2 Tim. 4:13, NRSV). From the beginnings of the church, the books and the people entrusted with them have had a special role. Today theological librarians are unique providers of religious and theological information access to schools that have as their purpose the training and educating of people for ministry. This paper will attempt to answer the question, "How do theological librarians perceive themselves as being involved in ministry?" The issue of theological librarianship as ministry will be considered and evaluated through the responses of theological librarians to a questionnaire that was mailed to 371 American members of the American Theological Library Association.[1] This paper will also draw upon the literature of theological librarianship that is concerned with various aspects of this question.[2] I will argue that the theological librarian's perception of ministry comes directly from his/her view of the nature and meaning of theological librarianship and how it relates to the nature and meaning of ministry.

The results of this survey suggest that many theological librarians see themselves as both doing ministry and participating in the educational process. On the other hand, a sizable minority viewed theological librarianship as simply an occupation that happens to be set within a theological institution. Overall, there are five broad questions of meaning that influence how a theological librarian views his/her work as ministry: (1) what it means to be involved in theological education, (2) what it means to develop personal relationships, (3) what it means to work with theological and religious materials, (4) what it means to be "called" into a particular ministry, and (5) what it means to be involved in ministry. Each of the different questions of meaning evoked responses that displayed the diversity of outlooks of theological librarians. Similarly, the importance of each question varied for each librarian. Each question, taken individually and collectively, can help to guide our understanding of theological librarianship as ministry.

Theological Education as Ministry
"If we agree that the seminary objective is to provide the means and opportunities for moral and spiritual development and intellectual and pastoral training, then the administration of the seminary should be built around these objectives, and each activity should be directed toward their fulfillment . . . ."[3]

Unfortunately, not all seminary faculty, administrators, and librarians agree on the "seminary objective." Some believe that the seminary should be an academic institution, while others maintain that the seminary should be a professional school for ministers. One of the survey's questions asked respondents about whether the main purpose of a theological school should be professional education or academic education. Over two-thirds (70.4%) indicated that the purpose should be a mixture; 21.3% favored professional education; and 8.3% favored academic education. A follow-up question asked about the main purpose of the institution supported by their library. Only half (50.0%) believed that their institutions provided a mixture of professional and academic education. Rather, 37.1% indicated a focus on professional education and 12.9% on academic education. Relatively few librarians advocated an exclusive focus on academic education. Although such a focus might theoretically strengthen the place of the library, it could undermine both the mission of the institution and the ministry of the librarians.

Some responses to the survey reflected a more academic view of theological education, which was also viewed as ministry. As the librarian enhances and adds to that education, he or she participates in that ministry. In response to the question on theological librarianship as ministry, one wrote, "It is a ministry because I am helping educate men and women to work in religious vocations—helping them develop skills which will aid them in life-long learning. My work parallels that of the classroom faculty." Many responses and much of the literature indicate that there is a strong desire among theological librarians to be educators foremost and not simply administrators of the library. This is reflected in Gamble's presentation for ATLA on contemporary challenges to theological librarianship (". . . the library is a central teaching agency of the seminary rather than a mere warehouse for book storage")[4] and in Mehl's dissertation dealing with ATLA and American Protestant libraries and librarianship (". . . those individuals responsible for planning the ATLA program should consider seriously the role of the librarian as teacher. The emphasis underscored in this recommendation goes beyond the teaching role of the librarian through his typical involvement in all aspects of the library program. The thrust being made here is the involvement of the librarian in the classroom.").[5]

Although the librarian as educator was an important theme, many also saw an important role for the librarian within professional training of ministers. In response to the question of how one saw theological librarianship as ministry, one person responded, "I see myself as helping to train young ministers and support established ones through my work." Responses like this one were also quite common in response to the question of what librarians liked best about theological librarianship. Many theological librarians gained personal satisfaction through their interactions that promoted the professional development of students. In advocating the extension services of a theological library, Gamble makes the following argument, "If the theological library has the capacity to serve an expanding church in its wide outreach, does this library not have an obligation to stretch its resources to make them available as broadly as possible? If it is the mission of the seminary graduate to serve others, it would appear to be incumbent upon the campus library likewise to be the servant of all . . . ."[6] There is often a desire for the library itself to be a model of service. In varying degrees, theological librarians identify with the mission of their institution of theological education and feel that they participate in that ministry.

Personal Relationships as Ministry
"The most rewarding and satisfying part of our strategy is our communi-

cation with students . . . our awareness and interest and a sensitivity to each [student] provides so many bridges of communication and opportunities for us to share our library treasures with them."[7]

These words were spoken by James Kortendick at the 1965 ATLA conference. Similar sentiments were expressed by many of the librarians who responded to the survey. The relationships with people within the seminary community were often touted as being a positive aspect of theological librarianship. One wrote, "I see it as ministry because I am called on to use my theological training and I do provide a needed service to the students. I help guide students in their research which has an influence on their faith development."

The survey dealt with this issue of the significance of personal relationships when it queried the importance of a theological librarian dealing pastorally with people. In this question, "dealing pastorally" was defined as providing spiritual care and guidance in the context of an ongoing personal relationship. Over half (52.5%) indicated that this type of care was very important; 23.5% moderately important; and 24.0% indicated that it was not important. As a follow up, librarians were then asked if they themselves dealt with patrons and colleagues pastorally. This time, less than half (47.7%) indicated that they behaved pastorally to a great degree; 23.0% in a moderate degree; and 29.4% responded that they did not. It is significant that around three-quarters of theological librarians responding believed that this type of activity was important.

Some respondents felt that although "dealing pastorally" was a good thing, there needed to be limitations. One person responded, "I am able to be involved with meeting personal/spiritual needs as well as information needs, and have a limiting context within which to do so, which protects against over-involvement." Over-involvement was occasionally a problem, as one person recounted an experience where a librarian had provided counseling to others to the extent of neglecting his other library duties. Another wrote, "I do not pastor employees or patrons—they have pastors for that." Not everyone felt comfortable in the role of librarian/pastor, and some expressed a desire to keep most personal relationships with patrons on a "professional level." One felt that although this kind of pastoral ministry was not necessary for every theological librarian, it should be available in every theological library: "A theological library staff probably should include someone (not necessarily everyone) with clergy background, especially if [the] position is a faculty one and involves ad-

175

vising students."

Although professors and courses change every semester, the librarian can be seen here as a constant during the length of theological education. Connolly Gamble once remarked, "many [graduate theological students] have come to feel that the library is one of their most dependable partners in the persistent pursuit of knowledge. Their rapport with the librarian continues after their graduation, and they maintain touch with him or her through correspondence and occasional personal visits."[8] Of course, much of this sense of ministry through personal relationships is apparent in library positions where there is a high degree of contact with patrons, especially students. "Through the [library] services, you build up deeper relationships with patrons. Watch[ing] them grow spiritually and mentally is a joy and reward – especially knowing that in some way you had helped." Perhaps Morris was correct when he wrote, "the thing which gives importance to our jobs is that they involve people and human destiny."[9]

Working with Religious Materials as Ministry

"The theological librarian, like a pastor, is a broker, a broker of a wide and not entirely predictable range of information and service . . . ."[10]

Although the librarian is a broker of information, the religious or theological information is not always simply understood as merchandise involved in an information exchange. Paraphrasing C. A. Cutter's statement, a librarian wrote, "Theological libraries are the parish churches of theological literature and learning." In some cases, there seems to be a close connection between the librarian and the information that he or she provides. One of the questions in the survey asked, "How much does the religious or theological nature of the information you work with impact on how you view your involvement in ministry?" For various reasons, this question was widely misunderstood and confusing to many respondents. The intention of the question was to get at the issue of how theological librarians felt about working with religious materials. Are they merely the raw tools and materials of the trade, or are they themselves significant in some way? In the responses that were received, there were two kinds of affirmative responses: (1) that the religious information was only significant when received by a seeking patron and (2) that the religious information was intrinsically significant.

One theological librarian wrote, "[I] use the religious/theological content of materials to minister to patron spiritual needs." Some took this view of the theological librarian as spiritual director, providing a kind of spiritual bibliotherapy. The theological library does not always just provide raw information to be churned into term papers and academic theses—the theological library is also a place to go for spiritual nourishment. Another related view was expressed by a theological librarian who wrote, "By providing books I in a sense provide communion of the saints between students/faculty and Christians from diverse times/places." The task of the theological librarian is more of a historian connecting the past to the present and the present to the past. This view was expressed again by another, "Theological librarianship is an ancient vocation within the Christian community as Christians have long theorized that they can learn much from their brothers and sisters in Christ past and present. The theological librarian is and has been the intermediary in this conversation and thus has a unique ministry in the body of Christ."

Although the religious information may eventually reach an anxious seeker, to hold and work with a text produced by a religious person of centuries or decades past was itself a religious experience for some. One cataloger wrote, "The material I encounter in my work has had a revolutionary impact on my faith, involvement in ministry, and concept of the church." A theological librarian involved in public services offered a similar view: "Dealing with questions of my religion and faith permits me to deal continually in spiritual questions and concerns—to be concerned about people's souls, not just minds."

Theological Librarianship as a Vocation
"If we are to make a contribution, there must be meaning for us in what we do."[11]

Few, if any, theological librarians originally set out in life to become theological librarians. An interesting study done by Stephen L. Peterson looks at the educational preparation of theological librarians. He notes that "few theological librarians apparently start their post-baccalaureate education with the unequivocal goal of serving in this particular capacity."[12] Indeed, analyzing the educational patterns of those surveyed yielded no one particular pattern. Some came to theological librarianship through theological study or preparation for ministry. Others came to theological librarianship from the general field of librarianship.

The survey did, however, ask about theological librarianship as a vocational calling: "Most clergy report a 'calling' to ministry. Is theological librarianship (rather than other types of librarianship) a vocational calling for you?" A little over two-thirds (67.8%) concluded that theological librarianship was a vocational calling; the remainder (32.2%) indicated that it was not. However, more than a few expressed some ambiguity in their answers when asked to provide further explanation.

Many wrote about vocational callings in terms of theological librarianship matching their gifts and talents. One wrote, "This job is where my gifts, interests, needs converge as an opportunity for community and service." Some were directed and affirmed by others in pursuing theological librarianship, and there was often a specific interest in the subject matter that was articulated. Not surprisingly, job satisfaction and happiness also were prominent responses. One person believed that he "would not be happy doing anything else." Another group held what was variously described as a "Reformed" or "Calvinist" view of vocation, whereby all are called to do whatever they do.

Many saw theological librarianship as a way of expressing their own call to ministry. One wrote, "I entered theological librarianship on my way to ministry and after 10 years I realized I was already there . . . ." Many responded that God has specifically called them to theological librarianship in some way. One person wished to make a distinction between "a call to ministry" and a call to a vocation, suggesting, "Theological librarianship is a call from the church, but other types of librarianship are vocational calls."

Among the respondents explaining why theological librarianship was not a vocational calling, I received the following response, "I do not believe people are 'called' but—I have a strong desire to be a theological librarian as opposed to an academic librarian, so it's a chosen profession." Many expressed the opinion that theological librarianship was a professional career choice and not a calling. Others wished to reserve the rhetoric of "calling" and "vocation" for those intending to become ordained clergy. Another suggested, "It's rather an occupation; there are several other occupations for which I am also well suited, I think. I do not sense the direction of God to do this work nor do I find myself specially ordained or enabled by God to do this work, so I do not consider it a calling."

Theological Librarianship as Ministry

"Effective theological librarians must have a sense of the church, whether

or not we are ourselves communicant members of it. Effective theological librarians must have a sense of the community of scholarship, whether or not we are ourselves scholars. Effective theological librarians must have a care for people . . . theological education can well be seen as ministry, and many theological librarians see their work in specific terms of vocation, in the theological sense . . . The recruitment and training of theological librarians should be set alongside the recruitment and training of theological teachers, or pastors, and of other ministries in the church and in the seminary."[13]

A remaining issue for considering theological librarianship ministry is the relationship between the theological librarian and the church. According to the survey results, only 11.3% were not involved in the religious activities of their local congregations. This group of theological librarians were the least likely to indicate that theological librarianship was ministry and least likely to view theological librarianship as a vocational calling. Most theological librarians, however, were involved in the religious activities of their local congregations: 65.2% indicated that they were moderately involved and 23.4% were very involved. Over one-third (34.6%) of the respondents indicated that they were ordained, yet only 14.2% of the respondents currently served as clergy of local churches. Many of those who claimed to be ordained are appointed by their denominations to the ministry of theological librarianship. Thus, a majority of theological librarians are involved in local churches, and a number are serving the church through their ordained work of theological librarianship.

The church and the theological librarian are also related through the service that a theological library provides: "Theological librarianship is done in the twofold setting of school and church . . . . The library is necessary to illuminate, sustain, and advance the relations between the church and the seminary, between the church and the field of theology, and between the church and the world of learning more generally."[14] The theological librarian is at the intersection of these relationships. In many cases, the theological librarian is not just an information broker but also an interpreter and promoter of that information. Ancient and contemporary religious expressions of faith, as well as materials on the relationship of theology to the larger world of learning, must be acquired and promoted by the librarian. The end of all this is also the end of all information transfer: comprehension and knowledge. As Crow suggests, "If we are not called to lead persons to a vital comprehension of the Christian message, then what is our unique business [?]"[15] The ministry of the theological librarian is ultimately related to the church and the "vital comprehension" of theology.

As Dunkly suggested above, the perceived ministry of the theological librarian should have an impact on how we recruit, educate, train, and even compensate theological librarians as compared to other librarians and other ministers. If theological librarianship is about ministry, theological librarians need to be more intentional about recruiting people to the profession from among the ranks of the faithful. Education should include training in theology and library science, as well as in the professional aspects of ministry. Moreover, the continuing education of theological librarians must indeed be ongoing—not just in technology but also in the ways in which theological librarianship is expressed as ministry.

The issue of compensation can be difficult to address when theological librarianship as ministry may seem to imply that there ought to be willingness to work for less money. Although over half of the respondents (52.2%) thought that their salaries were reasonable; 35.4% believed their salaries to be lower than they should be; and 4.2% believed their salaries to be outrageously lower than they should be. Lewis addressed this issue well when she wrote, "There are three professional traditions which combine in theological librarianship—ministry, education, and librarianship—three traditions which are not noted for monetary reward and are identified with serving. But serving should mean service, not servitude."[16]

Conclusion

Theological librarians understand their work as ministry for a variety of reasons. Many of these reasons focus on how both ministry and theological librarianship are understood and defined. A librarian's view of theological education, personal relationships, religious materials, vocation, and ministry are all factors in how theological librarianship is understood as a ministry. "I feel that anyone working in the library of a theological institution, other things being equal, will do better work and will be happier and more content in doing it if he feels a sense of commitment to the overall cause and purpose of the institution he serves. Theological librarianship is at its best a ministry."[17] Although theological librarians do not have to view their work as ministry, perhaps it may remain a ministry for those who receive their services. When theological librarians perceive themselves as being in ministry, there is a theological and spiritual focus to their work that adds to their satisfaction and contentment in that they are engaged in both the ministry of their institution and the ministry of service possible through theological librarianship.

Endnotes

1. A total of 278 responses were received, of which 243 were usable for statistical manipulation. Data from the open-ended questions were transcribed and analyzed.

2. Literature on theological librarianship is very scarce within the general literature of librarianship. Although some important information can be found within studies and survey's done of theological education, the main sources for information on theological librarianship come from the papers and proceedings of the ATLA.

3. James J. Kortendick, "The Theological Librarian—His Commitment and Strategy," *Summary of Proceedings* 19 (1965): 106.

4. Connolly C. Gamble Jr., "Contemporary Challenges to Theological Librarianship," *Summary of Proceedings* 16 (1962): 46.

5. Warren Roy Mehl, "The Role of the American Theological Library Association in American Protestant Theological Libraries and Librarianship, 1947-1970" (Ph.D. diss., Indiana University, 1973), 207-208.

6. Connolly C. Gamble Jr., "The Seminary Library and the Continuing Education of the Minister," *Library Trends : Current Trends in Theological Libraries* 9/2 (1960): 270-71.

7. Kortendick, "The Theological Librarian," 110.

8. Gamble, "The Seminary Library," 275.

9. Raymond P. Morris, "Theological Librarianship as a Ministry," *Summary of Proceedings* 7 (1953): 34.

10. James Dunkly, "Theological Libraries and Theological Librarians in Theological Education," *Summary of Proceedings* 45 (1991): 228.

11. Robert Gordon Collier, "Introduction" Panel Discussion: "The Vocation of the Theological Librarian," *Summary of Proceedings* 17 (1963): 114.

12. Stephen L. Peterson "Theological Libraries for the Twenty-First Century : Project 2000 Final Report," *Theological Education* 20 (Suppl. 1984): 59-60.

13. James Dunkly, "Theological Libraries," 230-31.

14. Ibid., 228.

15. Paul A. Crow, "Professors and Librarians—Partners in the Oikoumene," *Summary of Proceedings* 20 (1966): 75.

16. Rosalyn Lewis, "Theological Librarianship: Service, Not Servitude," *Summary of Proceedings* 42 (1988): 157.

17. Morris, "Theological Librarianship," 32.

Julia Pettee and Her Contribution to Theological Librarianship[1]

Richard D. Spoor

Introduction

There was a time—not long ago—when Julia Pettee's was a household name in theological libraries and in the precincts frequented by the grandees of American librarianship. Yet today she is hardly known by younger theological librarians; while among older theological librarians and those of the middle generation, she is largely of interest to that small number who still make use of her classification scheme and struggle to keep it alive. In the larger world of librarianship, her name, while honored, remains essentially buried in library catalogs and in the footnotes and bibliographies of often obscure publications. But Julia Pettee had a great influence on theological and academic libraries in general and on cataloging and classification theory and practice in particular. The time would seem right at this point in the lengthening career of the American Theological Library Association and the history of modern librarianship to take a fresh look at her accomplishments and to assess their significance.[2] Before turning to her achievements, however, it may be useful to review briefly what is known about Julia Pettee as a person.

Biographical Framework

If Julia Pettee were alive today, she would be one hundred and twenty-four years old, which helps to place her in the chronology of our times. She died nearly thirty years ago (1967) having spanned the formative years of American librarianship and exercised a well-nigh unique influence on both theological and general librarianship during the first half of the twentieth century. In 1955 at a dinner given in her honor, the American Theological Library Association saluted her "enduring contribution to theological librarianship" and her long career of devoted service to theology.[3]

Who was Julia Pettee? No definitive biography exists. The nearest thing we have to one is a study done by Lennart Pearson, then Librarian of Presbyterian College (Clinton, SC) in 1970.[4] Readers interested in biographical detail or in a bibliography of works by and about Julia Pettee should consult Pearson's now dated but still useful work. Late in her life, Miss Pettee composed an autobiographical sketch of her thirty years of work at Union Theological Seminary in the City of New York. The manuscript of this work—never published—has been dated 1962 and is housed in the Archives at Union's Burke Library.[5] Beyond the Pearson and Pettee works, however, there is little available to the researcher other than Miss Pettee's own papers and modest gatherings of Pettee-related material scattered here and there.[6] But this does not mean that the basic features of Miss Pettee's life and career are unknown to us. Except for a few minor details, the chronology, at least, is clear.

> 1872 Born in Lakeville, a village of the Town of Salisbury, CT, on August 23, 1872
>
> 1890 Completed studies at Mount Holyoke Seminary in South Hadley, MA
>
> 1891 Attended Mount Holyoke College in South Hadley
>
> 1895 Completed the course in library science at the Library School of Pratt Institute in Brooklyn, NY
>
> 1895-1899 Attended Vassar College in Poughkeepsie, NY, working as a cataloger in the college library on a half-time basis; graduated with an A.B. degree in 1899
>
> 1899-1909 Worked in the library of Vassar College as a full-time cataloger and classifier
>
> 1908-1909 Visited a number of theological libraries in the northeast, examining their catalogs and systems of classification; during a leave of absence from Vassar, reorganized the library (a collection of 50,000 volumes) of what was then the Rochester Theological Seminary

1909-1939 Served as the Chief Cataloger at Union Theological Seminary in the City of New York, devising a major classification scheme that was ultimately published as *Classification of the Library of Union Theological Seminary in the City of New York*, prepared by Julia Pettee, Chief Cataloger. . . Revised and enlarged edition (New York: Union Theological Seminary, 1939; subsequently republished by Union, with additions and corrections by Ruth C. Eisenhart, in 1967); recataloged and classed Union's collection of more than 165,000 volumes; during and after this time, Miss Pettee was actively involved in the larger concerns of general librarianship, including work on classification systems, catalog code revision, extensive committee work for the American Library Association, etc.; retired from Union in the summer of 1939

1939-1946 Worked at the Sterling Library at Yale University in New Haven, CT, on a half-time basis reclassifying religious books in the university library; worked out an adaptation of the Union classification scheme for use in a large general library

1946-1950 Remained in New Haven at Yale, working on a number of special projects, including the publication of her authoritative study, *Subject Headings* (1946), and the preparation of the second edition of her *List of Theological Subject Headings and Corporate Church Names* . . . (1947)

1950 Returned to Salisbury to live out her days at her home, Mayflower Farm, atop Selleck Hill, maintaining an avid interest in library matters and devoting attention to the researching and writing of local history (in which her family had played a considerable role)

1967 Died in Salisbury on May 30, 1967, at the age of ninety-four

Achievements

While theological librarians lay just claim to Julia Pettee as one of their own, her achievements were seminal for librarians serving non-theological libraries as well. Her unique contribution to the life of the seminary library at Union in New York benefited not only Union but theological and academic libraries everywhere. And her work on issues critical to the larger world of librarianship influenced librarians of every stripe. Thus, while she may have "belonged" to New York's Union and the world of theological librarianship in a special way, she was, in fact, a major force in the then emerging profession of academic librarianship. She was, first and foremost, a librarian, a cataloger, a classifier. That she was also a theologian of no mean ability and chief cataloger of Union's library appears, in retrospect, to be one of those happenstances that mark the careers of certain individuals who seem destined to succeed in their chosen fields, come what may.

It must be remembered that when Julia Pettee began her work as a librarian late in the last century, the dictionary catalog as we know it today did not exist (by and large only author catalogs and perhaps rudimentary subject arrangements were available). Moreover, most theological libraries—indeed, most libraries of every kind—were still organizing their collections according to the old system of fixed location—a situation in which shelves, not books, were classed and numbered. Relative classification was only beginning to make its way into libraries, and although a few theological libraries had already elected to adopt a relative scheme (most often some adaptation of the newly-minted Dewey Decimal Classification or the developing Cutter Expansive Classification or a redaction of Alfred Cave's popular late nineteenth-century encyclopedia, *An Introduction to Theology: Its Principles, Its Branches, Its Results and Its Literature*), none of these had proved to be ultimately satisfactory. The time was ripe for someone to take a fresh look at the way in which theological knowledge was organized and theological literature classified. Called to Union in New York to do just that—and to recatalog and class Union's sprawling collections in the process—Julia Pettee arrived in 1909 and set to work. It was almost certainly William Walker Rockwell, then Union's Librarian, who wrote an unsigned report to seminary authorities dated May 11, 1911, hailing Miss Pettee's efforts on behalf of Union as "a work which no other woman in America is fitted to accomplish, a work whose call is insistent and inevitable."[7] The task facing Miss Pettee was a formidable one. When she began, the seminary was located on the east side of Manhattan on Park Avenue, but was soon to move to upper Broadway on the west. The seminary library was well stocked with both theological and secular materials and was organized by the old system of fixed location. The books had long since outgrown their locations and were piled high and deep on shelves throughout the stacks. Everything now had to be moved, located on shelves in the new building on Morningside Heights, and then—once a new relative classification scheme could be devised by Miss Pettee—recataloged and classed. By 1939, when Miss Pettee retired from Union, she had virtually completed her task, having (1) established a modern dictionary catalog, shelf list, and authority file; (2) created and published a classification scheme that won the admiration of her peers and that would soon be adopted by more than fifty other theological libraries; and (3) recataloged and classed the entire collection of more than 165,000 volumes, "with the exception of a small remnant of sermons and devotional literature and, what I most regretted, a few volumes of the Van Ess Collection."[8]

In devising a classification scheme for Union, Julia Pettee drew upon her experience in working with the Dewey Decimal Classification, which had been adopted by Vassar, and in developing a classification scheme and dictionary catalog for Rochester Theological Seminary a few years earlier. She was also influenced by the classification of the sciences that had been devised by Professor Hugo Münsterberg of Harvard University for use by the International Congress of Arts and Science held in St. Louis in 1904. The theoretical basis for her work was explained by Miss Pettee in two articles: "A Classification for a Theological Library" (1911)[9] and "The Philosophy of the Maker of a Special Classification" (1937).[10] In addition to these two important pieces, Miss Pettee's own correspondence, notes, unpublished reviews and articles, etc. reveal much about the development of her thinking. "A Classification for a Theological Library" was published very shortly after Miss Pettee arrived at Union and long before she had had much experience working with Union's exceptionally large and complex collections. Still, it stands as a reliable guide to her ideas about classification and theological books. "The Philosophy of the Maker of a Special Classification" preserves the substance of a presentation that Miss Pettee gave to the general membership of the Special Library Association in New York two years before she completed her work at Union. It represents a useful summary of her position at that later date. It is, however, the unpublished Pettee materials at Union that the ardent researcher will find to be the richest source for tracing her ideas and their development during fifty years and more. It is these unpublished materials that have proved most useful to the writer of the present article.

In reviewing Julia Pettee's contribution to classification theory and the classification of theological books, we can observe the development of several significant principles. This article focuses on those having to do with the organization of knowledge, the design of classification schemes, the relationship between theoretical schemes and actual book collections, broad versus close classification, systems of notation, and the life expectancy of classification schemes. In reviewing her contributions to other areas of librarianship, one is reminded of her masterful work on subject headings, and her insistence, in her work on cataloging codes, on authorship as the keystone of cataloging work and on entry under author as the primary access point in library catalogs. As we look briefly as these principles, it is important to remember that many of Miss Pettee's ideas, while commonplace today, were by no means so common in her day. It was largely her careful thinking and solid craftsmanship that set the standard we have come to take for granted.

It was Julia Pettee's conviction that any library classification, if it is to be consistent and therefore useful, must be based on some theoretical classification of knowledge. Yet one must proceed carefully here, for theory can easily confound practice. Miss Pettee was enough of a philosopher to realize that the establishment of any order of knowledge rests on certain assumptions, on a theory of knowledge, and that this theory of knowledge will inevitably control the outcomes of the library classification that is based on it. Her convictions regarding the organization of knowledge are so fundamental to all that Miss Pettee accomplished in her work with library classifications that she deserves to be heard at some length on the subject. In a cogent review of Henry E. Bliss's important work, *The Organization of Knowledge and the System of the Sciences*[11]—the same Henry Bliss who would eventually create a scheme of his own, the Bibliographic Classification—Miss Pettee wrote:

> Without going into metaphysics, everyone will agree with Mr. Bliss' main proposition that the closer a library classification scheme conforms to a well established order of the sciences the more useful it will be. This rests upon the assumption that there is a progressive organization of knowledge to all practical purposes quite permanently valid upon which new accretions are based. It seems to me, however, that Mr. Bliss is over confident as to the extent of this permanently fixed area. It is the vast fringe of knowledge in the process of organization that troubles classifiers. This highly interesting fringe of experimentation and unproved theses is largely the subject matter of our current books. It is these books dealing with data which has not yet been thoroughly organized which confuses our older schemes and makes the repeated demand for a newer and more modern scheme into which this new

data will fit.

Librarians owe Mr. Bliss a debt of gratitude for informing the world of the magnitude of their task. Whether he wishes it or not the librarian should be a philosopher. His books must be placed somewhere and unless he is content merely to locate them without regard to logic, he must think out the relationships of groups and decide upon clear and consistent lines of cleavage between them. And when it comes to this ever present and perplexing fringe, his office goes beyond that of philosopher. He must prophesy, or guess, to use a much less dignified word. And as prophet or guesser his chances of error are large. Of course he would like a classification based upon a "real" order which would eliminate these chances of error. We are much hampered by the makeshifts which these inadequate guesses necessitate. No one more than the librarian has a right to be interested in the progressive organization of knowledge which is constantly working to establish the "real" order for this new material. But any library classification that follows this "real" order of nature *will necessarily follow considerably behind the philosophical attempts at restating the new order and be out of date for new books when that desired quality of permanent validity is assured.*[12]

With respect to her quibble with Bliss's own theory of knowledge, Miss Pettee invokes John Dewey's opinion as expressed in his *Certainty*:

John Dewey in his new volume . . . launches a head-on attack upon this "Newtonian theory" in which the natural order is affirmed to be something inherently fixed, a thing apart from and correlative with human knowledge, something the mind observes and reveals. Not so, says Mr. Dewey, nature is bound up in our very processes of knowing and is one with us, and we are all together in the process of becoming. The "real" order of today will be quite a different thing from the "real" order of another day when we have worked ourselves out a bit further. . . .[13]

Once questions regarding the organization of knowledge have been settled (to the extent that they *can* be settled!), the classifier must decide whether to make use of an existing classification scheme or create a new one. In either case, it then becomes necessary to decide whether the existing scheme or the new scheme should be a general or universal classification (in which no one subject is given prominence over other subjects) or a special classification (in which one subject is given prominence over other subjects, sometimes even to the exclusion of the other subjects). As we have seen, Julia Pettee found all standard classifications for general collections to be inadequate for her purposes—although she would later express the opinion that a reasonably well-constructed general scheme could probably be adapted to meet the needs of special libraries, much as Jeannette M. Lynn, in her *An Alternative Classification for Catholic Books*[14] would expand the tables of the Library of Congress scheme to meet the needs of Catholic libraries. In creating her own scheme, Miss Pettee concluded that what was not needed was another general scheme (Dewey and Cutter were readily available by that time and the Library of Congress had begun to work seriously on a general scheme of its own). She also concluded that a special classification dealing principally or exclusively with theology (of which a few were available at the time) was not called for, particularly in view of the fact that Union's collections contained many general and secular works that would not fit into a purely theological classification. What was needed, she felt, and what she finally came up with, was a hybrid scheme—one that encompassed both sacred and secular, but in a special way: rather than looking at theology from the perspective of the larger world of knowledge, her scheme looked at the world of knowledge from the perspective of theology. Despite her readiness to refer to her own scheme as a "special classification," it is not too far-fetched to argue that what Miss Pettee actually designed was a general scheme (necessarily thin in many places, to be sure) *for the theologian and student of theology*. Ruth Eisenhart, Miss Pettee's successor at Union, discussing the needs of a gathering of librarians from the law, journalism, and theology, expressed it in this way:

> At first glance it [the gathering] looked a rather mixed lot. But, almost at once, they discovered a common ground: there is no aspect of human experience to which the law, the press, and the church will admit indifference. The library serving one of these professions must be prepared to cover the whole range of knowledge, and its specialized classification must operate within the framework of a general classification. . . .[15]

Elsewhere in the same article, referring to the special character of the Union scheme, Miss Eisenhart observed that "although the Union Classification is comprehensive, providing for all departments of knowledge, theology does not take its place as a separate discipline but pervades the whole scheme."[16]

Perhaps more than any other classifier, Julia Pettee insisted that classification schemes be tested against real collections of books. Experience had convinced her that no classification of knowledge conceived in the philosopher's study could be applied successfully, as is, in the stacks. It was not, as we know, that she eschewed the classification of knowledge. For her, both knowledge classifications and book classifications were necessary. One "cannot sit down," she maintained, "and work out a scheme from his head that will fit the books. Neither can one sort books usefully without making a systematic scheme. You have to work from both ends."[17] Elsewhere she wrote:

> It may be said . . . that no theoretical classification of knowledge can be consistently applied to every detail of a book classification. The theoretical classification is a freelance bound by no utilitarian ideas of practical convenience. The book classification is slave to all sorts of practical considerations. It is hopelessly shackled to the past. Books written under antiquated categories still exist for the classifier to arrange, and nothing but antiquated categories will fit them. At best, a classification is a compromise between old systems and new, for the lines of cleavage which may be cut beautifully through ideas cannot be cut so easily through books. In spite of exceptions, however, a good book classification should, on the whole, conform to sound logic. We instinctively expect to find our books in the same pigeonholes into which we habitually sort our thoughts. For this reason, the more nearly its logic conforms to the philosophical tendencies of the times the more useful a classification will be. Knowledge will continue to be sorted and re-sorted, as it always has been, according to the prevailing Zeitgeist: the best that a book classification can do is to plan its outline with an eye prophetic, so that it will serve the coming as well as the present generation; and then to provide, by a flexible notation, for inevitable future readjustments.[18]

The maker of a classification scheme must also decide whether to favor broad or close classification—i.e., whether one should be satisfied with material organized on the shelves in larger, more general categories, or whether one should strive to organize the material in smaller, more specific and detailed categories. Julia Pettee's experience (and personal preference) led her to favor broad classification. She observes:

> I find that most people prefer a rather broad shelf classification. The eye takes in readily on the shelves a hundred books or more on one topic and as readers going to the shelves very frequently have a specific author in mind, a straight author arrangement rather than fine subdivisions is more convenient. I do not try to sort Psychology by special school, gestalt or behaviorist, or socialism by brand. Date divisions are more useful. Especially is this

true if you have collections of older literature. In very many classes I prefer date to topical divisions.[19]

At first glance, it may seem incongruous to suggest that Miss Pettee's comprehensive and weighty *Classification of the Library of Union Theological Seminary in the City of New York* represents a broad classification. Yet if one studies the scheme carefully—and especially if one notes how efficiently the notation carries the classes and subclasses and the ease with which the scheme can be abbreviated—it will be found to be, in fact, a particularly well-crafted example of broad classification, albeit one processing an impressive level of detail.

Allied to matters of broad versus close classification, it may be noted that Miss Pettee, in order to obtain a consistent and logical order of material in the classes and subclasses of her scheme, employed what she referred to as a fundamental law of classification. This law, she said, is "the simple rule of logic—arrange your groups in the order of progression from the more general to the more specific."[20] She was also, as one would expect, an advocate of short notation—the shorter the better. Those familiar with her scheme will attest to her success in achieving this end.

It is not surprising—given the great labor and cost involved in making changes, not to mention the general human resistance to change—that both the creator and the users of a classification often come to look upon their scheme as permanent, as embodying a state of knowledge that is universal and essentially complete. While classifiers may often make minor adjustments to the scheme to accommodate newer knowledge, they seldom resort to large-scale reorderings of classes and subclasses as a way of dealing with the situation. And outright shifts to "roomier" schemes or to new schemes that include the newer knowledge are almost never contemplated, unless one is prepared to reclassify or to impose a second classification scheme on a library's collection. Yet, as we have seen, Julia Pettee was firm in her conviction that no classification of knowledge or books can be expected to last for long. In her review of Bliss's *The Organization of Knowledge and the System of the Sciences*, referred to above, she held:

> In my opinion, in the very nature of things, neither a classification of knowledge nor a book classification can have more than a limited period of usefulness. Our library catalogues have much more chance of permanence than our library classifications and will probably be useful long after the present topical arrangement of our books has grown hopelessly out of date. . . .[21]

Julia Pettee's principal contributions to areas other than classification theory and practice have to do with her work on important cataloging questions. Her publication, in 1936, of a major article entitled "The Development of Authorship Entry and the Formulation of Authorship Rules as Found in the Anglo-American Code"[22] influenced all subsequent thinking on the subject and made a direct contribution, years later, to the International Conference on Cataloguing Principles in Paris in 1961 and to the development of the *Anglo-American Cataloguing Rules*. It is difficult for many of us today to remember how hotly the principle of authorship was debated in the earlier and middle years of this century, particularly in international discussions where participants were often wary of—and sometime hostile towards—the long-established Anglo-American tradition of using authorship (both personal and corporate) as the lodestar of cataloging work. In the area of subject analysis, the publication of Miss Pettee's *Subject Headings: The History and Theory of the Alphabetical Subject Approach to Books*[23] represented the culmination of a lifetime of reflection and experience in dealing with subject headings (her own *List of Theological Subject Headings and Corporate Church Names*[24] had been a "standard" for years) and laid out in definitive fashion her case for the dictionary catalog (versus the classified catalog) as the bibliographic tool of choice for librarians and researchers.

Conclusion

What may we conclude regarding Julia Pettee and her accomplishments? In a very real sense, her contribution to librarianship can be discerned clearly enough in the detail of her ideas and works, some of which we have explored in this article. Bibliographic organization and control was her great passion. Yet it was a passion steadied by the force of reason, for in spite of all the changes that have occurred in librarianship in the intervening years, those whose professional lives are today involved in dealing with issues of bibliographic organization and control pursue their endeavors—whether they realize it or not—in the light of her achievements. There is, however, one factor regarding her personality and her work that is easy to miss in an overview of the kind provided here. And that has to do with Miss Pettee's extraordinary capacity to sustain a profound engagement with the theoretical dimension of librarianship, while pursuing with patient diligence the practical demands of her craft as a cataloger. She was, simultaneously, a strong thinker and a vigorous practitioner—a rare breed in any field. That she elected to devote her life to theological librarianship can only be considered one of the great, good fortunes of the profession.

Endnotes

1.   I am deeply indebted to the Reverend Dr. Milton McCormick Gatch, Director of the Burke Library and Professor of Church History; Mr. Seth E. Kasten, Head of Reader Services; the Reverend Andrew G. Kadel, Reference and Collection Development Librarian; Ms. Cyndie Frame, Preservation and Collection Management Librarian; and the other staff of the Burke Library for their generous and gracious assistance in the use of the extensive body of Pettee materials housed in the Archives of the Burke Library of Union Theological Seminary in the City of New York.

2.   While Julia Pettee's major accomplishments predated the founding of the American Theological Library Association in 1946, she maintained an avid interest in the work of the association throughout the long years of her retirement in Connecticut.

3.   American Theological Library Association, *Summary of Proceedings* 9 (1955): 60.

4.   Lennart Pearson, "The Life and Work of Julia Pettee, 1872-1967," *ATLA Newsletter* 18/2 (November 14, 1970, Supplement): 25-92.

5.   Julia Pettee, "A Cataloger for More Than a Half a Century Takes a Backward Look at Her Profession and Reviews Her Thirty Years as Head Cataloger of the Union Theological Seminary Library, in Relation to It" [1962], Archives, The Burke Library, Union Theological Seminary, New York (hereafter cited as "Cataloger").

6.   The major deposit of Julia Pettee's papers relating to her interests in librarianship are housed in the Archives of the Burke Library of Union Theological Seminary, New York. Other deposits of Pettee material will be found in the libraries of Vassar College, Colgate Rochester Divinity School, New Brunswick Theological Seminary, Yale University, and the Scoville Memorial Library in Salisbury, CT.

7.   Report on the library and the work of Julia Pettee, May 11, 1911, Archives, The Burke Library, Union Theological Seminary in the City of New York.

8.   Pettee, "Cataloger."

9.   Julia Pettee, "A Classification for a Theological Library," *Library Journal* 36 (1911): 611-24.

10. Julia Pettee, "The Philosophy of the Maker of a Special Classification," *Special Libraries* 28 (1937): 254-59.

11. New York: Henry Holt and Co., 1929.

12. Julia Pettee, "The Organization of Knowledge and Its Bearing upon Library Classification," n.d., Archives, The Burke Library, Union Theological Seminary in the City of New York.

13. Pettee, "Organization."

14. Milwaukee: Bruce Publishing Co., 1937; subsequently revised several times.

15. Ruth C. Eisenhart, "The Classification of Theological Books," *Library Trends* 9/2 (1960): 257.

16. Eisenhart, "Classification," 264.

17. Pettee, "Philosophy," 258.

18. Pettee, "Classification," 623.

19. Pettee, "Philosophy," 258-59.

20. Pettee, "Philosophy," 257.

21. Pettee, "Organization."

22. Julia Pettee, "The Development of Authorship Entry and the Formulation of Authorship Rules as Found in the Anglo-American Code," *Library Quarterly* 6/3 (1936): 270-90.

23. New York: H.W. Wilson Co., 1946.

24. 2nd ed. (Chicago: American Library Association, 1947).

Theological Library Automation in 1995

James C. Pakala

The purpose of this article is to describe the state of automation in 1995 among libraries of the American Theological Library Association. Aside from serving certain historical interests, this piece may also assist efforts to draw comparisons between types of libraries, to assess patterns of system selection or of other implementation decisions, and to locate data which might inform planning.

In early 1995 a library automation questionnaire went to 152 ATLA libraries,[1] of which 140 responded. This astounding 92% return rate must be attributed in large part to the professionalism and collegiality of the Association's membership.[2] All but two responses were usable.[3] The instrument addressed eight automation-related issues: sources of cataloging, status of retroconversion, catalog status, circulation, interlibrary loan, acquisitions, reference, and automated security for library materials.

Cataloging Sources

OCLC is the cataloging source for 110 (80%) of the libraries.[4] Of these, 19 report using other sources as well, ranging from the National Union Catalog to RLIN.[5] Five non-OCLC libraries use RLIN, but four of them cited other sources as well.[6]

Only two libraries reported sole reliance on Library of Congress cards, but I gathered that two others fit this category as well. There were two libraries that simply put "in-house." The Seminario Evangelico de

Puerto Rico listed a combination of LC cards, CD MARC, the Internet, and data from "other libraries" (the last being important for some Spanish titles, they said). Four libraries rely solely on cataloging from Library Corporation's BiblioFile, and a few more use it along with something else. Several others said their only sources were some local system, CD-ROMs from LC, or Winnebago, LaserQuest, and the like. Of the few mentioning the Internet, none cited it as their primary source.

Retroconversion

Of the 138 libraries, retroconversion is complete at 57, in process at 57, and contemplated at 19. Of the remaining five libraries, two are maintaining a card catalog system of access for now;[7] one reports that retroconversion is "not contemplated at this time"; one was founded so recently that retroconversion does not apply; and another simply noted that retroconversion is not applicable. A few of the retroconversions that I counted as completed were in fact in their final stages in the first half of 1995. At least five of those that are listed as in-process are over 90% complete. Some libraries contemplating retroconversion indicated that they plan to have the project done by a vendor (e.g., by OCLC). On the other hand, some libraries whose retroconversions were done this way earlier are engaged in extensive clean-up work, depending on who did the work, the condition of the library's cataloging, etc.[8]

Of the 57 libraries with retroconversion completed, 11 have CD-ROM catalogs and 32 have online systems, ranging from Bib-Base to Horizon.[9] The other 14 still rely on card catalogs, except for the one that uses microfiche, but many of these libraries anticipate bringing up an online system within the next year or two.

Among the catalogs at the 57 retrocon-in-process libraries, 8 are CD-ROM, 16 are online, and 33 are card catalogs. Of the last group of 33, there are 13 definitely awaiting termination upon the completion of the retroconversion. In some cases system selection and/or funding delays may prolong the library's reliance on its card catalog. But among the 19 libraries only contemplating retroconversion, a very different situation obtains. Fully-active card catalogs function at all but three.[10]

Catalog

The survey instrument distinguished between card, online, CD-ROM, and "other" catalogs. "Online" in this context therefore signifies a range of computerized catalogs, excepting those on CD-ROM. The following figures reveal the situation among the 55 libraries reporting an active card catalog:

- 46 (83.6%) are on OCLC;
- 5 (9%) have an online catalog;
- 1 (1.8%) has a CD-ROM catalog;
- 8 (14.5%) have retroconversion completed;
- 22 (40%) have a retroconversion in process;
- 22 (40%) have plans to terminate the card catalog.

It would appear that a third of the 138 libraries still have OCLC supply them with cards to file, but that figure should decrease to one-sixth as 22 libraries' card-abandonment plans achieve fruition.[11] Here is a similar picture of the 17 libraries reporting maintenance of the card catalog indefinitely but only for access to older material:

- 11 (64.7%) are on OCLC;
- 8 (47%) have an online catalog;
- 5 (29.4%) have a CD-ROM catalog;
- 7 (41%) have retroconversion completed;
- 8 (47%) have a retroconversion in process;
- 2 (11.7%) have plans to terminate the card catalog.

Just over three-fourths of these 17 libraries have an automated catalog, but with under half having completed a retroconversion, the indefinite maintenance of their card catalog is understandable, especially with a good third not having OCLC.

A total of 52 libraries (37.6% of the 138) await termination of use of their card catalog as follows:

- 22 pending retronconversion completion;
- 5 pending funding;
- 5 pending system selection;
- 3 pending retroconversion and funding;
- 1 pending retroconversion and system selection;
- 6 pending funding and system selection;
- 5 pending retroconversion, funding, and system selection;
- 3 pending installation;
- 1 pending remodeling;
- 1 not specifying the reason.

In terms of the degree or sophistication of catalog automation, not too much should be made of the difference between online and CD-ROM libraries. Some online libraries have only stand-alone microcomputers running relatively plain software, whereas Union (NY) and Emmanuel School of Religion (TN), for example, have CD-ROM systems served on local area networks. Among the 22 libraries with a CD-ROM catalog:

- 10 (45%) are on OCLC (2 more are on RLIN);
- 12 (55%) have retroconversion completed;
- 9 (41%) have a retroconversion in process;
- 7 (32%) have plans to terminate a card catalog.

For whatever reason, Library Corporation's BiblioFile is clearly the system of choice among these libraries, though as we shall notice later, the preference does not extend to circulation and acquisitions modules.

- Library Corporation/BiblioFile - 16
- SWLI/LaserGuide - 2
- Autographics - 1
- Brodart/LePac - 1
- CPLI - 1
- Winnebago - 1

A few libraries that reported having an online catalog simply listed "OCLC" as it, so I reduced the number to 60 by omitting them. The list still includes quite a range. Before naming vendors, I shall provide information similar to that provided above:

- 51 (85%) are on OCLC;
- 30 (50%) have retroconversion completed;
- 30 (50%) have a retroconversion in process;
- 21 (35%) have plans to terminate a card catalog.

The above figures reflect the presence of university divinity schools and seminaries sharing library facilities with their denominational colleges. These institutions account for about half of the online libraries. In these settings retroconversion efforts apparently tended to begin earlier. Perhaps what is remarkable is the roughly comparable situation among the CD-ROM catalog libraries, despite only about half as many having OCLC compared with the online catalog libraries. Moreover, only a fourth of the CD-ROM libraries are college-connected in even a loose way.[12]

The following shows the names of systems as they were reported, together with the number of libraries reporting each. In a few cases the system was to come up by if not before the summer of 1995. Where there is only one, I provide the name of the seminary, and in certain cases some geographical information.[13]

- Ameritech/Dynix - 6
- Ameritech/Horizon - 6
- Ameritech/NOTIS - 5
- BEP (Proprietary) - 1 (Concordia)
- Bib-Base - 4
- Data Trek - 1 (Erskine College & Seminary)
- DRA - 4 (plus 3 via UTLink at Toronto)
- DRA/ATLAS - 2 (TX seminaries)
- DRA/Inlex - 1 (Virginia Theological)
- DRA/PALNI - 3 (IN seminaries)
- DRA/MultiLIS - 2 (Vancouver schools)
- Gaylord/Galaxy - 2
- Geac/Advance or 9000 - 3
- ILCSO - 1 (Catholic Theological Union)
- ILLINET - 1 (Lincoln Christian Coll. & Sem.)
- IME/Information Navigator - 1 (St. Patrick's)
- Innovative Interfaces, Inc./Innopac - 4
- MPALS - 1 (St. Joseph's, NY)
- Nicholas Technology/MOLLI - 1 (Westminster/CA)
- PALS (South Dakota) - 1 (North American Baptist)
- SIRSI/Unicorn - 4
- VTLS - 2
- System not specified - 1 (Seminario Ev. de PR)

Circulation

Over half the libraries (75, or 54%) still have manual circulation. Automated circulation exists at 63 libraries (46%), but this does include three institutions that intend to implement it in the spring of 1995 and three more reporting implementation in the summer. It also includes one institution reporting a home-grown "semi-automated" system. A few more libraries projected implementation in the fall of 1995 or during 1996, but these were counted among those with manual circulation. Significantly, those now projecting automated circulation do so as part of an integrated library system. The actual dates for implementation of components may or may not be the same. This is now a practical matter of staffing, training, payment-making, etc. Full integration is well along the road from dream to necessity. The challenges to this include major network maintenance and decisions concerning abandonment, stand-alone retention, or reconfiguration and integration of any existing automated operations.[14]

Here are the vendors and systems as the libraries reported them, with the number of libraries reporting each. Where there's only one or two I provide names, and in certain cases some geographical information.

- Ameritech/[unspecified] - 1 (St. Mary's/TX)
- Ameritech/Dynix - 4 (one specified "Classic")
- Ameritech/Horizon - 6
- Ameritech/NOTIS or just "NOTIS" - 5
- BEP (Proprietary) - 1 (Concordia)
- Data Trek - 2 (General and New York)
- DRA - 3 (plus 3 via UTLink/Toronto)
- DRA/ATLAS - 2 (TX seminaries)
- DRA/Inlex - 1 (Virginia Theological)
- DRA/PALNI - 3 (IN seminaries)
- DRA/MultiLIS - 1 (Regent)
- Gaylord/Galaxy - 2 (Ashland and Austin Presby.)
- Geac/Advance - 2 (Atlantic and Fresno/Mennonite)
- ILCSO - 1 (Catholic Theological Union)
- ILLINET - 1 (Lincoln Christian Coll. & Sem.)
- IME/Information Navigator - 1 (St. Patrick's)
- Innovative Interfaces, Inc./Innopac - 4
- Library Corporation/BiblioFile - 4
- Nicholas/MOLLI - 2 (Westm./CA and Wash. Th. Union)
- PALS - 1 (North American Baptist)
- Professional Software/Circ. Mgr. - 1 (St. Charles)
- Right-On Programs - 1 (St. Thomas Seminary)
- SIRSI/Unicorn - 4
- TIM - 1 (St. Mary's College/SS Cyril & Methodius)
- VTLS - 2 (Beeson/Samford and Univ. of the South)
- Winnebago - 2 (Covenant and Hartford)
- Unspecified/in-house–2 (EDS-Weston and St. Mary, OH)

Interlibrary Loan

Paper forms are still the Interlibrary Loan method at 31 libraries (22%). Several noted that they do facilitate with fax, phone, etc., and one indicated some use of e-mail. OCLC's Interlibrary Loan subsystem is used by 102 (74%) of the libraries.[15] Some indicated that they use paper forms for loans to (or borrowing from) libraries not on the OCLC ILL subsystem, and I suspect most others do this as well. Several libraries indicated use of fax, phone, local networks, etc. to facilitate loans. Vanderbilt specified ARIEL Internet transfer.

New York's Union Theological Seminary is the only one that specified using OCLC, RLIN, and paper forms. The Graduate Theological Union, New Brunswick Theological Seminary, and Yale Divinity School specified RLIN. Pope John XXIII National Seminary indicated the question was not applicable in their situation.

Acquisitions

Manual acquisitions procedures are still in place at 59 (43%) of the libraries, while 79 (57%) report automation. The vendor/system profile is markedly different from those for public access catalogs and circulation systems provided above. Bib-Base established an early and decisive lead, owing in part to its development by Bob Kepple, who combined astute programming skills with knowledge and experience as a theological librarian. Although some libraries will be leaving it as they migrate to a large integrated system, many remain committed.[16]

- Ameritech/Dynix - 4
- Ameritech/Horizon - 6
- Ameritech/NOTIS or just "NOTIS" - 4
- Baker & Taylor/BTLink - 5
- BEP (Proprietary) - 1
- Brodart/PCRose - 1
- DRA - 1 (Duke)
- DRA/ATLAS - 2
- DRA/PALNI - 1
- Geac/Advance - 1
- Innovative Interfaces, Inc./Innovacq - 5
- Library Technologies, Inc./Bib-Base - 33
- Library Corp./BiblioFile - 2
- Midwest/Acqcess or MATSS - 3
- PALS - 1
- SIRSI/Unicorn - 3
- VTLS - 1
- Winnebago/Lamp - 1
- In-house/Alpha Five, Quattro Pro, etc. - 6

Automation of acquisitions should witness dramatic change as direct electronic ordering replaces slower and more cumbersome "paper and postage" steps that now are still often involved. Some of the above systems are equipped for direct electronic ordering and may be performing it already. Others are not. In any case, the role of expert and enterprising book jobbers may have significant opportunity for growth in view of these developments.[17]

Reference

Only 18 (13%) of the libraries have no automation of any kind related to reference services, although another dozen checked the questionnaire line (under Reference) marked "No automation as yet." But ten of these have at least some sort of mediated online reference service such as DIALOG or OCLC's EPIC, and the remaining two at least have a periodical index on CD-ROM. Therefore, they are included in the figures below.

Periodical indexes/abstracts on CD-ROM are available at 103 (75%) of the libraries. One such index is found at 31 libraries, two at 35, three at 10, four at 12, five at 3, and six at 5 of the libraries. The following numbers of such indexes/abstracts are reported by one library each: 7, 8, 10, 12, 15, 30, and 35. Each of these last seven libraries also serves a college or university, with one exception.[18]

"Other reference resources on CD-ROM" gleaned responses from 59 (43%) of the libraries. One such CD-ROM reference resource is found at 15 libraries, two are found at 16, three at 6, four at 7, five at 5, six at 3, eight at 1, nine at 1, ten at 2, and thirteen, fifteen, and sixteen at 1 library each. Curiously, among the top seven owners of such resources, only one is among the top seven in ownership of CD-ROM periodical indexes/abstracts![19]

The American Theological Library Association seems to merit credit for so many of its members having CD-ROM reference technology. Although I avoided asking for specific titles, it is reasonable to assume that for most of the 66 libraries reporting just one or two CD-ROM periodical indexes/abstracts, ATLA is the exclusive or leading vendor!

Mediated online access to reference resources is available at 76 (55%) of the libraries. Here is a slightly abridged enumeration of what they reported:[20]

- ATLA Religion Database - 1
- BRS (now CDP) - 9
- Cetedoc - 1

- CompuServe - 1
- DIALOG - 28
- InfoGlobe - 1
- Internet - 21
- NLM - 2
- OCLC - 15
- OCLC's EPIC - 23
- OCLC's FirstSearch - 19
- RLIN - 3
- UNCOVER - 1

Online access unmediated by library staff is found at 43 (31%) of the libraries. Clearly libraries prefer mediated access for systems that are complex, costly, or both. And many of the unmediated resources appear to be that way simply because they have been mounted on the library's public access catalog or other local network. Therefore, to a greater extent than with the figures for mediated resources, I am limiting the enumeration below.

- Advance (by modem) - 1
- Dow Jones - 1
- ERIC - 4
- Expanded Academic Index - 2
- Internet - 7
- Internet (menu access to other catalogs) - 1
- Magazine Index - 2
- Medline - 3
- OCLC - 2
- OCLC's FirstSearch - 14
- Sociofile - 1
- UNCOVER - 1
- Wilson index(es) - 3

Combining the 19 mediated and 14 unmediated instances of OCLC's FirstSearch availability, one can safely conclude that it is the online reference tool of choice. When the 33 instances of FirstSearch are combined with the 23 for EPIC and the 17 libraries simply designating mediated or unmediated OCLC access, one can conclude that the cataloging supplier so widely benefiting theological libraries also has become the most preferred reference resource as well.

Security System

This final area treated by the survey instrument gleaned information about the protection of library materials through automated loss-detection systems. Of the 138 libraries responding, 81 (58.6%) have none, 35 (25%) have the 3M electro-magnetic system, 7 (5%) have the KNOGO electro-magnetic system, 2 others went with other electro-magnetic systems, and the School of Theology Library at University of the South is implementing one by September (vendor unspecified).[21] Of the remaining 14 libraries, 11 (8%) use CheckPoint's radio frequency system, St. John's (CA) uses Ademco's radio frequency system, and Eastern Baptist specified "exit door alarms."

Why are such systems needed at institutions preparing people for ministry? Apart from hamartological reasons that may be found in the collections needing the protection, answers may include viewing such security as an integral component of the efficient tracking and enhanced accountability that automation provides to library management. Theological libraries today often serve sizable and diverse constituencies including the public at large. Some have been visited by serious theft. But I suspect that for most the key benefit of automated security is reduced frustration at the inadvertent and temporary walk-away of material.

Concluding Remarks

The 91% return rate and the completeness and clarity of the responses have made this study both possible and significant. The American Theological Library Association is, frankly, a remarkable organization with highly professional, committed, and caring members. This is conveyed as well by the picture that the results give of the state of theological libraries in North America. What these libraries have accomplished with often meager financial resources is a credit to their staffs and in no small degree to the collective esprit of the Association. As I worked through the responses from libraries with even very minimal automation, I detected interest in reporting what they could and in making strides forward as best they could. I also detected in the aggregate a healthy spirit that recognizes that automation is neither a panacea nor a goal in itself. It is not for every purpose and situation, nor does it have some uniform timetable or agenda.

The foregoing description should indeed illuminate the status of automation in theological libraries in 1995, and comparisons between this sort of library and other types of special libraries may be feasible, at least to the extent comparable data from the other types of libraries is available. Moreover, the information outlined above may facilitate the assessment of patterns of system selection or of other implementation decisions, and although I drew some conclusions in presenting the data, I suspect that more are waiting to be garnered. Finally, it is hoped that the foregoing has provided data that might assist with the planning of library automation projects.

AN AUTOMATION SURVEY OF
AMERICAN THEOLOGICAL LIBRARY ASSOCIATION
LIBRARIES

Point of Contact: Jim Pakala
Covenant Seminary, 12330 Conway Rd., St. Louis, MO 63141
Phone: 314-434-4044 x240
FAX: 314-434-4819
Internet E-MAIL: 75662.2277@COMPUSERVE.COM
CompuServe address: 75662,2277

The purpose of this questionnaire is to glean data from which to provide a snapshot of the stage of automation among ATLA libraries as of early 1995. Historical interest, comparison with other types of libraries, considerations of system selection, and ATLA planning are among the areas of interest which may be served.

In each case check as many as apply.

I. Cataloguing <u>SOURCES</u>:
    ____LC (cards)
    ____OCLC
    ____Other sources (please specify):

                _____

                _____

II. RETROCONVERSION:
    ____Completed
    ____In process
    ____Contemplated
    ____Other:

III. Catalogue (again, check as many as apply):
    ____Card catalogue:
    ____Fully active
    ____Maintained permanently/indefinitely but only for access to
        older material
    ____Awaiting termination of use pending:
        ____Completion of in-progress retroconversion
        ____Funding
        ____Selection of system

_____CD-ROM catalogue:
        Source/Vendor:
        Specific system?:
_____On line catalogue:
        Source/Vendor:
        Specific system?:
_____Other (specify):
        Source/Vendor:
        Specific system?:

IV. CIRCULATION:
    _____Manual system
    _____Automated system:
        Source/Vendor:
        Specific system?:

V. INTERLIBRARY LOAN:
    _____Paper forms only
    _____OCLC's ILL subsystem
    _____Other:

VI. ACQUISITIONS:
    _____Manual system
    _____Automated (or partly automated) system
        Source/Vendor:
        Specific system?:

VII. REFERENCE:
    _____No automation as yet
    _____Periodical indexes/abstracts on CD-ROM:
        Number_____ (e.g., ERIC on 3 discs and Religion Indexes on 1 disc would total 2)
    _____Other reference resources on CD-ROM
        Number_____ (e.g. QED would = 1)
    _____On line access mediated by library staff:
        Access to:

    _____On line access not mediated by library staff:
        Access to:

VIII. SECURITY SYSTEM FOR LIBRARY MATERIALS:
Vendor:

Type:

_____Electro-magnetic

_____Radio frequency

_____Other:

Person completing this survey:

Institution:

Familiarity with the American Theological Library Association membership may help account for certain universities appearing below, despite the survey's exclusion of certain others that appear in the membership directory of the 1994 ATLA *Summary of Proceedings.* Having said that, I apologize to Southern Methodist University's Bridwell Library, for example, which should have been included and was not. And in retrospect, I think that some more Canadian libraries should have been included. On the other hand, four institutions appear below, but are not in the member list.[22] I deemed it appropriate to include them as I used ATLA exchange list labels for mailing the survey. The exchange and membership lists are not identical, but at least one or two of these schools should appear in the next *Proceedings.*

Anderson University, Theology Library
Andover-Harvard Theological Library (see Harvard)
Andover Newton Theological School
Asbury Theological Seminary
Ashland Theological Seminary
Associated Mennonite Biblical Seminary
Athenaeum of Ohio
Atlantic School of Theology
Austin Presbyterian Theological Seminary
Bangor Theological Seminary
Baptist Missionary Association Theological Seminary
Beeson Divinity School, Samford University
Bethel Theological Seminary
Biblical Theological Seminary
Biblioteca Central, Padres Dominicos
Boston University School of Theology
Brite Divinity School, Texas Christian University
Calvary Baptist Theological Seminary
Calvin College & Calvin Theological Seminary
Canadian Theological Seminary
Cardinal Beran Library (see St. Mary's, Houston)
Catholic Theological Union
Chesapeake Theological Seminary
Chicago Theological Seminary
Christ the King Seminary
Christian Theological Seminary
Cincinnati Bible College and Seminary
Claremont, School of Theology at

Colgate Rochester Divinity School
Columbia Theological Seminary
Conception Abbey & Seminary
Concordia Lutheran Seminary (Edmonton)
Concordia Seminary (St. Louis)
Covenant Theological Seminary
Dallas Theological Seminary
Denver Seminary
Duke University Divinity School
Eastern Baptist Theological Seminary
Eastern Mennonite College and Seminary (now University)
Eden Theological Seminary (with library of Webster University)
Emmanuel College (Toronto)
Emmanuel School of Religion
Emory University (Pitts Theology Library)
Episcopal Divinity School/Weston School of Theology
Episcopal Theological Seminary of the Southwest
Erskine College and Theological Seminary
Evangelical School of Theology
Fuller Theological Seminary
Garrett-Evangelical/Seabury-Western Seminaries (United Library)
General Theological Seminary
Golden Gate Baptist Theological Seminary
Gordon-Conwell Theological Seminary
Grace Theological Seminary
Graduate Theological Union
Harding Graduate School of Religion
Hartford Seminary
Harvard Divinity School (Andover-Harvard Theological Library)
Holy Name College
Iliff School of Theology
International School of Theology
Jesuit/Krauss/McCormick Library
Kenrick-Glennon Seminary
Lancaster Theological Seminary
Lexington Theological Seminary
Lincoln Christian College and Lincoln Christian Seminary
Louisville Presbyterian Theological Seminary
Luther Seminary (St. Paul)
Lutheran Theological Seminary (Gettysburg, PA)
Lutheran Theological Seminary (Philadelphia)
Lutheran Theological Southern Seminary
Mary Immaculate Seminary
Meadville/Lombard Theological School
Memphis Theological Seminary

Mennonite Brethren Biblical Seminary (Fresno Pacific College)
Methodist Theological School in Ohio
Mid-America Baptist Theological Seminary
Midwestern Baptist Theological Seminary
Moravian College and Moravian Theological Seminary
Mt. St. Alphonsus Seminary
Nashotah House
Nazarene Theological Seminary
New Brunswick Theological Seminary
New Orleans Baptist Theological Seminary
New York Theological Seminary
North American Baptist Seminary
Northern Baptist Theological Seminary
Oblate School of Theology
Phillips Graduate Seminary Library
Pittsburgh Theological Seminary
Pontifical College Josephinum
Pope John XXIII National Seminary
Princeton Theological Seminary
Providence College and Providence Theological Seminary
Reformed Presybterian Theological Seminary
Reformed Theological Seminary (Jackson)
Reformed Theological Seminary (Orlando)
Regent College & Carey Theological College
Sacred Heart Major Seminary
Sacred Heart School of Theology
School of Theology at Claremont (see Claremont)
Seminario Evangelico de Puerto Rico
Southeastern Baptist Theological Seminary
Southern Baptist Theological Seminary
Southwestern Baptist Theological Seminary
St. Augustine's Seminary
St. Charles Borromeo Seminary
St. Francis Seminary
St. John's Seminary (Brighton, MA)
St. John's Seminary (Camarillo, CA)
St. Joseph's Seminary
St. Mary's College & SS Cyril & Methodius Seminary
St. Mary Seminary (Wickliffe, OH) [*Proceedings* list as St. Mary's]
St. Mary's Seminary and Univ., School of Theology (Baltimore)
St. Mary's (Houston) [under Cardinal Beran Library in *Proceedings*]
St. Meinrad School of Theology
St. Patrick's Seminary
St. Paul School of Theology

St. Paul Seminary and Univ. of St. Thomas [under Univ. in *Proceedings*]

St. Peter's Seminary

St. Thomas Theological Seminary

St. Vincent de Paul Regional Seminary

Trinity College (Toronto)

Trinity Episcopal School for Ministry

Trinity Evangelical Divinity School (Trinity International University)

Trinity Lutheran Seminary

Union Theological Seminary (New York)

Union Theological Seminary in Virginia

United Theological Seminary (Dayton)

United Theological Seminary of the Twin Cities

University of Dubuque

University of the South

Vancouver School of Theology

Vanderbilt Divinity School

Virginia Theological Seminary

Wartburg Theological Seminary

Washington Theological Union

Wesley Theological Seminary

Western Conservative Baptist Seminary

Westminster Theological Seminary (Philadelphia)

Westminster Theological Seminary in California

Weston School of Theology (see Episcopal Divinity School)

Winebrenner Theological Seminary

Wycliffe College

Yale Divinity School

Endnotes

1.   The first appendix is a copy of the instrument; the second lists respondents. I constructed it in late 1994 with encouragement from Patrick Graham who, as Director of the Pitts Theology Library at Emory University, also offered to facilitate the effort by placing my questionnaire on ATLANTIS, the ATLA listserv on the Internet. (Most ATLA libraries are not yet on ATLANTIS, but many are.) My February 1995 mail-out omitted ATLA members such as archives and universities, i.e. those appearing not to be seminary libraries or equivalent. I also omitted libraries outside the United States and Puerto Rico, though some Canadian ones were included.

2.   The survey was not mailed to the 14 libraries that already had responded via the note posted on ATLANTIS in late 1994 by Robert L. Craigmile, Reference Librarian at the Pitts Theology Library. I thank him as well as M. Patrick Graham for this kind facilitation.   By February 1995, when I mailed the instrument, I was on ATLANTIS myself, and one additional library responded directly to me thereby. Craigmile had forwarded on diskette the 14 earlier e-mail responses that he had received directly. In retrospect, I see merit in distributing the instrument both ways in a coordinated fashion and without preconceptions as to which means a respondent will prefer.

3.   Hereafter the percentages are based on 138 responses. Holy Name College's status is now that of a "house library," following a move and new theological library access for their students. St. Paul (Kansas City) responded too late to be included, but in brief, they are on OCLC, have a retroconversion in process, pending completion will terminate their card catalog, use DRA via consortium, have BTLink and Alpha Four for acquisitions, and have three periodical indexes on CD-ROM plus one other CD-ROM tool.

4.   Only one of the 110 libraries reported using OCLC through a neighboring seminary.

5.   Duke, Emory, Fuller, the Graduate Theological Union, and Yale report using RLIN in addition to OCLC.

6.   Emmanuel and Trinity in Toronto, as well as Luther, New Brunswick, and Union (NY) were those that listed RLIN but not OCLC. Also listed by Emmanuel were LC(DRANET) and CDN MARC; by Trinity, ISM (formerly UTLAS) and DRANET; by Luther, BiblioFile; and by New Brunswick, LCMARC/CD-ROM. Of the 19 OCLC libraries reporting other sources, only Harvard Divinity cited LC MARC tapes per se.

7.   St. Mary's College/SS Cyril & Methodius Seminary is on OCLC and St. Vincent de Paul uses LC cards, BiblioFile, and the British Library National Bibliographic Service as their cataloging sources.

8.   My own experience suggests that medium-sized theological libraries may be in a better position to do their own retroconversion than those with collections too large or staffs too small to allow for a rigorously conceived and executed project. The advantages of an in-house project include detection of cataloging curiosities and weeding of items that do not merit retroconversion. However, provided such a library is on OCLC, it is the speed, acuity, and discretion of the cataloger(s) that should serve as the deciding factors in whether to conduct such a project in-house.

9.   Library Technologies, Inc. has not developed Bib-Base into a full-blown automated system, owing to their focus on database clean-up projects and the like, as well as to Bib-Base's original and abiding technical processing purposes. The Ameritech takeover of Dynix and

NOTIS is well known. Many consider their minicomputer-based systems to be outstanding.

10. In some cases, card catalogs may merit retention as historical documents. Yale Divinity Library may retain theirs for this reason.

11. The one-third of 138 is reached by assuming that the 46 OCLC libraries with fully-active card catalogs are filing cards from OCLC, even in the case of the 6 with automated catalogs. The reduction by about one-half is reached by assuming that the 22 libraries planning to terminate the card catalog are among the 46 on OCLC.

12. I hesitate to comment on other patterns that might be perceived, such as denominational ones. I can safely observe that Roman Catholic seminaries, in general, seem to be slower at automating.

13. I have not listed a system being evaluated by the Biblioteca Central, Padres Dominicos library in Puerto Rico, but it is Siabnc 4.0 developed by the Universidad de Colima in Mexico. I also should note that under Ameritech/NOTIS one library each specified NOTIS 5.1, 5.1.2, and LMS 5.0. Princeton Seminary listed simply NOTIS and Harvard indicated a modified NOTIS. In this and similar lists of vendors/systems I have for curiosity's sake tried to provide what libraries actually recorded, but this was not always feasible (e.g., "Dynix Marquis/Notis Horizon" in a few responses).

14. Covenant Theological Seminary brought up Library Corporation's BiblioFile because of its user-friendliness, cost, and ease of maintenance, and it has not been a disappointment. However, our test of their initial acquisitions system proved a disaster, and so we used Alpha Four to program our own. We later chose Winnebago's sophisticated but easy-to-use CIRC system, because it had an excellent platform (Btrieve), which Library Corporation was just adopting. Now we may buy Winnebago's CAT system, as well, to mount on the campus ethernet. Besides wider access, this would inform patrons about the availability of the item and update the catalog daily (versus monthly CD-ROM remasterings with BiblioFile). With each system having merits, we may use both, at least until a future migration.

15. One library accepts paper forms only, but uses OCLC for its own borrowing. Two specified that they did their OCLC interlibrary loan through arrangements with another institution.

16. Phillips Graduate Seminary Library reports using Bib-Base for budget control and Baker & Taylor for ordering, and so I counted them under each. I also did this for Erskine College and Seminary, which uses both Baker & Taylor's BTLink and Brodart's PCRose. The list therefore tallies 81.

17. Acquiring materials may be fraught with publisher incompetence at handling certain library standing or individual orders. At Covenant Seminary we now usually verify existence, edition, etc. on

OCLC before placing an order, and try to use a competent jobber. The extra cost is offset by regaining staff time lost to correspondence, returns, etc., not to mention satisfied patrons. As for electronic orders, proficient jobbers are among those leading the way.

18. Asbury Seminary has its own library, which houses more volumes than that of Asbury College, located in the same town. The other six are Brite, Calvin, Eden-Webster, Emory, Moravian, and Trinity International University (the former Trinity Evangelical Divinity School and Trinity College/IL). At this juncture I also should note that in both my tallies related to CD-ROM titles it is possible that a few responses reflect a count based on discs rather than titles, despite my specification. There also may have been difficulty on the part of a few respondents in determining what counted as strictly a periodical index/abstract on CD-ROM.

19. Brite Divinity School. The other six in this case are Cincinnati Bible College and Seminary, Duke Divinity School, Emmanuel School of Religion, Lincoln Christian College and Seminary, Southeastern Baptist Seminary, and Yale Divinity School.

20. Eight libraries reported mediated access to state or local library networks, catalogs, etc., ranging from URSUS in Maine to Melvyl in California (and sometimes not named). The tally omits these data.

21. Emmanuel College at Toronto uses ID Systems and Union (VA) uses ADT.

22. Beeson Divinity School, Conception Abbey & Seminary, International School of Theology, and Reformed Theological Seminary (Orlando) are the four.

The Only Thing

Louis Charles Willard

When Red Sanders of Vanderbilt University said, "Winning isn't everything; it's the only thing," libraries probably ranked low, if at all, on his list of possible games. The notion of winning, or losing, really is missing from the discourse of librarians, who have traditionally taken a passive role in the learning process. In a way, maybe such a role is inevitable for members of almost any helping profession. Whether by necessity or because it just seems better, we tend to shun competition. We also disdain entrepreneurial endeavors and are uncomfortable with commercially oriented language and concepts, such as manage, customers, and business purpose.

This passivity has a down side, though. The heavier players in our educational game, namely the faculty, never really view us helpers as peers. Our role, even though acknowledged as important in prefaces to books and in introductions to school catalogs, is subservient. Members of the faculty view us as clerks in a big warehouse. We might be good clerks, thoughtful clerks, even smart clerks, but we are still clerks.

Although we dislike our assigned role, at least it has been secure. Some, to be sure, have sought full faculty status, but not having it means that our job is not in jeopardy of a tenure decision. Deans and presidents, in welcoming addresses to incoming classes, piously declare the library the heart of the school. This is changing. The relentless tide—no, "tide" implies a return—the relentless, irresistible onslaught of technology is transforming the playing field.

The Business of Books

Railroads almost went out of business earlier in this century because the owners thought of themselves too narrowly, as being in the railroad business instead of the transportation business. Although I confess that I prefer to describe myself as "the librarian" rather than "the director of the library," it is very clear that a sea change is occurring in our work, in our business. Ever since Alexandria, perhaps even before, we have considered ourselves to be in the book business. Gutenberg's invention, dramatic as it was, did not really alter all that much the fundamental business of libraries. They remained collections of books, tended by well-informed clerks. Even as other intellectual containers (i.e., formats) modified the singular role of the book in our collections, the book continued to assert its predominance through the generic definition of all the other formats as "non-book." The customer, moreover, has had to come to our store—rather literally, our store of books—in order to do intellectual business. The weakly supported interlibrary loan process, which reaches out to other collections in acknowledgement of the incompleteness of any particular collection, also functions out of our store. The card catalog, which replaced the (distributable) book catalog, serves as the on-site index to the store. It really is a unique tool, created and maintained by highly trained, professional clerks, whose job includes adjusting standard records to their particular store's unique idiosyncrasies.

All this has always been very labor intensive and expensive. Up to this point, fortunately, the library has been relatively sacrosanct. Deans, presidents, and other administrators have tended to leave the library pretty much alone, in part because there is widespread agreement that the library is a good thing, in part because external standards exist that mandate certain levels of financial support, and perhaps in part because the inner workings and hidden mechanisms of libraries are mysterious to deans, presidents, and other administrators. And it has been to our advantage as under-acknowledged clerks to keep it that way.

Change Agents

The conjunction of several events, however, is already eroding our insular security, even as I write. By the time conventional processes publish these words, the transition will very likely be much advanced.

Automation

Only in the last quarter century has the computer infiltrated the library. We have not resisted this tireless *Gastarbeiter*, though in common with most folks, our initial applications merely assisted us to do better what we were already doing, without asking whether the computer might actually enable us to do something quite different. The first successful, multi-library computer system, created by Frederick Kilgour as the Ohio College Library Center (now the less parochial acronym OCLC), functioned initially as a shared cataloging and card production system. Libraries, much more rapidly than anyone could rationally have predicted, moved from using the computer to create and maintain the labor intensive card catalog to using the computer to create and to maintain the electronic catalog, as an online tool. By way of a side note, some librarians formatted these online catalogs so that the information appeared formatted like the cards in the card catalogs they replaced. These librarians, probably unwittingly, replicated the earliest printers, who designed fonts for the new moveable type so that the resulting printed book resembled the manuscript, which it too was replacing.

Computer Conferencing

I consciously choose an old fashioned term rather than the language that is more common as I write, namely, the Internet and the Worldwide Web, since the old fashioned term at least has the virtue of conveying accurately a sense of what it is about, while the newer, more contemporary terms may have vanished by the time this appears. That term itself, computer conferencing, is a useful example of the accelerating pace of technology. When it came into vogue, in the sixties, it was really nothing more than e-mail. That changed abruptly with the advent of the microcomputer. The Internet and the Worldwide Web have produced, or are the products of, yet another seismic shift in the technology of communication and information transfer.

Scanning, Digitizing, and Interpreting

Microforms ought to have had a leveling effect among research libraries. As I thought about the completion of the STC and Wing collections by UMI, I realized that any library in the world for not all that much cash outlay can acquire a early English collection that is more comprehensive than the Bodleian or the British Library. I believed this fact would enhance, promote, and invigorate sixteenth and seventeenth century research anywhere and everywhere. The micropublications of the AAS make possible a similar collection of early Americana. It never turned out that way because the medium is the message, and no one is listening to microforms.

Scanning and digitizing, though, perform significant value-added functions. At the outset, they followed the same replicative path of computer assisted cataloging—do what I already do, perhaps a little faster or a little better—and the scanning/digitizing devices are linked to printers to produce a faster, sharper photocopy. A digitized text, though, whether it began as a paper copy that was scanned or whether its original and only format is electronic, is a far more efficient, flexible, and useful document.

The third facet is interpreting. By interpreting, I mean the conversion of the digitized images of an original printed document to machine-readable texts. As I write, it is too early to predict how conventional publishers are going to make peace with this new technology. At first blush, it is a mortal threat. In a privately circulated paper, "The Problem of the One and the Many," I have already asked why the intellectual world needs to subsidize the production of many copies of an electronic text when a single copy can suffice. Very few scholars make significant amounts of money from their publications, and the few who do should be reluctant to insist that the funding of their personal activities ought to take precedence over the advance of scholarship.

Right now, all these forces, together with our old friends, insufficient money and insufficient time, are buffeting our familiar, comfortable world. We ought to be very worried because probably for the first time, there is going to be evidence increasingly available for the faculty to interpret—wrongly in my opinion but nevertheless convincingly—to mean they no longer need us. Not only do they not need our clerkly guidance and support any more; they do not need our store either. It bids to be all available online.

Fast Knowledge

Imagine with me for a moment, a newcomer who happens upon a modern grocery store. This stranger happens first upon the frozen food section; the stranger is amazed and pleased. Everything one could possibly want or need is available here: orange juice, waffles, bagels, starters, entrees, vegetables, pizzas, and desserts. The stranger fills a cart and departs the market. The stranger is satisfied. The stranger has also doubtless paid more for less nutritious, less appetizing, and less varied food than was available elsewhere in the store. The stranger, though, has no notion that there is any more to the market than the frozen food section. We are heading, in my opinion, for a frozen food, fast food, convenience store approach to research that is unreflectively, indeed unconsciously, developing. This approach is inevitably superficial, though it has a veneer of quality and depth. Two examples may illustrate the reality and the problem.

Convenience Notes

First, the photocopy machine is a remarkable and irreversible boon to research in innumerable ways. For some, perhaps many, it has sharply reduced and even eliminated the process of thoughtful engagement with the text. Before photocopy machines made possible the reproduction of entire articles, chapters, and books, the scholar actually had to read and, generally, understand the text in order to make notes, the preferred alternative to transcribing the whole text. (Some, of course, solved this problem in a less socially acceptable way by surreptitiously cutting out the article or chapter or by simply stealing the book.)

My perception is that for some, making the photocopy completes the intellectual process. Since notes are no longer required to capture or to summarize the intellectual content of printed texts, the nascent scholar has "done the job" by achieving possession of the text. The fact the copier—however understood—has not thought through or even engaged the text is irrelevant to the fact of mere possession. The electronic catalog, which makes it possible for the nascent scholar to search library catalogs and other bibliographic databases worldwide, now facilitates the creation of electronic and eclectic bibliographies. The would-be scholar is further distanced from the reality of intellectual exchange, and the computer-assisted bibliography has an elegant appearance, through the magic of desktop publishing software, though it has not required understanding, evaluating, or even reading the citations.

New Wineskins

A second example concerns existing card catalogs, which were about to collapse from their own size and complexity. Studies demonstrated that researchers as well as casual users simply ran out of steam early in the alphabet when confronted with a subject file comprising hundreds of cards. Much evidence shows that most users avoided subject searches, and even locating known items in lengthy files was often frustrating. We have been able to show our users that the electronic catalog has overcome most of these difficulties. The problem is that the electronic catalog has, itself, become an increasingly complex research tool, with its own myths and unexamined assumptions.

First, we tend to transfer to the new, the characteristics and limitations of the old. In the electronic catalog, this means that the newly initiated researcher, be that researcher an entering student or a full professor, is going to do author and title searches. The results are usually immediate and startling. The most difficult job is getting the resister to the keyboard. Once there, it does not take much to convince even the most reluctant user that the electronic catalog is a giant improvement over the unwieldy card catalog. The transition from skittish to over-confident is also rapid, especially when the scholar learns that the catalog is accessible from the office and home.

Second, we confer upon computers, the systems they operate, and the products they produce, a quality of omniscience. If a user does a title search in the electronic catalog and the response is, "No Hits," the inclination of the majority is to accept the response as an accurate answer to the question that we thought we were asking. No matter that our recollection of the title varies slightly from its published form; no matter that a minor typo has crept into our search; no matter that our library's retrospective conversion program has not yet incorporated the title into the electronic catalog; no matter that we are searching in a periodical index rather than in the main catalog. We interpret the response of the computer to be conclusive, comprehensive, and unarguable. The response may be relieving or perturbing but in either case, it is convincing.

Third, the developers and maintainers of our electronic catalogs cannot leave well-enough alone. Perhaps just because it is possible, perhaps pressed by a need continually to revise and to improve, perhaps encouraged by user requests for systemic as well as cosmetic improvements, the programmers are constantly tinkering, constantly adding, to use the more fashionable term, functionality. Our users, whose initial needs seemed satisfied with a simple-minded transfer of inquiries based on the card catalog model, consider themselves expert practitioners when they can recreate those types of inquiries in the electronic catalog. We use our funds to support the extension, expansion, and increase in the number and modes of access to our catalog. We choose improvements instead of using our funds to support the improved and wider utilization of existing functionality. This choice of priorities, which I consider misguided, is understandable inasmuch as it is possible to list, enumerate, and display added functionalities. Measuring degree of improvement in the mastery of the skills required fully to exploit the electronic catalog is not so easy as listing new search gambits. I am convinced, though, that at the point the electronic catalog was made publicly available to my scholarly community, only a tiny fraction of the faculty was conscious of as much as 75% of the system's capabilities. The working knowledge, those capabilities that are actively and regularly used, of this tiny, well-informed fraction, was about 30%. Over the course of the years, the percentage of the faculty actually using the electronic catalog is certainly well over 95%, but as the back room programmers have more cleverly outfitted the catalog, the average user's working knowledge, as a percentage of the system's capabilities as a whole, has certainly dropped.

So, what do we have? Well, we have a constituency that is under-informed but is confident that it knows what it is doing. This constituency is learning that the institution's electronic catalog is accessible from a distance. This constituency is learning that texts, new publications, and whole dialogues are accessible over long distances. This constituency is learning that you can even shop for frozen food from a distance. Furthermore, this constituency is learning that you can search the frozen food lockers of many other, distant supermarkets. The likely result of this trend is that our constituency will cease coming to the library. They no longer require our mediation either for identifying information they need or for acquiring that information. Of course, what they identify and acquire will constitute an increasingly small fraction of the potentially relevant information. They are unconscious of this deficiency, and since they no longer interact with the clerks, they will discover this deficiency only serendipitously.

Initiative

The alternative to despair is initiative. To take the initiative, though, is contrary to our learned, passive behavior. We need retraining, which is to say, we have to learn how to speak, and we have to incorporate relevant, meaningful content in what we say. In a way, it is a symbol of our own arrogance that we have never learned how to converse with the faculty. If someone had recently asked us, what is your mission, we would have promptly responded with something like, "Our mission is to serve the information needs of our scholarly community." But in our arrogance, or maybe fear, we never really bothered to ask the faculty what they wanted. We assumed that we knew. First of all then, we have to learn how to be engaging conversationalists. Part of the art of dialog is active listening to the other, who is speaking about (1) the scholarly process of research and teaching, as that other undertakes it, and (2) what are the material (or information) resources that the process requires. It is this information, rather than our self-created criteria for collection development and resource allocation, that should inform how we stock and operate the store.

Earlier in this essay, I implicitly criticized library operations as being labor intensive and expensive. The dialogical process that I have proposed in the preceding paragraph is also exceedingly labor intensive and expensive, especially if we act on the basis of the information about practices, wants, and needs we collect. One of the difficulties with transferring business models into the library environment is the distinction between for-profit and non-profit enterprises. Although pressure to economize is undeniable—by the way, it is also appropriate—academic/research libraries do not yet operate with the bottom-line driven motivation that energizes the commercial sector. In spite of this, our financial officers are anxious to reduce our costs, or at least to reduce their rate of increase. They are not going to be pleased with a program that adds significantly to the cost of operating the library.

Precision Cataloging

There are two moderating factors to consider here. The first is that, with the level of interaction and responsiveness I am proposing, the faculty will shift from nominal to ardent, zealous supporters, based on significant, direct improvement in the way that the library works for them. The second factor is that we can meet the information needs of the faculty with a dramatic reduction in two of our present major cost centers, personnel and collection development. In an earlier published article, titled somewhat colorlessly, "The Library Yet to Come,"[1] I included the outline of a strategy that we are using to move some monographs through the cataloging process here more rapidly and efficiently. We devised the strategy by asking, "How are our catalog records actually going to be used, and are there differences among titles, rather than forcing every title, regardless of language and predictable audience, through the same routine." Though the term was not available to us at the time, we were, in fact, "re-engineering" that aspect of the library operation.

Precision Collection Development

The Machine That Changed the World : How Japan's Secret Weapon in the Global Auto Wars Will Revolutionize Western Industry by James Womack, Daniel Jones, and Daniel Roos[2] is a review of the way that the innovative business strategy of Japanese automobile manufacturers enabled them to produce cars that were better, more reliable, and less expensive than cars rolling off Western mass production lines. One—by no means the only—of these strategies focused on inventory. The successful alternative to the capital-intensive, "just-in-case" approach traditionally required by the mass production method, became the "just-in-time" approach, which produced a dramatic, and significantly cost saving, reduction in on-hand inventory required.

In a curious way, we can characterize the collection development policies of research libraries as mirroring the "just-in-case" inventory strategy of Western mass production. My education as a librarian included the lesson that this is the way of research libraries, and I learned my lesson well. But perhaps it is time to unlearn it. I am not intending, here, to leap on the faddish and fashionable access-instead-of-ownership bandwagon. In my opinion, the access practice has always assumed there would always be an "owner" somewhere, with no reliable evidence or plan in place to assure that. This bandwagon, moreover, has always operated at the fringes of collection development and without any structure of coordination.

The model that I have in mind is much more aggressive. It is also risky. I propose at least a 50% reduction in the collection development expenditures of research libraries. Abandon as unrealistic and no longer appropriate the "just-in-case" approach to collecting. Buy those items for which there is a reasonably clear and present demand. Our automated circulation systems, in addition to our dialogue with faculty, students, and other users, will inform us how accurate our collection decisions are. Err on the over-buy side in the area of bibliographic access tools (e.g., reference works, indices, and bibliographies, especially those in an electronic form), and enhance the importance and responsiveness of our interlibrary loan systems.

There are several major, possibly fatal, problems with the just-in-time approach. One is that it assumes our user can access the item, which means that it has to exist somewhere and that it has a bibliographic pointer that is available to our user. If the access-over-ownership argument were to achieve its logical extreme, no one would own marginal or even merely moderately important titles, and research libraries would become mediocre, essentially duplicate, collections. A second problem is that the success of the access model is that it assumes that each owner of this literature, which is being accessed rather than owned by some other library, will promptly provide it. The plain truth is that the current interlibrary loan system would never support the level and quality of exchange that this model envisions. At least one reason for the low priority that interlibrary loan activity has at most net-lending libraries is that the beneficiaries are, by definition, not their primary patrons.

Old Partners with a Difference

Perhaps the solution is to look elsewhere. The "elsewhere" that I have in mind consists of our international book vendors. If we librarians are headed for extinction by continuing to think of ourselves as being in the business of warehousing books, our vendors might be unnecessarily limiting their future survival if their self-perception is the business of providing current imprints. Although some international vendors undertake searches for out-of-print items, these focus on obtaining used or hoarded copies of original publications and such searches are usually a sideline.

I am proposing that my major vendors become information purveyors, without limit as to imprint. We want to be able to order a title when we discover we need it. For our vendor, addressing our order has a much higher priority than it would for a holding library, since we are the vendor's primary patrons. There is, furthermore, no longer the issue of providing an unused original. The vendor can borrow on our behalf or supply a reproduction, in a paper or (more likely) an electronic form.

To be sure, the cost of this item is considerably more than it would have been if we had acquired the title when it first appeared. This calculation shifts, though, when we factor in other relevant costs. These other relevant costs include cataloging and maintaining the title. More significantly, these other relevant costs include the likely expense of acquiring the dozens, if not hundreds, of other, similar titles that the collection development policy would have had to have picked up in order to have included this particular title. For example, if the title in question were the church history of a small village in Denmark, our library would have to have been collecting European city and regional church histories generally and would have acquired, cataloged, and maintained hundreds—even thousands—in order to have this particular one in the collection.

The Only Thing

Winning is the only thing, to return to where we began. Fortunately, in this game, it is possible for everyone to win.

Endnotes

[1] In *Reference Services in the Humanties*, ed. Judy Reynolds (New York: Haworth Press, 1994), pp. 193-200.

[2] New York: Harper Perennial, 1991.

List of Contributors

John A. Bollier: Director of Development, ATLA, 1 July 1991–29 February 1996. Formerly, Head of Public Services, Yale Divinity School Library.

Brian Carter: Antiquarian Book Dealer. Oxford, United Kingdom.

Myron B. Chace: Head of Special Services Section (Photoduplication Service), Library of Congress.

Diane Choquette: Head Public Services, Graduate Theological Union.

Stephen D. Crocco: Librarian, Clifford E. Barbour Library, Pittsburgh Theological Seminary.

Cindy Derrenbacker: Librarian, Wycliffe College, Toronto, Canada.

Milton McC. Gatch: Director, The Burke Library, Union Theological Seminary (NY).

M. Patrick Graham: Director, Pitts Theology Library, Emory University.

Albert E. Hurd: Executive Director/CEO, The American Theological Library Association, 1 July 1991–23 February 1996.

Andrew J. Keck: Acquisitions Assistant, Clifford E. Barbour Library, Pittsburgh Theological Seminary.

Alan D. Krieger: Theology Bibliographer, University of Notre Dame.

Betty A. O'Brien: Retired. Formerly United Theological Seminary, Dayton, Ohio.

Elmer J. O'Brien: Librarian, United Theological Seminary, Dayton, Ohio.

James C. Pakala: Director, Library, Covenant Theological Seminary.

Paul Schrodt: Director, Library , Methodist School of Theology in Ohio.

Martha Lund Smalley: Archivist, Day Missions Collection, Yale Divinity School Library.

Newland F. Smith: Librarian for Collection Management, United Library of Garrett-Evangelical and Seabury-Western Theological Seminaries.

Richard D. Spoor: Retired. Formerly Director, The Burke Library, Union Theological Seminary (NY).

Paul F. Stuehrenberg: Director, Yale Divinity School Library.

Louis Charles: Willard: Librarian, Andover-Harvard Theological Library, Harvard University.